From the Page to the Stage

From the Page to the Stage

The Educator's Complete Guide to Readers' Theatre

Shirlee Sloyer

Professor, Speech Communications and Rhetorical Studies
Hofstra University, New York

2003
Teacher Ideas Press
Libraries Unlimited
A Division of Greenwood Publishing Group, Inc.
Westport, Connecticut

TEACHER IDEAS PRESS
Libraries Unlimited
A Division of Greenwood Publishing Group, Inc.
88 Post Road West
Westport, CT 06881
1-800-225-5800
www.lu.com/tips

Library of Congress Cataloging-in-Publication Data

ISBN 1-56308-897-5

Acknowledgments

Selections from IT'S MINE by Leo Lionni, copyright © 1985, 1986 by Leo Lionni. Used by permission of Alfred A. Knopf Children's Books, a division of Random House, Inc.

Selections from THE FORTUNE-TELLERS by Lloyd Alexander, copyright © 1992 by Lloyd Alexander, text. Used by permission of Dutton Children's Books, an imprint of Penguin Putnam Books for Young Readers, a division of Penguin Putnam Inc. All rights reserved.

Selections from THE TRUE STORY OF THE THREE LITTLE PIGS by Jon Scieszka, copyright © 1989 by Jon Scieszka, text. Used by permission of Viking Penguin, an imprint of Penguin Putnam Books for Young Readers, a division of Penguin Putnam Inc. All rights reserved.

Selections from THE FROG PRINCE CONTINUED by Jon Scieszka, copyright © 1991 by Jon Scieszka, text. Used by permission of Viking Penguin, an imprint of Penguin Putnam Books for Young Readers, a division of Penguin Putnam Inc. All rights reserved.

Selections from MATH CURSE by Jon Scieszka, copyright © 1995 by Jon Scieszka, text. Used by permission of Viking Penguin, an imprint of Penguin Putnam Books for Young Readers, a division of Penguin Putnam Inc. All rights reserved.

Selections from WHY THE SEA IS SALT. Text Copyright © 1993 Vivian French; Illustrations Copyright © 1993 Patrice Aggs. Reproduced by permission of the publisher Candlewick Press, Inc., Cambridge, MA., on behalf of Walker Books Ltd., London.

Selections from "The Moth and the Star" and "The Little Girl and the Wolf." From FABLES FOR OUR TIME. Copyright © 1940 by James Thurber. Copyright © renewed 1968 by Helen Thurber and Rosemary A. Thurber. Reprinted by arrangement with Rosemary A. Thurber and The Barbara Hogenson Agency. All rights reserved.

Selections from JUST JUICE by Karen Hesse. Copyright © 1998 by Karen Hesse. Reprinted by permission of Scholastic Inc.

Excerpt from THE TOP-SECRET JOURNAL OF FIONA CLAIRE JARDIN, copyright © 1998 by Roberta Ann Cruise, reprinted by permission of Harcourt, Inc.

Selections from MANIAC MAGEE by Jerry Spinelli, copyright © 1990 Jerry Spinelli. Reprinted by permission of HarperCollins Publishers Inc.

Excerpt from THE HOBBIT by J.R.R. Tolkien. Copyright © 1966 by J.R.R. Tolkien. Copyright © Renewed 1994 by Christopher R. Tolkien, John F.R. Tolkien and Priscilla M.A.R. Tolkien. Reprinted by permission of Houghton Mifflin Company. All rights reserved.

"Invitation" and "Us," in WHERE THE SIDEWALK ENDS, by Shel Silverstein. Copyright © 1974 BY EVIL EYE MUSIC, INC. Used by permission of HarperCollins Publishers.

"Messy Room" and "Hug-o-War," in A LIGHT IN THE ATTIC, by Shel Silverstein. Copyright © 1981 BY EVIL EYE MUSIC, INC. Used by permission of HarperCollins Publishers.

"Remote-A-Dad" and "No Grown-Ups," in FALLING UP, by Shel Silverstein. Copyright © 1996 BY EVIL EYE MUSIC, INC. Used by permission of HarperCollins Publishers.

Selections from "basketball" from SPIN A SOFT BLACK SONG by Nikki Giovanni. Copyright © 1971, 1985 by Nikki Giovanni. Reprinted by permission of Hill and Wang, a division of Farrar, Straus and Giroux, LLC.

"The Skier" by Robert Francis, from *Come Out into the Sun* © 1965. Used by permission of University of Massachusetts Press.

Selections from "YOU'RE A GOOD MAN, CHARLIE BROWN" by Clark Gesner, copyright ©1967 by Clark Gesner. Used by permission of Random House, Inc.

Excerpt from ANASTASIA HAS THE ANSWERS by Lois Lowry. Copyright © 1986 by Lois Lowry. Reprinted by permission of Houghton Mifflin Company. All rights reserved.

Selections from . . . AND NOW MIGUEL, by Joseph Krumgold. Copyright © 1953 BY JOSEPH KRUMGOLD. Used by permission of HarperCollins Publishers.

Selections from TO KILL A MOCKINGBIRD, by Harper Lee, copyright © 1982 by Harper Lee. Reprinted by permission of HarperCollins Publishers Inc.

Selections from "Mother to Son," from THE COLLECTED POEMS OF LANGSTON HUGHES by Langston Hughes, copyright © 1994 by The Estate of Langston Hughes. Used by permission of Alfred A. Knopf, a division of Random House, Inc.

Selections from "Jazz Fantasia" from SMOKE AND STEEL by Carl Sandburg, copyright 1920 by Harcourt, Inc. and renewed 1948 by Carl Sandburg, reprinted by permission of the publisher.

Selections from "Inside a Poem," from IT DOESN'T ALWAYS HAVE TO RHYME by Eve Merriam. Copyright © 1964, 1992 Eve Merriam. Used by permission of Marian Reiner.

Selections from THE FANTASTICKS. Words by Tom Jones. Music by Harvey Schmidt. Reprinted by permission.

Selections from TALES OF FARAWAY FOLK by Babette Deutsch and Avrahm Yarmolinsky. Copyright © 1952 BY HARPERCOLLINS PUBLISHERS. Reprinted by permission of HarperCollins Publisher.

"The Legend of Lightning Larry" (script). Story copyright © 1993, Aaron Shepard. Script copyright © 1993, 1996 Aaron Shepard. Reprinted by permission of the author.

"Housework," from FREE TO BE YOU AND ME by Sheldon Harnick. © 1972 Free To Be Foundation, Inc. Used by permission.

"He Mail She Mail" used by permission of Ted K. Hechtman.

Selections from THE D-POEMS OF JEREMY BLOOM by Gordon Korman and Bernice Korman. Used by permission of Curtis Brown, Ltd. Copyright © 1992 by Gordon Korman & Bernice Korman. All Rights reserved.

Selections adapted from NOTHING BUT THE TRUTH by Avi. Published by Orchard Books, an imprint of Scholastic Inc. Copyright © 1991 by Avi. Reprinted by permission.

Selections from HEY WORLD, HERE I AM! by Jean Little. TEXT COPYRIGHT © 1986 BY JEAN LITTLE. Used by permission of HarperCollins Publishers.

Selections from HOW TO EAT LIKE A CHILD by Delia Ephron. Reprinted by permission of International Creative Management, Inc. Copyright © 1978 Delia Ephron.

Selections from *Class Dismissed!* and *My Friend's Got This Problem, Mr. Candler*, by Mel Glenn, reprinted by permission of Mel Glenn.

Selections excerpted and reprinted from FOR YOUR EYES ONLY, by Joanne Rocklin, copyright © 1997 by Joanne Rocklin, published by Scholastic Press. All rights are reserved by the Author.

Selections reprinted with the permission of Simon & Schuster, Inc., from UP THE DOWN STAIRCASE by Bel Kaufman. Copyright © 1964 by Bel Kaufman; copyright renewed © 1992.

For Seymour, he with the quiet demeanor and the keen mind,
who inspired us all to love books. The baton is passed.
It is up to the children now.

Contents

Part 1: Selecting, Analyzing, Adapting, and Performing

Part 2: Model Readers Theatre and Sample Scripts

PART 1

Selecting, Analyzing, Adapting, and Performing

Rehearsing "The Clever Judge"

Chapter 1

THE PROLOGUE

STUDENT 1: Ladies and gentlemen,
I am the prologue.
The readers have sent me to introduce the program.
It's called "People Are Only Human . . . "
All the stories tell about what people are like.

STUDENT 2: Some are wise.

STUDENT 3: Some are foolish.

STUDENT 4: Some are greedy.

STUDENT 5: Some are heroic.

STUDENT 6: Some are prideful.

STUDENT 1: But enough—you will see for yourself.

ENTIRE CAST: Our book is open . . .

STUDENT 1: Listen . . . . Once upon a time . . .

(Readers theatre begins . . .)

Yes, readers theatre has begun. It is not a play. There are no elaborate stage sets, no ornate costumes, no need for memorized lines. It is an activity that calls on the imagination. But it is not ordinary reading with dull, word-by-word reciting. Leslie Coger and Melvin White, authors of a practical readers theatre guidebook, suggest that both "readers" and "theatre" are crucial elements in this art form. The *readers* are interpreters who bring characters to life through their voices and gestures, whereas the literature contains the *theatre,* which will be "animated in performance for an audience."[1] Readers theatre is a shared happening between performers and audience. Each has a part in the transaction.

Used in the classroom or the library, readers theatre becomes an integrated language arts event centering on the oral interpretation of literature. Students adapt and present the material of their choice. A story, a poem, a scene from a play, a letter, even a song lyric provide the ingredients for the script. As a reading, thinking, writing, speaking, and listening experience, readers theatre makes a unique contribution to our English language arts curriculum.

An Overview

This book is intended for teachers and librarians. Teachers of elementary and middle school grades will find it a valuable resource for enriching the English language arts curriculum. School and public librarians will discover readers theatre to be a natural activity for the library as a creative approach to guiding and teaching young people about literature. The chapters that follow offer the educator comprehensive instructions for selecting and adapting literature, staging, directing, and evaluating the presentation. A segment on the often-neglected area of improving students' voice and diction is incorporated. *Specific* suggestions for enhancing the language arts can be found in the chapters under that heading. Also, instructors may be guided by an account of a model readers theatre program as it was done in a fifth-grade class. Sample scripts provide typically adapted material for use and study. A reference list and a bibliography of relevant books and articles for teachers, librarians, resource personnel, and students are included.

Benefits of Readers Theatre

The benefits that accrue from incorporating readers theatre into the classroom are many. Engaging students in the art form of dramatizing literature motivates them to read willingly, think critically, write creatively, speak correctly, listen intently, and work together productively. In this regard, readers theatre activities are compatible with the standards set by the International Reading Association (IRA) and the National Council of Teachers of English (NCTE), which emphasize the need for developing reading, writing, and oral skills.[2] In addition, readers theatre reinforces learning in content areas. By preparing and performing scenes adapted from social studies texts and books from other areas of study, students relate to otherwise remote ideas in a realistic and exciting fashion.

Readers Theatre Is a Reading Motivator: "Get thee to the library!"

If we look in a thesaurus for additional meanings of the word *motivation,* we come up with *drive, impetus,* and *incentive.* All these words have significance for us. As educators we must recognize that what drives our students is not only to be *able* to read but to *want* to read. The research of Carole Ames and Jennifer Archer, published in the *Journal of Educational Psychology,* tells us that students who perceive reading as valuable and important and who have good reasons for reading will engage in reading more often and more meaningfully.[3] Providing a classroom culture that includes a goal-centered activity such as readers theatre gives students a reason to interact with books in a purposeful way. After all, they will eventually become part of the literature. "It's like a treasure hunt," exclaims Ginny, a sixth grader, "I love reading to find a story that we can turn into a script."

Julianne Turner and Scott Paris, researchers of children's motivation for literacy, explain that students want to see themselves as originators of plans and ideas, not as followers in a grand scheme they may not understand.[4] Readers theatre activities allow children to share in controlling their learning. With some guidance from the teacher, they make their own choices about the texts they want to dramatize. They are eager to find appropriate material and hence engage in reading many books, stories, poems, and plays to discover the literature they wish to put on stage. Being involved with literate projects, students learn that reading can be a joyful and useful experience. The sense of independence that is engendered in this way serves as motivation for students to read. It becomes obvious that creative activities, such as readers theatre, should no longer be reserved for special occasions.

Readers Theatre Promotes Critical Thinking: "Rev up the mental motor!"

Young people growing up in the twenty-first century need to sharpen their thinking skills more than ever before. Larry Johannessen and Elizabeth Kahn, specialists in English and communication skills, assert that teaching language arts must be designed to prepare students for the unique demands of life and work in the technological age. To do this, they add, teaching should be focused on problem solving and inquiry.[5] When students are confronted with a situation that is important to them and that demands a decision, they will struggle to unearth a solution and determine a course of action. This kind of experience serves as a practice round for the higher order thinking required in adulthood.

How can teachers meet the challenge of preparing students to think? One method is to provide pupils with small-group collaboration activities, the goals of which depend on student decision making. This assumption is built into the planning of a successful readers theatre program. Involved students must make informed decisions all along the way. Which story or poem or play works best as a dramatized reading? How should such material be adapted? Who will read what part? How must the script be staged and rehearsed? What needs to be done for the presentation? A myriad of questions arise during the preparation stages of the activity. The anticipation of a performance for an audience is an unrivaled force that maintains motivation for thinking. The show must go on!

Readers Theatre Encourages Writing: "Click on that word processor!"

Let's face it, most children do not like to write. This negative attitude about writing generally stems from a fear of being judged or graded. "I have good ideas," says Adam, a pupil in the fifth grade, "but I'm afraid to write them 'cause the teacher will think I'm dumb." What a pity to squelch the free and imaginative spirit of a young student! The implication for educators is clear: less *telling* and more *doing*. We must give our children many opportunities to use their creative skills in a setting that is not judgmental.

Loretta Stewart, a sixth-grade language arts teacher and a co-director of the Central Virginia Writing project, describes how readers theatre helps to teach writing in the classroom. She explains the benefits of having students examine well-written pieces of literature: "I think of it as having them *crawl* around in the text, and I find success in using good literature as models for student writing."[6] She adds that students' close attention to the conventions of dialogue required in readers theatre carry over to their own writing.[7] Children are inspired to add and recreate lines in a story. Often they must provide introductory and transitional details as they adapt literature into dramatic form. Sometimes whole blocks of original material written by the students appear in the final script. One can only imagine the joy a child must feel seeing his or her work performed by fellow classmates.

Readers Theatre Improves Oral Skills: "Speak the speech I pray you . . ."

A word is dead
When it is said
Some say.

I say it just
Begins to live
That day.

—Emily Dickinson, 1872[8]

The benefits of a readers theatre project as it relates to oral skills are readily seen. Since this venture calls for only a suggestion of a story's action, readers must rely on their vocal abilities to portray a character. To obtain the desired response from an audience, students work to develop voice flexibility, good articulation, proper pronunciation, and projection. Teachers can take advantage of their enthusiasm by providing "warm up" speech exercises, which will add needed proficiency and confidence. (See Chapter 6 for appropriate exercises.)

Reading aloud has other advantages. Children who have difficulty when they read silently often find material easier to understand when they read it aloud or when they hear it read to them. By participating in the program or by listening to it, students make close contact with the text and can see more easily how a story builds to its climax and how the characters relate to one another.

At the heart of readers theatre is the performance itself. Here is a rich and vital occasion when even the most reluctant speakers willingly perform in front of an audience. Perhaps it is the taking on of another's voice, becoming another person, that promotes the courage to perform. But whatever inspirational muse is at play, there is nothing that has more appeal than "show biz."

Readers Theatre Creates Good Listeners: "Hear ye! Hear ye!"

Readers theatre is incomplete without an audience. The players speak to be heard, and audience members listen to respond. This is not careless listening, no "tune in" and "tune out" kind of listening such as commercial television produces. This audience is involved. They are *living* the literature along with the players. Coger and White maintain that hearing well-written stories extends the listener's capacity to imagine and stimulates concentrated listening.[9] As a result something unexpected happens. Often listeners who hear dramatized material are inspired to seek out the selections for recreational reading on their own.[10] As Jim Trelease states in *The Read Aloud Handbook*: "The listening vocabulary is the reservoir of words that feeds the reading vocabulary pool."[11] He concludes that listening to other readers stimulates growth and understanding of language patterns.[12]

As a follow-up activity, students may lead discussions and share personal interpretations of the events and characters as they were presented in the program. They can also be asked to write down their reactions to what they saw and heard.

Readers Theatre Advances Personal and Social Growth: "Let's get together!"

A very important dimension of instruction, according to Johannessen and Kahn, "is the use of small-group collaboration to promote high levels of student-to-student interaction."[13] They add that such collaborative efforts help students gain a better understanding of other viewpoints, which enables them to revise and refine their thinking. This provides *scaffolding* for children who will ultimately become proficient at tackling tasks on their own.[14]

Readers theatre provides many occasions for students to interact socially with others. The entire activity is a group effort around a shared goal. They will discuss their choices about selection of texts, adaptations, staging, and performing. This is teamwork personified! The children understand that they need each other if the program is to succeed. They see themselves as vital to that accomplishment. This perspective gives each person in the group a sense of pride and self-worth.

Readers Theatre Rewards Educators: "Put the show on the road!"

"What shall I do for an assembly program?" Teachers grapple with this frustrating question every term. With limited time it is not always possible to find something new, something different.

Ready-made plays are often not suitable or do not have enough parts for the entire class. Readers theatre provides an unusual and creative approach to producing the class play and at the same time illuminates some of the finest examples of children's literature. The technique allows every member of the class to participate, no matter the range of abilities. In a relatively short time, with a minimum of effort and a maximum of student enthusiasm, a full-blown production is ready for an assembly or the library.

Standards for the English Language Arts: Sponsored by NCTE and IRA

The vision guiding the NCTE/IRA standards is that all students must have the opportunities and resources to develop the language skills they need to pursue life's goals and to participate fully as informed, productive members of society. These standards assume that literacy growth begins before children enter school as they experience and experiment with literacy activities: reading and writing and associating spoken words with their graphic representations. Recognizing this fact, these standards encourage the development of curriculum and instruction that make productive use of the emerging literacy abilities that children bring to school. Furthermore, the standards provide ample room for the innovation and creativity essential to teaching and learning. They are not prescriptions for particular curricula or instruction. Although we present these standards as a list, we want to emphasize that they are not distinct and separable; they are, in fact, interrelated and should be considered as a whole.

1.   Students read a wide range of print and nonprint texts to build an understanding of texts, of themselves, and of the cultures of the United States and the world; to acquire new information; to respond to the needs and demands of society and the workplace; and for personal fulfillment. Among these texts are fiction and nonfiction, classic and contemporary works.

2. Students read a wide range of literature from many periods in many genres to build an understanding of the many dimensions (e.g., philosophical, ethical, aesthetic) of human experience.

3. Students apply a wide range of strategies to comprehend, interpret, evaluate, and appreciate texts. They draw on their prior experience, their interactions with other readers and writers, their knowledge of word meaning and of other texts, their word identification strategies, and their understanding of the textual features (e.g., sound-letter correspondence, sentence structure, context, graphics).

4. Students adjust their use of spoken, written, and visual language (e.g., conventions, style, vocabulary) to communicate effectively with a variety of audiences and for different purposes.

5. Students employ a wide range of strategies as they write and use different writing process elements appropriately to communicate with different audiences for a variety of purposes.

6. Students apply knowledge of language structure, language conventions (e.g., spelling and punctuation), media techniques, figurative language, and genre to create, critique, and discuss print and nonprint texts.

7. Students conduct research on issues and interests by generating ideas and questions and by posing problems. They gather, evaluate, and synthesize data from a variety of sources (e.g., print and nonprint texts, artifacts, people) to communicate their discoveries in ways that suit their purpose and audience.

8. Students use a variety of technological and information resources (e.g., libraries, databases, computer networks, video) to gather and synthesize information and to create and communicate knowledge

9. Students develop an understanding of and respect for diversity in language use, patterns, and dialects across cultures, ethnic groups, geographic regions, and social roles.

10. Students whose first language is not English make use of their first language to develop competency in the English language arts and to develop understanding of content across the curriculum.

11. Students participate as knowledgeable, reflective, creative, and critical members of a variety of literacy communities.

12. Students use spoken, written, and visual language to accomplish their own purposes (e.g., for learning, enjoyment, persuasion, and the exchange of information).[15]

Notes

1. Leslie Irene Coger and Melvin R. White, *Readers Theatre Handbook*, 3rd ed. rev. (Glenview, IL: Scott Foresman, 1982), 11.

2. A list of standards published by the NCTE/IRA can be found at the end of this chapter.

3. Carole Ames and Jennifer Archer, "Achievement Goals in the Classroom: Students' Learning Strategies and Motivation Processes," *Journal of Educational Psychology* 80, no. 3 (1988): 264–265.

4. Julianne C. Turner and Scott G. Paris, "How Literacy Tasks Influence Children's Motivation for Literacy," *The Reading Teacher* 40 (1995): 662–675.

5. Larry R. Johannessen and Elizabeth A. Kahn, "Teaching English Language Arts for a Technological Age," *The Clearing House* 70, no.6 (1997): 305.

6. Loretta Steward, "Readers Theatre and the Writing Workshop: Using Children's Literature to Prompt Student Writing," *The Reading Teacher* 51, no. 2 (1999): 174.

7. Ibid., 175.

8. *The Complete Works of Emily Dickinson,* ed. Thomas H. Johnson (Boston: Little, Brown, 1957), 534.

9. Coger and White, *Readers Theatre Handbook,* 169–170.

10. Shirlee Sloyer, "Show on the Road: Oral Performers as Reading Motivators," *Oral English* 1, no. 1 (1972): 13–15.

11. Jim Trelease, *The Read Aloud Handbook,* 4th ed. (New York: Penguin Books, 1995), 11.

12. Ibid., 26.

13. Johannessen and Kahn, "Teaching English Language Arts," 306.

14. Ibid., 307.

15. *Standards for the English Language Arts* (Urbana, IL.: National Council of Teachers of English and the International Reading Association, 1996), 3.

Chapter 2

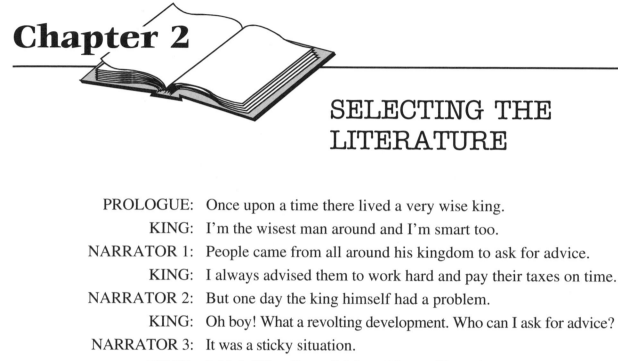

SELECTING THE LITERATURE

PROLOGUE:	Once upon a time there lived a very wise king.
KING:	I'm the wisest man around and I'm smart too.
NARRATOR 1:	People came from all around his kingdom to ask for advice.
KING:	I always advised them to work hard and pay their taxes on time.
NARRATOR 2:	But one day the king himself had a problem.
KING:	Oh boy! What a revolting development. Who can I ask for advice?
NARRATOR 3:	It was a sticky situation.
KING:	I think I'll poll my Cabinet. They will surely come up with a final answer.
NARRATOR 4:	So the king called his Cabinet together to tell them about his dilemma.

(Readers theatre continues . . .)

Where to Look for Material

There are no boundaries when it comes to selecting literature to adapt for readers theatre. Novels, short stories, poems, letters, and plays can all be used. The goal is to find material that interests the students who perform it and the audience who come to see it. This may seem a daunting task. But by breaking down the material into categories—picture storybooks, fairy tales and folk tales, fables, realistic stories, fantasy and science fiction, poetry, and plays—the assignment becomes easier to carry out.

In the library to select the literature.

Picture Storybooks

Gaily illustrated picture books often contain material for readers theatre. Many are sophisticated enough to be performed *by* and *for* any age group. Best of all, students can easily engage in the selection process.

Storybooks make good scripts because they are written to be read aloud to children. The words and phrases follow the rhythmic pattern of conversation. Books designed for beginning readers also work well. When an author writes within the limits of an easy-to-read storybook, he or she makes the sentences short, the plot taut, and the characters lifelike. A dose of humor not found in longer books is often found in these. Children need not grapple with difficult vocabulary before having the pleasure of adapting and performing a script.

Leo Lionni's beautiful storybook, *It's Mine!,* tells of three frogs, Milton, Rupert, and Lydia, who quarreled and quibbled from dawn to dusk:

> "Stay out of the pond!" yelled Milton. "The water is mine."
> "Get off the island!" shouted Rupert. "The earth is mine."
> "The air is mine!" screamed Lydia as she leaped to catch a butterfly.[1]

On and on the squabbling goes until a storm and a large toad show the frogs the value and the benefits of sharing. In a simple yet prophetic tale, Leo Lionni makes it possible for us to learn that we must get along in this world or suffer the consequences. By the same author and equally appealing, *Fish Is Fish* makes a good companion piece.

In *The True Story of the 3 Little Pigs!* Jon Scieszka writes about what really happened to the Three Little Pigs as told by the only person who knows the true story—the wolf himself:

> I'm the wolf. Alexander T. Wolf.
> You can call me Al.
> I don't know how this whole Big Bad Wolf thing got started, but it's all wrong.[2]

Al, the wolf, explains how it happened that he got a bad rap. He was framed! So Mr. Alexander T. Wolf ends up in the big house, the "pig penn."

For more fun, add to the script Mr. Scieszka's other droll tale, *The Frog Prince, Continued,* about what happened to the Princess *after* she kissed the frog who turned into a prince. Did they live happily ever after?

> Well, let's just say they lived sort of happily for a long time.
> Okay, so they weren't so happy. In fact they were miserable.
> "Stop sticking your tongue out like that," nagged the Princess.
> "How come you never want to go down to the pond anymore?" whined the
>   prince.
> The Prince and Princess were so unhappy. They didn't know what to do.[3]

The Princess cannot tolerate the Prince's frog-like habits. The Prince hates hearing the Princess nag all the time. He decides to find a witch who will change him back into a frog. Of course, they finally find love and happiness and *do* live happily ever after—as frogs.

Many of Scieszka's books, as a group, including *The Stinky Cheese Man and Other Fairly Stupid Tales, Knights of the Kitchen Table, The Not-So-Jolly Roger,* and *Squids Will Be Squids,* will make a delightful readers theatre production. Especially relevant and fun to adapt into a script is *Math Curse,* in which Scieszka's central character sees her entire life as a math problem:

> I wake up at 7:15. It takes me 10 minutes to get dressed, 15 minutes to eat my breakfast, and 1 minute to brush my teeth.
> SUDDENLY, IT'S A PROBLEM:
> 1. If my bus leaves at 8:00, will I make it on time?
> 2. How many minutes in 1 hour?
> 3. How many teeth in 1 mouth?[4]

The girl in the story is plagued with questions like this throughout her day. And just when she thinks she has broken the curse, her science teacher explains that everything in life can be seen as a science experiment. Obviously a new curse is visited upon her. This is a great place to begin a creative writing project resulting in an original readers theatre script about how our everyday lives are involved with science.

Picture Books for Beginning Readers

For beginning readers or others struggling with reading problems, there are many easy storybooks suitable for adaptation. Particularly clever are the Marjorie Weinman Sharmat stories about Nate the Great, the Henry and Mudge series by Cynthia Rylant, and the Encyclopedia Brown tales by Donald J. Sobol. Most of these books contain large blocks of dialogue that offer a rewarding script-writing and reading experience, and all can be effortlessly dramatized by even the youngest reader.

Trisha is in fifth grade, and she still cannot read. Kids call her "dummy" and "toad." This is the problem presented in Patricia Polacco's *Thank You Mr. Falker.* But then the tide turns when a new teacher, a real character, comes into Trisha's life. "You're going to read—I promise you that," says Mr. Falker. Trisha does learn, and the audience is surprised to learn that this story is autobiographical. The author, Patricia Polacco, ultimately confesses that she is the little girl portrayed in the book.

Picture Books for Older Students

Older students enjoy working on a theme. Eve Bunting, in *Smoky Night,* explores race relations as she tells of the Los Angeles riots and the children who lived through them. Concerns about who we are and how we are shaped by the perceptions of others are well handled by Allen Say in *Stranger in the Mirror.* A poignant story about a Jewish girl, *Raisel's Riddle* by Erica Silverman, includes elements of courage and romance. A sensitive story of Mary Antin's difficult life in Russia and her eventual immigration to Boston is told in lyrical fashion by Rosemary Wells in *Streets of Gold.* Extending the theme of immigration from the perils of the Cossacks in Russia is Elvira Woodruff's *The Memory Coat.* This charming storybook tells about Rachel and Grisha's escape to the United States and of their grandmother, who wants to make a good impression at Ellis Island. Facts about immigration and Ellis Island are included at the close of the book.

Humorous Picture Books

For humor, guide students to *The King's Trousers* by Robert Kraus. The king's disgruntled subjects want to remove him from office because, of all things, he puts his trousers on one leg at a time just as they do. But in the end the villagers are foiled when the king announces that he doesn't wear trousers since he wears royal robes. The villain, Slammo McJock, and his motley crew see that they cannot win and leave, deflated and defeated.

Another king, in William Wise's *Perfect Pancakes, If You Please,* loves pancakes so much that he promises his daughter's hand in marriage to the man who can make the perfect pancake. Maximilian, the Evil Inventor, shows up with a recipe for winning the contest. Princess Elizabeth is devastated. But in the end Roderick, the hero, foils Maximilian's plans and wins the princess.

A unique storybook in the "witty" category is *The Fortune-Tellers* by Lloyd Alexander. The story, set in the country of Cameroon, concerns a young carpenter who sets off to see a fortune teller and learn about his future:

> "My first prediction is this," the fortune-teller said before the carpenter could begin. "You're going to pay me a nice fee. But that's a mere trifle to someone destined for wealth."
>
> "Do you see me rich then?" exclaimed the carpenter, gladly handing over the coins the fortune-teller demanded.
>
> "Rich you will surely be," answered the fortune-teller, settling his magic cap on his head and gazing into the crystal ball on the table.
>
> "On one condition: that you can earn large sums of money."[5]

Strangely enough, the promising predictions come true and the West African carpenter becomes wealthy and famous.

It Happened in Chelm, a story about the legendary town of fools, is retold by Florence B. Freedman. In this story, the inhabitants of a mythical mid-European town seek advice from seven wise men about what to do when evil bandits come to rob their shops. They solve their problems in fanciful ways. These tall tales never fail to evoke laughter from even the most sophisticated listener, perhaps, says the author, "because there is a little bit of Chelm in each of us."

"How To" Books

"How to" picture books can be adapted with exciting results. Take, for example, books on story writing. *The Young Author's Do-It-Yourself Book* by Donna Guthrie, Nancy Bentley, and Katy Keck Arnstein; *Write Your Own Story* by Vivian Dubrovin; and *Thinking Like a Writer* by Lou Willett Stanek, are not only workable for readers theatre but are relevant for writing exercises as well. Culled from these step-by-step illustrated manuals, a script can be developed in which students play the different facets involved in writing. For instance, one could represent "ideas," another "character creations," still another "plot," and finally, "editing and publishing."

Books on how to write letters can be used also. See *Putting It in Writing* by Steve Otfinosksi, *How to Write a Letter* by Florence D. Mischel, and *Messages in the Mailbox* by Loreen Leedy. Again, players may take on the different parts of the letter.

I am the heading.
789 Fantasy Street
New York, NY 11120
September 2002

I am the salutation.
Dear Mrs. Johnson,

I am the body.
    I was thrilled to receive the book I inquired about, *How to Write Poetry.* I didn't expect that you would remember me, much less send the book. I have always been interested in writing poetry and I know that reading this book will help me. Perhaps one day I will be published and it will be my pleasure to send you *my* book. Thanks again.

I am the complimentary close.
Sincerely yours,
I am the signature.
Dina Resmun

I am the postscript.
P. S. If you send me your e-mail address we can correspond online too. Mine is resmun3@aol.com.

Letter writing is becoming a lost art thanks to the computer, but stressing the importance of learning to write a good letter as a means of in-depth communication can be accomplished painlessly in a readers theatre program. Follow the example with a dramatization of the occasions that require a letter. One player hears of a friend's illness, another plans a party, a third is away at camp, while a fourth applies for a job. Each situation is augmented by the reading of an appropriate letter. Original correspondence can come from a class assignment.

Also in the information-book category is Harvey Weiss's *How to Be a Hero.* Mr. Weiss provides us with a series of comic situations about the most heroic ways to solve problems. These incidents are presented in the realm of fantasy, but the solutions make real sense. A class divided into groups, each presenting one segment of the book, will enjoy playing characters such as mean gorillas who hijack a dirigible on the way to a zoo in Budapest.

How to Take Your Grandmother to the Museum by Lois Wyse and Molly Rose Goldman presents an unusual way to learn about the contents of the Museum of Natural History in New York. A grandmother and granddaughter inspect the bones of *Apatosaurus* (older even than grandma's), the mouth of *Anatotitian,* and the twenty-three-foot wingspan of *Pteranodon.* The Ice Age exhibit gives them the shivers and the African Hall feels like a safari. This book not only gives students interesting facts about the history of the world but also explores that very special relationship between grandparent and grandchild. It would make a unique readers theatre presentation.

Fairy Tales and Folk Tales

> In olden times when wishing still helped one there lived a king whose daughters were all beautiful, but the youngest was so beautiful that the sun itself, which has seen so much, was astonished whenever it shone in her face.[6]

Set a young student reading on a classroom stage and the king's daughter stands before us. The language of the fairy tale begins to do its work. Imagination soars! Everyday expectations are suspended in favor of the make believe. The spell is cast!

May Hill Arbuthnot tells us that fairy tales "are a legacy from anonymous artists of the past, the old wives and grannies as well as the professional storytellers. They were first created orally and passed on by word of mouth for generations before the printing press caught up with them."[7] Indeed, fairy tales were the entertainment of their times. They sustained interest then and survive to this day for the same reasons: A fairy tale starts swiftly, moves directly through its magical episodes, and ends with a gratifying finale. Universal themes—love, courage, goodness, wickedness—around which the story is built develop through the deeds of the characters, not through idle talk.

A fairy tale satisfies a child's need to fantasize. The dramatization gives shape to these fantasies. A boy dreams of overcoming a powerful enemy; he becomes the valiant little tailor outmaneuvering two giants. A girl imagines herself with magical powers; she is transformed into the miller's daughter spinning straw into gold for the king's heart. The young readers create a fabulous world and allow the spectators to inhabit it.

A well-liked tale is "The Fisherman and His Wife" by the Brothers Grimm. Students will find this one easy to prepare for presentation. The beginning of the story is assigned to a narrator, who sets the scene, introduces the characters, and describes the first action:

> *Narrator*: There was once a fisherman, who lived with his wife in a miserable hovel close to the sea. He went to fish every day, and he fished and fished. One day, as he was sitting looking deep down into the shining water, he felt something on his line. When he hauled it up there was a big flounder on the end of his line.

Three characters, the obedient fisherman, his greedy wife Isabel, and an enchanted flounder, advance the plot:

> *Flounder*: Listen, fisherman, I beg you not to kill me; I am no common flounder, I am an enchanted prince!
> *Fisherman*: Ho! Ho! You need not make so many words about it. I am quite ready to put back a flounder that can talk.
> *Wife*: Husband, have you caught nothing today?

The wife learns about the enchanted flounder and persuades her husband to go back to the sea and wish for better circumstances. This he does. Joining the others, the narrator supplies transitions:

> *Narrator*: The man went home and found his wife no longer in the old hut, but sitting on a bench in front of a pretty little cottage.

The plot speeds along. Isabel will not be satisfied, not with a cottage nor a great stone castle. She wants to be King, Emperor, Pope. The end comes with no more fanfare than the beginning:

> *Flounder*: Now what does she want?
> *Fisherman*: Alas, she wants to be Lord of the Universe.
> *Flounder*: You have asked too much. Now she must go back to her old hovel.
> *Narrator*: So there they are to this very day.[8]

There is magic here, but not without logic. Each event follows in understandable sequence. The plot unfolds through plain spoken dialogue and direct narrative passages. Engrossed in this fantasy demonstrating the foolishness of greed, student adapters will have a good time rewriting and reading "The Fisherman and His Wife" for the readers theatre stage.

Other exciting and suitable tales from the Brothers Grimm are "The Frog Prince," "The Brave Little Tailor," "The Four Musicians," "Clever Elsie," "Rumpelstiltskin," and "The Goose Girl." All of these and more are available in *Tales from Grimm* and *More Tales from Grimm,* translated by Wanda Gag, and *Grimm's Household Tales,* translated by Margaret Hunt. Hans Christian Andersen's best stories are "The Emperor's New Clothes," "The Ugly Duckling," and "The Princess and the Pea." These can be found in *Hans Christian Andersen: The Complete Fairy Tales and Stories,* translated from the Danish by Erik Christian Haugaard, and *Time for Fairy Tales Old and New,* compiled by May Hill Arbuthnot. All of these old, classic fairy tales and fables are in the public domain and can be used without royalty fees.

Some popular folk stories workable for readers theatre have been singled out and updated in picture books. *Why the Sea Is Salt* is a retelling of a Norwegian folk tale in which Matilda and her family will have a hungry Christmas unless her rich uncle helps out. But he is much too stingy to deliver even a crumb. However, Matilda, because of her kindness to a stranger, is rewarded with a magic churn, which gives her anything she wants. This does not sit well with the greedy uncle, and he manages to steal the churn. He gloats:

> "I will make sure that I fill my houses and cellars and barns with gold—yes, and with rubies, too. This time the churn will make me the richest man in the world."[9]

The plot becomes intriguing when the uncle, on board ship, wishes for a little more table salt. The churn does its work and delivers the salt. But because the uncle does not know how to stop the magic churn, it continues to deliver salt until the sea is full of it, and his ship sinks to the very bottom of the ocean. A tale with numbers of characters, exciting dialogue, and a dramatic plot, this story is perfect for readers theatre.

Over 100 years ago, Oscar Wilde wrote nine fairy tales for his sons. Stories such as "The Remarkable Rocket," "The Happy Prince," and "The Selfish Giant" are filled with passion, friendship, suffering, and joy. They span the range of human emotions, which will engage children of all ages. Oscar Wilde's contribution to English literature is legion. Not so well known is his writing for young people. This collection, *The Fairy Tales of Oscar Wilde,* presents a wonderful opportunity to dramatize his work and introduce the author via readers theatre.

International Folk Stories

For an international program, include folk tales from around the world. *Mysterious Tales of Japan* by Rafe Martin is a collection of Japanese stories that are spiritual and evocative; ghostly and serene; tender, gentle, and mysterious. Also from Japan, a haunting, ancient folk tale entitled *The Stonecutter,* adapted by Gerald McDermott, creates an unusual dramatization. Six or seven students participate in the reading by representing the central character, Tasaku, as he changes from a lowly stonecutter into a wealthy prince, a burning sun, a treacherous storm cloud, and a mighty mountain. The spirit who lives in the mountains is yet another character who comes to life as a mysterious disembodied voice (reading into a megaphone, perhaps), granting Tasaku's every foolish longing.

From China come two stories: *Ten Suns,* retold by Eric A. Kimmel, about ten sons of Di Jun who almost burn up the earth, and *The Seven Chinese Brothers,* by Margaret Mahy, about seven brothers who elude execution by virtue of their individual characteristics. An Armenian tale, *A Weave of Words,* retold by Robert D. San Souci, is the story of a lazy prince who learns to read, write, and weave to win his love. *East O' the Sun and West O' the Moon,* a Norwegian story, translated by Sir George Webbe Dasent, is an exciting and romantic tale about a poor man who is promised riches by a white bear in exchange for his most beautiful daughter. A Russian story by Patricia Polacco, *Luba and the Wren,* centers around a young girl who saves a bird. For this she can ask for anything she wants. The girl asks for nothing, but her greedy parents will not rest until they get everything they long for. Finally, *Wisdom Tales from Around the World* by Heather Forest contains fifty stories from such diverse traditions as Sufi, Zen, Christian, Jewish, Buddhist, and Native American.

Fables

Fables are compact stories that illustrate one aspect of human behavior and provide a lesson. These tales unfold simply in a way children understand. Characters, usually animals with human qualities, are taught a lesson because of their selfishness, greed, or stupidity. A frog, trying to be as big as an ox, blows himself up until he bursts. A foolish lamb follows a wolf in sheep's clothing. After playing a trick on a crow, a fox is repaid with dinner served in a long-necked jar with a narrow mouth. Each brief story ends with an appropriate moral: "Self-conceit may lead to self-destruction," "Appearances are deceptive," "One bad turn deserves another."

Because fables are written in only two or three paragraphs, they are quickly adapted in one class session. Working together, the class can create an entire script. Students and teachers change some of the narrative passages into dialogue. New characters are invented. Lines are parceled out. Snatches of action and vocal sound effects are suggested. The finished script may look like the following.

The Fox and the Cat

Narrator:	A fox was boasting to a Cat of its clever devices for escaping its enemies.
Cat:	I have only one, but I generally manage with that.
Narrator:	Just at that moment they heard the cry of a pack of hounds coming towards them.
Hounds:	oo-oo-oo-oo
Narrator:	The Cat immediately scampered up a tree and hid himself in the boughs.
Cat:	This is my plan. What are you going to do?
Narrator:	The Fox thought first of one way, then the other.
Fox: (Dashing about.)	Well, maybe I could run under a bush, or perhaps dive down a hole, or more likely dash down the path.
Narrator:	While the fox was debating the hounds came nearer and nearer.
Hounds:	oo-oo-oo-oo-OO-OO-OO

> *Narrator*: At last the Fox, in his confusion, was caught up by the hounds and soon killed by the huntsman. The cat looked on.
>
> *Cat*: BETTER ONE SAFE WAY THAN A HUNDRED ON WHICH YOU CANNOT DEPEND.

With open-classroom practice, students will soon be able to work on their own, or in groups, to script longer and more complex stories.

Collecting five or six fables for a readers theatre presentation may be enough to involve all the children in a class. Fables can also be added to a compiled script with other kinds of literature—poems, play excerpts, riddles—for a diversified finished product. In keeping with a theme of brotherhood, for instance, a poignant fable to include is Aesop's "The Lion and the Mouse." In this tale a little mouse who is spared by a lion repays him by gnawing through ropes to free the huge beast from hunters. Moral: "Little friends may prove great friends."

Another story illustrating the same theme is "The Bundle of Sticks." Here a dying man asks his sons to break a bundle of sticks. When they are unable to do so, he has the bundle untied and asks the sons to break each stick separately. This they are able to do. Moral: "Union gives strength."

Aesop, according to some sources, may never have existed at all. He may be as much of a legend as the stories attributed to him. Aesop most likely is a collective name, a device for bringing together some of the earliest fables into one volume.[10] There are many editions of these popular fables. Over 100 are included in *The Fables of Aesop,* retold by Frances Barnes-Murphy. Particularly interesting is *Birds of a Feather and Other Aesop's Fables,* retold in verse by singer-songwriter Tom Paxton. In this volume Paxton puts together ten wise and witty fables waiting to be dramatized.

Using Aesop as his inspiration, La Fontaine, a brilliant seventeenth-century French classicist, turned many of the fables into verse. Both the French and English translations can be found in *The Complete Fables of Jean de la Fontaine,* edited and translated by Norman B. Spector. The book's introduction contains an appropriate statement by La Fontaine:

> The fables are not limited to moral behavior; they provide other kinds of enlightenment. The properties of animals and their various characteristics are presented in them. Consequently ours are too, since we're the epitome of good and evil among irrational creatures.[11]

Fables already scripted for readers theatre can be found in Suzanne I. Barchers's *Fifty Fabulous Fables: Beginning Readers Theatre.* Also, twenty original fables about an array of animal characters from crocodile to ostrich are beautifully written and illustrated by Arnold Lobel in *Fables.*

Although James Thurber's *Fables for Our Time* was written for adults, young people enjoy these zany tales because of the surprise endings to familiar situations. Three of the best are "The Moth and the Star," "The Unicorn in the Garden," and "The Little Girl and the Wolf." In the latter, an updated Red Riding Hood shoots the wolf because she decides he really does not look like her grandmother, even in a nightgown. Moral: "It is not so easy to fool little girls nowadays, as it used to be."[12]

Realistic Stories

Readers theatre becomes a unique event when it dramatizes life as it really is. Students, struggling with the problems of school and family life, are drawn into a story portraying characters with similar difficulties. They are exposed to the conflicts and concerns of others. Captivated by the personal nature of realistic stories, young people empathize with the oral reading, discovering more about life and themselves.

For realistic fiction to succeed as dramatization, it must be a candid exploration of events that are meaningful to children. Andrew Clements's *The Janitor's Boy* fills this requirement by reflecting on the real problems that beset kids in school. When Jack enters middle school, he and his friends learn that Jack's father is the janitor there, and the teasing begins. Clements makes his characters come alive. Not only will young audiences begin to think about their own parents and the jobs they do, but they will come to understand that many good folks are behind the scenes doing necessary work. This book is particularly appropriate when developing a theme centering on occupations and professions. Also look into the same author's *The Jacket,* which confronts racial discrimination head on. With their many realistic characters and dramatic sequences, these books are perfect for readers theatre.

The award-winning author Karen Hesse has written a first-person story, *Just Juice,* narrated by a nine-year-old girl who does not go to school often because kids are mean to her. The result is that she cannot read:

 I wish I could read the letter to Pa. That would fix everything. But I can't. I am plain stupid when it comes to reading. Everybody else gets it. But reading is pure torture for me.[13]

The letter that Juice speaks about claims that the town has sold their house out from under them because taxes were not paid. The house is saved, but the heroine decides to return to school to help the family survive.

Stories for Older Students

For older students, also by Karen Hesse is *Out of the Dust,* winner of the Newbery Medal. Fifteen-year-old Billie Jo describes her life on the family's wheat farm in Oklahoma. An accident, caused by her father, killed her mother. She cannot forgive him for this, and these are the years when she needs her mother the most. Yet she must come to terms with what happened and with all the hardships she encounters on the way to growing up. The book is written in a series of poems that would make a richly textured script for readers theatre. Several students can be assigned the role of Billie Jo. Each will read one or more selections. Dividing up a script in this fashion, where more than one person plays the same character, allows for greater participation and adds an interesting component to the composition.

In the same vein, also by Karen Hesse is *Letters from Rifka.* This book presents a history lesson as we learn about the Russians who sought to drive the Jews from the country by making their lives wretched. The story chronicles the day-to-day trials and horrors Rifka meets as she makes her way from the Ukraine to the United States. The letters make this novel easy to adapt for a dramatic presentation.

Louis Sacher's *Holes,* features a male voice, Stanley Yelnats. He is sent to Camp Green Lake Juvenile Correctional Facility for a crime he did not commit. Here the inmates dig holes in the Texas desert. This book contains wicked villainy, but there is no shortage of comic elements. Such a mix makes it a suitable selection for readers theatre. Parts of this hard-hitting, realistic novel can be adapted for a narrator who relates the story around segments of exciting dialogue.

Jacob Have I Loved, by Katherine Patterson, is a book about twin sisters. The title, based on the biblical phrase, "Jacob have I loved, but Esau have I hated . . ." reveals at the outset that this is a story of Louise who, like Esau, felt herself deprived because of her twin. In her first-person voice, Louise tells how she was robbed of all the things she hoped for: school, friends, family, and love. Before the story ends, however, we know she has found her own identity.

School Stories

For good-natured fun go to the Wayside School, where kids and teachers provide sequence after sequence of wacky antics waiting to be dramatized. Louis Sacher, in *Sideways Stories from Wayside School, Wayside School Gets a Little Stranger,* and *Wayside School Is Falling Down,* gives us humor along with familiar situations that children sometimes find themselves in (or would like to). There are twenty-six kids in Mrs. Jewl's class, all of whom can come to life on a classroom stage.

A fast-paced, amusing book about school is *Starting School with an Enemy* by Elisa Carbone. After a family move, Sarah has to start school hardly knowing anybody. She meets Christina Perez, but she already has a best friend. And on top of this Sarah has a run-in with a boy named Eric Bardo, who becomes her enemy. Surviving in a new community is not easy, but the author creates outrageously funny lines along the way. Adapting this book, or several of its chapters, will provide joy and laughter for all audiences.

Divorce is a sensitive subject that concerns many boys and girls these days. *The Divorce Express* by Paula Danziger, Beverly Cleary's *Dear Mr. Henshaw,* and *The Comeback Challenge* by Matt Christopher treat divorce in an empathetic manner that helps children understand the issue and overcome the inherent obstacles. *The Top-Secret Journal of Fiona Claire Jardin* is especially appropriate for oral reading; it tells a story in the form of journal entries:

> Sunday, February 16
> I never really knew about Joint Custody until last year. It means that if you're a kid whose parents are Divorced, both your mom and dad take care of you.[14]

A story that can take place in any inner city and about any ethnic group is *Make Lemonade* by Virginia Euwer Wolff. The novel develops the dramatic pace necessary for a readers theatre presentation. The richly textured characters provide emotional experiences with which teenagers identify. Verna LaVaughn is a fourteen-year-old who needs money to help her mother and to pay for her college education. The account of the job she takes and how she changes is both moving and engrossing. "When life gives you lemons, you make lemonade," is the familiar aphorism behind the title of this poetic book. The girls who populate the text make the best of the "lemons" they were given.

Jerry Spinelli's *Maniac Magee* is a favorite of kids everywhere. Jeffrey Lionel Magee is a grungy twelve-year-old who can run fast, hit a home-run bunt, score forty-nine touchdowns, and accomplish other miraculous feats. And, "while nobody knows who said it first," Jeffrey had a new name:

> "Kid's gotta be a maniac."
> And somebody else must have said: "Yeah, reg'lar maniac."
> And somebody else: "Yeah."
> And that was it. . . . When they wanted to talk about the new kid, that's what they called him: Maniac.[15]

It is not difficult to see what a delightful and fun-filled script this book, or selected chapters, would make.

Basal readers, textbooks, and even newspapers can supply material for readers theatre. For example, *Mr. Lincoln's Whiskers* by Karen Winnick is a true account of Grace Bedell, who wrote a letter to Abraham Lincoln suggesting he grow whiskers. To her surprise he answered her letter and grew the beard. This selection, coupled with more material about Lincoln or other U.S. presidents, would create an interesting compiled script for presentation. Similarly, social studies texts containing accounts of historical personalities and adventures can provide opportunities for rewriting and adapting material to be used in a production.

Fantasy and Science Fiction

Children (and adults, too) of all ages and stages long to escape to the world of daydreams and fantasies. Filled with marvels and unfamiliar terrors, fantasy stories power the mind to form images for a readers theatre that can hardly be duplicated by any other genre. Long ago J. R. R. Tolkien's *The Hobbit,* the enchanting prelude to *The Lord of the Rings,* became a classic, and it is still read and enjoyed by millions. Consider how a segment of this appealing thriller, as part of a full-blown fantasy script, would excite any audience. A narrator might begin by answering the question, "What is a hobbit?":

> I suppose hobbits need some description nowadays, since they have become rare and shy of the Big People, as they call us. They are (or were) a little people about half our height. . . . There is little or no magic about them, except the ordinary everyday sort which helps them to disappear quietly and quickly when large stupid folk like you and me come blundering along.[16]

A more recent, provocative novel that balances the values of freedom and security is *The Giver* by Lois Lowry. This Newbery Medal winner is written in simple language that lends itself to adaptation. Jonas, the protagonist, who lives in a perfect world, is singled out to receive special training from The Giver, who holds the power to remember all the emotions inherent in a not-so-perfect world, including the true pain and pleasure of life. Jonas does not know what his selection means and is afraid of what will become of him. The story is tightly plotted and the characters are believable. The excitement builds to a riveting climax: the flight for survival. This stirring book, or selected chapters from it, is ready for dramatization.

The popular Harry Potter books by J. K. Rowling provide a delightful romp through sequences of enchantment, suspense, and danger. Children will enjoy turning any one of Harry's exploits into a script while performing as their favorite characters. Other series include Bruce Coville's Aliens Adventures, Brian Jaques's Tales from Redwall, and Lynne Reid Banks's Indian in the Cupboard books.

More books in this category are *Mrs. Frisby and the Rats of Nimh* by Robert C. O'Brien, *Dragonsong* by Anne McCaffrey, *The Wringer* by Jerry Spinelli, and *The Bogart* by Susan Cooper. For original tales of suspense and the supernatural inspired by African-American history that range from the time of slavery to the civil rights era, see Patricia C. McKissack's *The Dark-Thirty.* Some of the aforementioned books and/or chapters, coupled with stories from the past, would make a memorable and unique presentation. Imagine it! The readers theatre presents "Fairy Tales and Fantasies."

Longer books can also be a source for a readers theatre production. Scripting the first few chapters of a novel introduces students to the story. Or a *Readers Digest* version can be developed to give children the basic plot. Developing scripts from long novels serves as an inducement for performers and listeners alike to seek out and read the entire book.

Poetry

If you are a dreamer, come in,
If you are a dreamer, a wisher, a liar,
A hope-er, a pray-er, a magic bean buyer . . .
If you're a pretender, come sit by my fire
For we have some flax-golden tales to spin.
Come in!
Come in![17]

This poem, "Invitation," begins Shel Silverstein's collection of poems, *Where the Sidewalk Ends.* This book and his later works, *A Light in the Attic* and *Falling Up,* provide a reservoir of out-of-the-ordinary verse for children. An entire program can be developed using Silverstein's imaginative verse. A poem such as "Messy Room," which follows, could be included in a program entitled "A Kid's Life." Here the main character reads the first line and the last four lines, while other segments are divided up among several other readers:

> *Whosever room this is should be ashamed!*
> *His underwear is hanging on the lamp.*
> *His raincoat is there in the overstuffed chair,*
> *And the chair is becoming quite mucky and damp.*
> *His workbook is wedged in the window,*
> *His sweater's been thrown on the floor.*
> *His scarf and one ski are beneath the TV,*
> *And his pants have been carelessly hung on the door.*
> *His books are all jammed in the closet,*
> *His vest has been left in the hall.*
> *A lizard named Ed is asleep in his bed,*
> *And his smelly old sock has been stuck to the wall.*
> *Whosever room this is should be ashamed!*
> *Donald or Robert or Willie or—*
> *Huh? You say it's mine? Oh dear,*
> *I knew it looked familiar!*[18]

Continuing the program, the instructor may wish to include the following mischievous poem, "Remote-A-Dad." For this poem, one student reads the first four lines, then, in quick succession, six readers take the next six lines. This is followed by the first student again reading lines eleven, twelve, and thirteen. Finally, the entire group shouts out the very last line of the poem:

> *It's just like a TV remote control,*
> *Except that it works on fathers.*
> *You push the thing that you want him to do*
> *And he does it—without any bother.*
> *You want him to dance? Push number five.*
> *You want him to sing? Push seven.*
> *You want him to raise your allowance a bit?*
> *You simply push eleven.*
> *You want him quiet? Just hit Mute.*
> *Fourteen will make him cough.*
> *You want him to stop picking on you?*
> *Yelling and telling you what not to do?*
> *And stop bossing you for an hour or two?*
> *Just push Power—Off.*[19]

For the same program Silverstein's delightful "No Grown-Ups," which follows, adds a familiar note for kids everywhere. This poem works very well as a choral reading. In unison, two students read two lines each until the next-to-the-last line. One reader, alone, takes the line, "Oh, now it's time to pay?" followed by the entire group reading the very last line together:

> *No grown-ups allowed.*
> *We're playin' a game,*
> *And we don't need*
> *"Be-carefuls" or "don'ts."*
> *No grown-ups allowed.*
> *We're formin' a club,*
> *And the secret oath*
> *Must not be shown.*
> *No grown-ups allowed.*
> *We're goin' out for pizza—*
> *No, no one but me and my crowd.*
> *So just stay away.*
> *Oh, now it's time to pay?*
> *Grown-ups allowed.*[20]

The following verse, "Hug O' War," provides a wonderful ending to the program, with everyone taking part:

> *I will not play at tug o' war.*
> *I'd rather play at hug o' war,*
> *Where everyone hugs*
> *Instead of tugs,*
> *Where everyone giggles*
> *And rolls on the rug,*
> *Where everyone kisses,*
> *And everyone grins,*
> *And everyone cuddles,*
> *And everyone wins.*[21]

Equally amusing and irresistible are Jack Prelutsky's poems in *The New Kids on the Block* and *Something Big Has Been Here.* Eve Merriam's *Chortles* contains highly imaginative wordplay poems, many of which have the rhythmic pattern, replete with puns, that children love. Four books of high school poems by Mel Glenn are *Class Dismissed, Class Dismissed II, Back to Class,* and *My Friend's Got This Problem, Mr. Candler.* All the poems in these volumes evoke a panoply of emotions that high school students experience at school, with friends, and at home. They are written in blank verse and present universal problems recognizable even by younger students: parents who don't understand, a little brother who's a pest, the realization that one is in love with a fellow classmate. Readers need not be poetry enthusiasts to find meaning in these poignant poems.

Spin a Soft Black Song by Nikki Giovanni includes a variety of poems for and about black children. "Basketball" fits nicely into a sports theme:

when spanky goes
to the playground all the big boys say
hey big time—what's happenin"
'cause his big brother plays basketball for their
high school
and he gives them the power sign and says
you got it
but when I go and say
what's the word
they just say
your nose is running junior

one day I'll be seven feet tall
even if I never get a big brother
and I'll stuff that sweaty ball down
their laughing throats[22]

A full-length program can be developed around the work of one author. Edgar Allan Poe's *Poetry for Young People*: *Edgar Allan Poe,* contains famous selections that create fear, horror, suspense, and other moods that make for a well-rounded readers theatre presentation. A spine-tingling poem such as "The Raven" can incorporate a chorus that utters the tormenting "Nevermore" over and over again. "The Bells," a poem in four parts, each representing a different set of bells—silver bells, sleigh bells, wedding bells, and alarm bells—is a natural to be read aloud by several groups of students, who may use their voices to create appropriate effects. Poems of love and friendship—"For Annie" and "To Helen"—may be included for a change of pace. A reading from Poe's fascinating biography, which appears in the book, will unite the script in the introduction, transitions, and conclusion.

When selections from two books, *You Come Too,* the poems of Robert Frost, and *Poetry for Young People*: *Carl Sandburg,* are read together, a unique readers theatre program evolves. Sandburg traveled across America as a hobo, writing poetry about his experiences. Many of his poems, such as "Plowboy," and "Summer Grass," can be linked with Frost's poetry about nature and people who work outdoors. This is a pleasurable way to introduce the great poets to students who otherwise may never hear "Mending Wall" or "The Road Not Taken."

Cynthia Rylant's book of poems, *Soda Jerk,* is about a young man who works in Maywell's Drugstore. Twenty-eight poems relate the soda jerk's observations about the people around him. As the boy creates sundaes and serves coffee, he is watching and listening to the rich kids, the law officers, the parents, the children, and others. He gets to know the secrets of the small town of Cheston, Virginia, and tells all in this series of poems written appropriately in free verse.

"And Mr. Maxwell thinks I've just been making sodas," says the boy at the close of the book. The selections, taken together, make up a fascinating story and as such can become a complete script.

The poet Robert Francis writes about sports in *The Orb Weaver* and *Come Out into the Sun.* Use his poem "Skier" as a beautiful descriptive interlude in a program with a sports theme:

He swings down like the flourish of a pen
Signing a signature in the white on white.

The silence of his skis reciprocates
The silence of the world around him

Wind is his one competitor
In the cool winding and unwinding down.

On incandescent feet he falls
Unfalling, trailing white foam, white fire.[23]

Other selections on the same theme are Francis's "Base Stealer" (see Chapter 4) and Ernest Lawrence Thayer's famous "Casey at the Bat." The latter piece builds in momentum as Casey, star of the Mudville nine, with two strikes against him, waits for the next pitch. The crowd and our audience watch expectantly:

They saw his face grow stern and cold; they saw his muscles strain,
And they knew that Casey would not let that ball go by again.
The sneer is gone from Casey's lips, his teeth are clenched with hate,
He pounds with cruel violence his bat upon the plate;
And now the pitcher holds the ball, and now he lets it go,
And now the air is shattered by the force of Casey's blow.

To the very last line the poet keeps us waiting for the call. Then it comes:

And somewhere men are laughing, and somewhere children shout;
But there is no joy in Mudville—mighty Casey has Struck Out.[24]

"The Pied Piper of Hamelin" by Robert Browning furnishes material for a lively program all by itself. The poem tells about a mysterious musician who is hired to rid a small town of its rats. Using one or two narrators, several small groups, and some solo readers, an entire class can be involved in the delivery. An excerpt illustrates a possible adaptation:

> *Narrator A*: At last the people in a body to the Town Hall came flocking:
> *Group I*: 'Tis clear,
> *Narrator B*: Cried they,
> *Group II*: Our Mayor's a noddy;
> *Group III*: And as for our Corporation—
> *Man*: To think that we buy gowns lined with ermine
> *Woman*: For dolts that can't or won't determine
> *All*: What's best to rid us of our vermin![25]

Other narrative poems that work well are Alfred Noyes's "The Highwayman" and Henry Wadsworth Longfellow's "Paul Revere's Ride."

There are a number of poetry anthologies in which poems are often categorized by subject. A good one is *The 20th Century Children's Poetry Treasury,* edited by Jack Prelutsky. Here one will find poems about monsters, outer space, animals, food fights, sports, and sibling rivalry. There are selections by Ogden Nash, William Jay Smith, A. A. Milne, and Walter R. Brooks, who wrote the joyful poem "Ants, Although Admirable, Are Awfully Aggravating." More traditional collections can be found in *The Oxford Illustrated Book of Children's Poems,* edited by Donald Hall, and *A Child's Anthology of Poetry,* edited by Elizabeth Hauge Sword and Victoria Fournoy McCarthy. The latter includes "Life Doesn't Frighten Me" by Maya Angelou.

Plays

In full costume for a reading of *Fiddler on the Roof.*

A play has all the obvious ingredients needed for readers theatre. Characters and action are defined through dialogue. The best plays are those that do not rely too much on staging and those that can be shortened without losing the author's intent. As with full-length books and long stories, the part of a narrator may be written into the script to fill in the needed details. We can also extract short scenes or sequences from plays to be used as independent units.

A scene from Mary Chase's two-act play *Mrs. McThing* can be developed into an exciting and funny readers theatre script. The story is about a spoiled, rich boy who finds himself involved with gangsters. Poison Eddie, the chief gangster, speaks:

Eddie: How wah yuh boys? Don't answer. The cops are out like flies. I'm hotter than a firecracker but they can't prove a thing. There's ice in this town but it's all behind glass. I've cased this burg from end to end and all I bring home is alibis. What's on the agenda? Call a meeting! Call a meeting!

Stinker: That's what I'm gonna do. I'm gonna call a meeting.

Eddie: Call it then and don't just stand there sayin' you're gonna call it—call it.

Stinker: I'm not gonna just stand there sayin' I'm gonna call it—I'm gonna call it. (*Whistles*) I called it.

Eddie: Boys, the question before us at this meeting is this one: Do we take this boy we call the squirt out of the dishwashing department and promote him to the mobster department?[26]

Escape to Freedom: *A Play About Young Frederick Douglass* by Ossie Davis is about young Douglass's escape from slavery. The play presents songs, narrative, and dialogue. Readers may assume the various roles with ease in a readers theatre adaptation. Also by Ossie Davis is *Langston: A Play* about the poet Langston Hughes who was the first to cry out "Black is Beautiful!" Consistent with the theme of courage and commitment is a play by Alice Childress, *When the Rattlesnake Sounds.* This inspiring drama portrays one summer in Harriet Tubman's life when she worked as a laundress to raise money for the abolitionist cause.

Theatre for Young Audiences, edited by Coleman A. Jennings, contains twenty plays, including Maurice Sendak's "Really Rosie" and other original scripts for children. Lowell Swortzell edited *All the World's a Stage,* in which many of the great dramatists are represented. Plays by such notables as William Saroyan, Ruth Krauss, Thornton Wilder, Luigi Pirandello, Gertrude Stein, and Bertolt Brecht are found in this fine collection.

Broadway musical comedies can be used as well. Story lines of these plays are often simple and imaginative, appealing to children as well as adults. A perennial favorite, "*You're a Good Man, Charlie Brown*" by Clark Gesner, is based on Charles Schultz's comic strip "Peanuts." Although the play is in two acts, continuity is not an essential feature. Any of the amusing fragments can be extracted and combined with other material for use in readers theatre. The well-known characters describe their problems in a whimsical, philosophical dialogue:

Charlie Brown: I think lunchtime is about the worst time of day for me. Always having to sit here alone. Of course, sometimes mornings aren't so pleasant either—waking up and wondering if anyone would really miss me if I never got our of bed.[27]

Other popular musicals, parts of which can be used to flesh out a compiled script, are *1776* by Sherman Edward and Peter Stone; *The Fantasticks* by Tom Jones; Rodgers and Hammerstein's *The King and I; Annie Get Your Gun* by Herbert Fields and Dorothy Fields and Irving Berlin; *Beauty and the Beast* by Howard Ashman, Tim Rice, and Alan Menken; and *The Lion King* by Tim Rice and Elton John. *Once Upon a Mattress* by Jay Thomson, Marshall Burer, and Deal Fuller is a witty version of Hans Christian Andersen's "The Princess and the Pea," which is particularly well suited for readers theatre.

Enhancing the Language Arts

Finding the *right* book or poem to dramatize presents a wonderful opportunity to discuss the questions, "What makes a good book?" and "What makes a poem great?" There are many ways to evaluate literature. By "webbing," that is by analyzing and identifying the various literary characteristics of selected texts, students will gain new insights into and understanding and appreciation of the material. A discussion of the integration of the elements in a book is useful in determining the quality of the work. Students can be guided to critically separate the whole into its parts for study. Find the central theme: What is the story about? Locate the setting: Where does the story take place? Analyze the characters: Who are the people in the story? Study the plot structure: What happens to move the story toward its climax? Look at the use of language: Do the words adequately relate the way the author wants his or her readers to feel?

Students' reactions to the literature are also part of the analysis process. Are the events in the book similar to those one experiences or dreams of experiencing? Do the children find *themselves* in the narrative? Does the story take them away from the ordinary concerns of real life? Is this transport, although fantasy, made to seem possible? Would they like to read the book again? Would they advise others to read it? And finally, would they like to read it aloud for listeners? These questions and others help students to view literature in a unique way, to interact with the material, and to learn to recognize a good book and the value of reading for enjoyment.

The ideal way to introduce poetry to young people is to read the poems aloud. As children listen, they are encouraged to hear the melody and feel the rhythm of the verse, create mental images of the contents, and respond subjectively to the emotions evoked. Dana Gioia, writing in *The Atlantic Monthly,* states, "Poetry is the art of using words charged with their utmost meaning."[28] Since the language of poetry is often eloquent and pithy, rereading a poem is essential to understanding the author's intent and shedding light on hidden meanings. Encouraging young people to memorize favorite poems is an old idea that still has merit.

After discussing stories and poems, inviting students to write creatively generates imaginative and often unpredictably fine results. Once again, many of the works produced by students can be used for readers theatre.

Let's Review

Appropriate literature for readers theatre can be found in all categories: picture books, fairy and folk tales, fables, fantasy and science fiction, poetry, and plays:

- Picture books are suitable for older students as well as beginning readers. "How-to" and humorous stories are often found in this division.

- Fairy and folk tales provide a rich reservoir of material for dramatization. These old tales satisfy a child's need to fantasize. Educators should also look into the fairy tales written by Oscar Wilde, who wrote stories for his young sons.

- Fables, usually about animals, are compact stories that illustrate human behavior while delivering a lesson. Short and to the point, they are easy to dramatize and to include in a compiled script.

- Realistic stories are favorites of both younger and older students because they portray characters facing difficulties similar to those experienced by the readers themselves.

- Fantasy and science fiction are filled with marvels and terrors. These stories appeal to all who want to escape into the fantasy world.

- Poetry can be enjoyable when dramatized. Readers theatre is the perfect art form to make poetry palatable. Full-length programs can be developed around the work of one author. Narrative poems are particularly suitable for dramatization.

• Plays have all the obvious ingredients for a readers theatre production. There are several good plays written for children. Musical comedies also lend themselves to adaptation.

Selecting material for readers theatre provides the ideal opportunity for teachers and librarians to discuss the attributes of good literature.

Notes

1. Leo Lionni, *It's Mine!* (New York: Alfred A. Knopf, 1985), unpaged.

2. Jon Scieszka, *The True Story of the 3 Little Pigs!* (New York: Penguin, 1989).

3. Jon Scieszka, *The Frog Prince, Continued* (New York: Penguin, 1991), unpaged.

4. Jon Scieszka, *Math Curse* (New York: Penguin, 1995), unpaged.

5. Lloyd Alexander, *The Fortune-Tellers* (New York: Penguin, 1992), unpaged.

6. May Hill Arbuthnut, comp., "The Frog King," in *Time for Fairy Tales* (Chicago: Scott, Foresman, 1952), 41.

7. Arbuthnot, *Time for Fairy Tales,* 4.

8. "The Fisherman and His Wife," in *Grimm's Household Tales,* trans. Margaret Hunt (New York: Pantheon Books, 1944), 103.

9. Vivian French, *Why the Sea Is Salt* (Cambridge, MA: Candlewick Press, 1993), unpaged.

10. Patricia Barrett Perkins, "Introduction," in *Aesop's Fables* (New York: Jellybean Press Division, Dilithium Press, 1988), ix.

11. Jean de la Fontaine, "Introduction," in *The Complete Fables of Jean de la Fontaine,* ed. Norman B Spector (Evanston, IL: Northwestern University Press, 1988), xxxiii.

12. James Thurber, *Fables for Our Time and Famous Poems* (New York: Harper & Brothers, 1940), 5.

13. Karen Hesse, *Just Juice* (New York: Scholastic, 1998), 20.

14. Robin Cruise, *The Top Secret Journal of Fiona Claire Jardian* (New York: Harcourt Brace, 1998), 28.

15. Jerry Spinelli, *Maniac Magee* (New York: HarperCollins, 1990), 28-29.

16. J. R. R. Tolkien, *The Hobbit* (New York: Random House, 1966), 2.

17. Shel Silverstein, *Where the Sidewalk Ends* (New York: HarperCollins, 1974), 9.

18. Shel Silverstein, *A Light in the Attic* (New York: Harper & Row, 1981), 35.

19. Shel Silverstein, *Falling Up* (New York: HarperCollins, 1996), 113.

20. Ibid., 113.

21. Silverstein, *Where the Sidewalk Ends,* 19.

22. Nikki Giovanni, *Spin a Soft Black Song,* rev. ed. (New York: Hill and Wang, 1985), 45.

23. Robert Francis, *Come Out into the Sun* (Boston: University of Massachusetts Press, 1965), 38.

24. Ernest Lawrence Thayer, "Casey at the Bat," in *Hold Fast to Dreams,* ed. Arna Bontemps (Chicago: Follett, 1966), 100.

25. Robert Browning, "The Pied Piper of Hamelin," in *The Arbuthnot Anthology of Children's Literature,* 4th ed., rev. Zena Sutherland (New York: Scott, Foresman, 1976), 16.

26. Mary Chase, *Mrs. McThing,* 1st ed. rev. (New York: Oxford University Press, 1952), I, ii, 49.

27. Clark Gesner, *"You're a Good Man, Charlie Brown"* (New York: Random House, 1967), I, 7-8.

28. Dana Gioia, "Can Poetry Matter?" *The Atlantic Monthly* 267, no. 5 (May 1991): 94.

Chapter 3

EXPLORING KEY LITERARY ELEMENTS

NARRATOR	1: Now listeners, please note that the folks in the king's Cabinet were fiercely competitive.
NARRATOR 2:	Each wanted to be the favorite.
JESTER:	I am the king's Jester. My training? Class clown!
FINANCE MAN:	I am the king's Minister of Finance. My motto? Show me the money!
PUBLICIST:	I am the king's P.R. man. More about this? Log on to www.kingdom.com.
MUSIC MAN:	I am the king's Minstrel. Sample? (*Sings*) Doo wop, doo wop, doo wop . . .
All:	**Ugh!!! Give me a break!**

(*Readers theatre continues . . .*)

What to Look for When Exploring

When looking for appropriate literature to dramatize for readers theatre, educators should be aware of the key literary elements that make for successful productions. The plot, characters, dialogue, and narration are the fundamental constituents of all selections and as such deserve our attention. Students, preparing for performance, become aware of the part these elements play in their scripts and thereby gain insights into the structure of good literature.

Librarian helps students identify key literary elements.

Plot

According to E. M. Forster, there is a difference between a story and a plot. A *story* is a narrative of events arranged in their time sequence. A *plot* is also a narrative of events, the emphasis falling on causality. *The king died and then the queen died*, is a story. *The king died and then the queen died of grief*, is a plot. A story keeps the audience curious. What will happen next? A plot gets them thinking: Why did it happen?[1]

To capture children's attention, present a suspenseful story. To have them use their heads, give them a well-designed plot. Propose an imaginative tale that presents characters in a series of events complicated by problems. The situation is ripe for something to happen. The action is quick and uninterrupted. The interest turns on some dramatic moment. The ending is clear cut and satisfying.

When students are ready to select material for readers theatre, a fairy tale is a good place to start. For example, give them "The Emperor's New Clothes" by Hans Christian Andersen as a possible candidate. It is easy to see how it shapes up. The story begins with a short introduction:

> Many years ago there was an Emperor who was so extremely fond of new clothes that he spent all his money on them.

We learn quickly that although the Emperor has a costume for every hour of the day, he still wants more outfits. The scene is set for trouble. Events follow logically. Two slick imposters tell the Emperor about the magical quality of garments that in reality do not exist at all. The Emperor is fooled. Out of fear, everyone else in the kingdom plays along.

The plot is hatched. Suspense builds. Will the Emperor continue to trust the double-talking swindlers? Will the great ruler walk naked in the procession? Will no one, not even his loyal officials, stop him? The big moment arrives. His majesty will march in the parade without clothes. The ending is at hand. It is uncluttered and surprising:

"But the Emperor has nothing at all on!" said a little child.

"Listen to the voice of innocence!" exclaimed his father; and what the child had said was whispered from one to another.

"But he has nothing at all on!" At last cried all the people.

The Emperor was vexed, for he knew that the people were right; but he thought the procession must go on now! And the lords of the bedchamber took greater pains than ever to appear holding up a train, although in reality, there was no train to hold.[2]

The point becomes clear: All concerned, including the Emperor, allow themselves to be duped for fear of being thought foolish and incompetent. Perfect! Here is drama at work. There are no subplots, no long descriptions. The language is lively and economical. In a few short pages we understand the wickedness of the tailors, the vanity of the king, the innocence of a little child. "The Emperor's New Clothes" is an engrossing story with an inventive plot. It needs little more than several scripts to bring it to life in the classroom.

Novels provide fertile ground for a good story and plot. It is fun for students to face the challenge of condensing a book or at least dramatizing a chapter or two to illuminate the author's intent and language. For example, consider Mark Twain's *The Adventures of Huckleberry Finn*. As the title implies, the book is filled with adventures. The first chapter develops the exposition. Huck tells us that he was a character in *The Adventures of Tom Sawyer*. But even if one had not read that book, he explains:

 That ain't no matter. That book was made by Mr. Mark Twain, and he told the truth, mainly. There was things which he stretched, but mainly he told the truth.

With this as a start, Huck himself gives us a précis of the previous book:

Now the way that book winds up is this: Tom and me found the money that the robbers hid in the cave, and it made us rich. We got six thousand dollars apiece—all gold. It was an awful sight of money when it was piled up. Well, Judge Thatcher he took it and put it out at interest, and it fetched us a dollar a day apiece all the year round—more than a body could tell what to do with.[3]

The introduction is in progress. Huck reveals that the Widow Douglas is about to "sivilize" him and he finds that "rough." He prefers the free life. His adventures begin. His father, a brutal drunkard, finds out about the money and goes to see Huck. Their conversation is dramatic as Pap, Huck's father, speaks to his son:

"Starchy clothes—very. You think you're a good deal of a big-bug, don't you?"

"Maybe I am, maybe I ain't," I says.

"Don't you give me none o' your lip," says he. "You've put on considerable many frills since I been away. I'll take you down a peg before I get done with you. You're educated, too, they say—can read and write. You think you're better'n your father, now, don't you, because he can't? I'll take it out of you."[4]

The audience is completely captivated. Who can resist discovering what happens next? Any one of Huck and Tom's exciting escapades that run throughout the book is well plotted and would make a thrilling segment for readers theatre. The novel is full of colorful characters too, twenty-nine to be exact, all of whom are anxious to populate the script.

Story Formula

This is a good time to discuss "story formula" with the class. Using the previous examples, it is not difficult to explain that a good story has five parts: a beginning, a problem, a highpoint or climax, a following action or solution, and a satisfactory ending.[5]

Critical thinking skills come into play when students recognize the essence of a problem or disharmony in a story. Teachers can delve more deeply into the conflict by asking, "What's the problem here?" "What do you think is wrong?" "What would *you* do in this situation?"[6]

Finally, a story-writing exercise can be incorporated in the session to give students a chance to create a tale of their own, perhaps one to be chosen for readers theatre.

Characters

Characters often remain fresh in one's memory long after a story is forgotten. This is especially true for dramatized literature. Players and spectators alike are deeply involved with the personalities in a script. The readers become the characters they portray; the listeners imagine themselves in the roles and they too are united with them. Thus, the characters in a tale are readers theatre stock in trade.

A character must be compelling and must be understood quickly through the dialogue. There is no place in a dramatization for long stretches of narration describing a character's nature or qualities. In Louisa May Alcott's *Little Women*, we learn much about the girls right from the start:

"Christmas won't be Christmas without any presents," grumbled Jo, lying on the rug.

"It's so dreadful to be poor!" sighed Meg, looking down at her old dress.

"I don't think it's fair for some girls to have plenty of pretty things, and other girls nothing at all," added little Amy, with an injured sniff.

"We've got Father and Mother and each other," said Beth contentedly from her corner.

It is clear at the outset that these are very special little women. They are normal girls who want pretty things like girls everywhere, but they recognize the importance of family. As we read on we learn about Mother from Meg:

"You know the reason Mother proposed not having presents this Christmas was because it is going to be a hard winter for everyone, and she thinks we ought not to spend money for pleasure, when our men are suffering in the army."[7]

With very little narration through this interchange, we discover a great deal about the nature of Alcott's characters, quickly and succinctly,

Children enjoy finding people like themselves in the stories they read. Many series books present characters who are of school age, facing some of the same problems as our students. These fictitious youngsters who portray adolescents and their problems in episode after episode are generally stock characters, appealing because of the familiar obstacles they encounter and ultimately overcome. Anastasia Krupnik, Lois Lowry's title character, sits in the middle of her parents' king-sized bed and has the following conversation with her mom:

"I wish they'd assign *Gone with the Wind* in seventh-grade English," she said. Her mother looked over from where she was folding a nightgown. "They couldn't," she said. "It's too risqué."

"*Mom*," Anastasia said, "there isn't a single sex scene in *Gone with the Wind*. And only one 'damn.' Remember when Rhett Butler says to Scarlett—" 'Frankly, my dear, I don't give a damn,' " Mrs. Krupnik said in a deep voice along with Anastasia, and they both laughed.[8]

The kings, beggars, princes, thieves, giants, and dwarfs who inhabit folk tales are usually stereotypes or archetypes of the human condition. Each represents a trait: virtue, greed, generosity, beauty, compassion. Children easily understand these kinds of people. They provide excellent subjects for dramatized stories. A sentence or two is all that is needed to breathe life into the characters for action on stage. Following are two examples from the Brothers Grimm:

There was once a widow who had two daughters—one of whom was pretty and industrious, whilst the other was ugly and idle.[9]

There was once a shoemaker who worked very hard and was very honest; but still could not earn enough to live upon, and at last all he had in the world was gone, except just leather enough to make one pair of shoes.[10]

That is all we want to know about these personalities. Now they must provide the action and suspense the audience demands. No one will be satisfied until the good are richly rewarded and the wicked are punished.

Sometimes a small measure of introspection reveals so much about a character that it may be included to round out characterization. In Joseph Krumgold's . . . *And Now Miguel*, Miguel introduces himself:

I am Miguel. For most people it does not make so much difference that I am Miguel. But for me, often, it is a very great trouble.

It would be different if I were Pedro. He is my younger brother, only seven years old. For Pedro everything is simple. Almost all the things that Pedro wants, he had—without much worry.[11]

Animal characters have delighted young children ever since they first listened to "The Three Bears" at bedtime. Fish and talking horses are as readily accepted as fairy tale or fantasy personalities. They are viewed as typifying human behavior. Animals, like other characters, must pass the test of credibility. Their reactions to situations should be consistent with what we know about them and reveal their true strengths and weaknesses. Consider Kenneth Grahame's classic *The Reluctant Dragon* as the dragon explains to the Boy why he has come to the Downs:

"—fact is, I'm such a confoundedly lazy beggar!"

"You surprise me," said the Boy, civilly.

"It's the sad truth," the dragon went on, settling down between his paws and evidently delighted to have found a listener at last; "and I fancy that's really how I came to be here. You see all the other fellows were so active and *earnest* and all that sort of thing—always rampaging, and skirmishing, and scouring the desert sands, and pacing the margin of the sea, and chasing knights all over the place, and devouring damsels, and going on generally—whereas I liked to get my meals regular and then to prop my back against a bit of a rock and snooze."[12]

The dragon is believable. We sympathize with his fear of being outgoing and chuckle at his desire for creature comforts. His wish to dodge his traditional role occurs to us all, but coming from a dragon, it makes us laugh.

Characterization

Before students decide on the characters who will populate their scripts, the time is ripe to exchange ideas about characterization. The analysis of a story allows us to learn about a personality, either directly as the character speaks and acts, or indirectly through the comments of others or the narrator. We say a character is three-dimensional when his or her past, future, hopes, fears, strengths, and weaknesses are developed by the author in detail throughout the story.[13] Why does the protagonist say the things he or she says? What are the reasons for his or her actions? A character can change before the story is over, but what motivates him or her to do so? When the many sides of an individual are revealed in the literature, it is then that we can admire, love, hate, or identify with him or her. It is then we truly know that character.

Thus, for a successful story dramatization, guide students to look for a cast of characters, whether flat or well rounded, who relate consistently to one another and to the action of the plot; characters who have spunk; and especially those who grow because of what happens to them in the story.

Dialogue

When choosing a story to dramatize, advise students to glance at the pattern the print makes on the page. Are there plenty of quotes? Are the prose paragraphs brief? Good readers theatre material emphasizes dialogue interspersed with spare narrative passages. L. Frank Baum's *The Wizard of Oz* is a fine choice. The book contains a generous measure of conversation. When Dorothy meets the scarecrow, they have the following exchange:

> "Who are you?" asked the Scarecrow when he had stretched himself and
>   yawned. "And where are you going?"
> "My name is Dorothy," said the girl, "and I am going to the Emerald City , to
>   ask the great Oz to send me back to Kansas."
> "Where is the Emerald City?" he inquired. "And who is Oz?"
> "Why don't you know?" she returned, in surprise.
> "No, indeed; I don't know anything. You see, I am stuffed, so I have no brains
>   at all," he answered sadly.
> "Oh," said Dorothy, "I'm awfully sorry for you."[14]

An author with a sense of drama will use dialogue to accomplish what descriptive passages do: create moods, set scenes, and depict actions. In *Alice's Adventures in Wonderland* by Lewis Carroll the conversation between Alice and the Caterpillar is a case in point:

> "Who are *you*?" said the Caterpillar.
> This was not an encouraging opening for a conversation.
> Alice replied, rather shyly, "I hardly know, sir, just at present—at least I know
>   who I *was* when I got up this morning, but I think I must have been
>   changed several times since then."
> "What do you mean by that?" said the Caterpillar sternly. "Explain yourself!"
> "I can't explain *myself,* I'm afraid, sir, " said Alice, "because I'm not myself,
>   you see."
> "I don't see," said the Caterpillar.

"I'm afraid I can't put it more clearly," Alice replied very politely, "for I can't understand it myself to begin with."[15]

Mazel, the spirit of good luck, and Shlimazel, the spirit of bad luck, set the scene for action in *Mazel and Shlimazel* by Isaac Bashevis Singer. Mazel claims he knows millions of ways to make people happy, whereas Shlimazel brags that he has *billions* of ways to make people *unhappy*. Mazel insists Shlimazel is up to his old tricks. Finally they make a bet. If Shlimazel can find one new way of spoiling something nice that Mazel has done, he will receive a bottle of fine wine. If not, Shlimazel must keep his "red nose" out of Mazel's business for fifty years. Select this delightful story and others by Singer for a readers theatre production that prompts laughter and interesting philosophical discussions.

Straight talk is easy to adapt. In Harper Lee's *To Kill a Mockingbird*, when the Finch children, Scout and Jem, meet their summer neighbor, Charles Baker Harris (Dill), the dialogue makes its impact on the audience, who are not told *about* what happens but see for themselves. The staccato-like conversation creates an atmosphere of intensity:

"Hey."
"Hey yourself," said Jem pleasantly.
"I'm Charles Baker Harris," he said. "I can read."
"So what?" I said.
" I just thought you'd like to know I can read. You got anything needs readin' I
    can do it . . . "
"How old are you," asked Jem, "four-and-a-half?"
"Goin' on seven."
"Shoot no wonder, then," said Jem, jerking his thumb at me. "Scout yonder's
    been readin' ever since she was born, and she ain't even started to school
    yet. You look right puny for goin' on seven."
"I'm little but I'm old," he said.[16]

When read aloud, repetition of words and phrases produce rhythm patterns that everyone enjoys. Cumulative stories containing passages recited over and over again make good listening. Expecting a familiar portion of the script, listeners become part of the performance as they mouth the lines. At the same time repetition encourages mental pictures that underscore the meaning of the language. Who can resist the sheer fun of exaggeration that occurs in Dr. Seuss's sentimental story, *Horton Hatches the Egg*? Horton, a compassionate elephant, helps out a Lazy Bird by vowing to sit on her nest until her baby is born. He claims over and over again that he means what he says because an elephant is 100 percent faithful.

Stories like *The Teeny Tiny Woman* and *The Gingerbread Man* also contain repeated words and phrases that enchant young people and are particularly good for beginning and remedial readers.

Narration

Narrators are an integral part of a readers theatre production. When a story is "up on its feet," they are speaking characters. Descriptive passages that are essential to the story are generally assigned to the narrators to read. These sections are as important to the production as the dialogue. They should help create believable characters and vivid settings. Consider James Thurber's fable "The Moth and the Star," about an obdurate moth who would not stop trying to reach a star. Imagine the narrator reading aloud with the other characters:

A young and impressionable moth once set his heart on a certain star. He told his mother about this and she counseled him to set his heart on a bridge lamp instead.

"Stars aren't the thing to hang around," she said; "lamps are the thing to hang around."

"You get somewhere that way," said the moth's father. "You don't get anywhere chasing stars."

But the moth would not heed the words of either parent. Every evening at dusk when the star came he would start flying toward it and every morning at dawn he would crawl back home worn out with his vain endeavor.

One day his father said to him, "You haven't burned a wing in months, boy, and it looks to me as if you were never going to. All your brothers and sisters have been terribly singed flying around house lamps. Come on, now, get out and get yourself scorched! A big strapping moth like you without a mark on him!"

The moth left his father's house, but he would not fly around street lamps and he would not fly around house lamps. He went right on trying to reach the star, which was four and one-third light years, or twenty-five trillion miles, away. The moth thought it was just caught in the top branches of an elm.

He never did reach the star, but he went right on trying, night after night, and when he was a very, very old moth he began to think that he really had reached the star and he went around saying sol this gave him a deep and lasting pleasure, and he lived to a great old age. His parents and his brothers and sisters had all been burned to death when they were quite young.

Moral: Who flies afar from the sphere of our sorrow is here today, and here tomorrow.[17]

In Caroline B. Cooney's *The Face on the Milk Carton*, we need the narration to learn how Janie *feels* when she learns she was kidnapped many years before:

She did not turn on the lights. The room was entirely dark except for the faint-blue glow from the digital clock. Yet she knew every object in the room; everything around her was normal. She did not feel kidnapped. She felt chosen. Adopted. Needed so desperately by Frank and Miranda that perhaps they didn't even know what they'd done to acquire a second daughter. Temporary insanity.[18]

When using stories having little dialogue, such as the one above, the script can be divided up for several readers, who become storytellers in the old tradition of *reading* a story aloud to others using their oral interpretation skills.

Enhancing the Language Arts

"*How* an author says something as opposed to *what* he or she says," is Rebecca J. Lukens's definition of *style*. And how the author conveys *feelings* about his or her subject is referred to as *tone*.[19] When students meet words on a printed page, whether dialogue or narrative, they make an important connection with a language-rich environment. This is especially true when they are planning a readers theatre program. Motivated to think about the sentences they will eventually utter, students are ready to analyze the wonderful attributes of style and tone of language.

Ask the students: How does the author create the effect and the mood he or she wants? Does the writing conjure up fear in the audience when the protagonist is locked in a dungeon? Consider figurative language: metaphors and similes. Is a mood of sadness evoked when the hero's mother dies? Let's have a conversation about word choices and sentence lengths. Do the words in the poem sound like the thing or the action described? Let's talk about alliteration and onomatopoeia. Has the author engaged in gross exaggeration? Let's think about hyperbole.

When planning to use narrative passages in the script, students will be interested to learn about *point of view*. Arthur W. Heilman and others sum it up as follows: "Authors may use first person, which allows them to speak through the 'I' of one of the characters; an objective point of view, which lets the actions speak for themselves; an omniscient point of view, which allows the author to tell the story in third person and be all-knowing about the characters; or a limited omniscient point of view, which allows the author to concentrate on one character but still be all-knowing about other characters."[20] Excellent examples that illustrate point of view are Paul Fleischman's *Bull Run* and his multicultural *Seedfolks*.

Let's Review

It is important to explore key literary elements when selecting literature for readers theatre. Plot, characters, dialogue, and narrative are worthy of study and discussion.

E.M. Foster explains that there is a difference between a *story* and a *plot*. A story is a narrative of events. A plot is a narrative of events with the emphasis on causality. Fairy tales provide exciting plots that develop quickly. These tales are a good place to start when planning a readers theatre production. The plots in novels can be condensed for presentation.

Before going on to the other elements, educators are advised to explain "story formula" to students. A good story has five parts: a beginning, a problem, a climax, a solution, and a satisfying ending.

It is important to find compelling characters to populate readers theatre scripts. Characters should be readily understood by readers and spectators alike. In some stories the personae are animals who have human characteristics. In others, the characters are realistic, resembling everyday people like ourselves. But no matter what they are like, characters that deliver action and suspense are best for readers theatre.

Before deciding on the characters for their scripts, students will benefit from an exchange of ideas about characterization. Instructors should hold a discussion about flat and well-rounded characters and what motivates them to act as they do.

Notes

1. E. M. Forster, *Aspects of the Novel* (New York,: Harcourt, Brace & World, 1954), 86.

2. Hans Christian Andersen, *Hans Andersen's Fairy Tales* (London: Constable, 1913).

3. Mark Twain, *The Adventures of Huckleberry Finn* (New York: World, 1947), 17–18.

4. Ibid., 42.

5. Paul S. Anderson and Diane Lapp, *Language Skills in Elementary Education,* 4th cd. (New York: Macmillan, 1988), 319.

6. Trelease, *Handbook,* p. 86.

7. Louisa May Alcott, *Little Women* (New York: Pocket Books, 1994), 3.

8. Lois Lowry, *Anastasia Has the Answers*, Yearling Books (New York: Dell, 1986), 7–8.

9. May Hill Arbuthnot, comp., "Mother Holle," in *Time for Fairy Tales* (Chicago: Scott, Foresman, 1952), 37.

10. Arbuthnot, "The Elves and the Shoemaker, in *Time for Fairy Tales,* 33.

11. Joseph Krumbold, . . . *And Now Miguel* (New York: Thomas Y. Crowell, 1953), 1.

12. Kenneth Grahame, *The Reluctant Dragon* (New York: Holiday House, 1953), 10–11.

13. Arthur W. Heilman, Timothy R. Blair, and William H. Rupley, *Principles and Practices of Teaching Reading,* 9th ed. (Englewood Cliffs, NJ: Prentice–Hall, 1998), 384.

14. L. Frank Baum, *The Wizard of Oz* (New York: Puffin Books, 1994), 23.

15. Lewis Carroll, *Alice's Adventures in Wonderland* (New York: Weathervane Books, 1978), 49.

16. Harper Lee, *To Kill a Mockingbird* (New York: Warner Books, 1982), 7.

17. James Thurber, " The Moth and the Star," in *The Thurber Carnival* (New York: Harper & Brothers, 1945), 261.

18. Caroline B. Cooney, *The Face on the Milk Carton* (New York: Bantam Books for Young Readers, 1990), 125.

19. Rebecca J. Lukens, *A Critical Handbook of Children's Literature,* 5th ed. (Glenview, IL: Scott, Foresman, 1995), 160.

20. Heilman et al., *Teaching Reading,* 385.

Chapter 4

COMPILING AND ADAPTING MATERIAL

NARRATOR 1: Yes, of all things the great adviser king now needed advice.

NARRATOR 2: Reluctantly, the king sought the counsel of his cabinet.

NARRATOR 3: Something he rarely had to do—being himself all knowing.

NARRATOR 4: Nevertheless, the members of the cabinet were told the king was coming.

JESTER: The king seeks advice because he lost his funny bone. He needs a good punch line.

FINANCE MAN: Nonsense! It's the financial state of the union. The king invested in Lucent. I told him to stick to the Blue Chips.

PUBLICIST: Not so. The scandal published in *The National Enquirer* did nothing for his image. I will develop his new persona.

MUSIC MAN: You are all mistaken. The king must have more music in his life. (*Sings*) doo wop, doo wop, doo wop . . .

ALL: Again with the doo wop? Cut it out!!!

NARRATOR I: But what *was* the king's problem?

(*Readers theatre continues . . .*)

Compiling a Script

A script can be developed from a single work of prose, poetry, or drama. Some of the most interesting programs, however, result from a collection of various kinds of literature organized to tell a story, illustrate a point, or create a mood. A complete presentation may contain adaptations of a short story, a scene from a play , a book excerpt, and one or two poems. According to Leslie Coger and Melvin White, this collection of materials, called a compiled script, can work as a dramatic whole when the segments have a common center and there is character interaction.[1] The script is then a definable unit consolidated around a theme that includes the appropriate introduction, transitions, and conclusion.

Creating Themes

The cohesive element of a compiled script is its central theme or idea. A workable theme is a packaged expression of some aspect of life. It has universal appeal and affords the widest latitude for selecting material. Themes such as "Love Is Everywhere," "Silly Situations Sometimes Surface," "Be Careful When You Make a Wish," "Friends Come in All Sizes," and "Growing Up Is Hard to Do" are broad enough to include many applicable stories and poems yet focused enough to provide a framework for an imaginative, interactive presentation.

Sometimes a title of one of the selections within the program may serve as its theme. *How to Be a Hero*, the title of a picture storybook by Harvey Weiss, is such an example, setting the scene for a script about heroes. In the same way Eve Merriam's "Inside a Poem" lends itself as a theme for a poetry program. Kathlyn Gay's *They Don't Wash Their Socks!* is a book about superstitions in the sports world. This theme prompts a fascinating glimpse into some funny and strange things people do because they are superstitious.

Scripts that tell a story about a figure from the past or a period of history have a narrower focus and naturally require stricter research. Finding material about Abraham Lincoln or the Civil War poses more difficulty than compiling material around a general theme, but there is a great deal of literature to be found on popular historical figures, and with creative handling of the selections and transitions the total effect can provide insights into a person and the times in which he or she lived. The same results can be had with more specific themes such as "Folk Tales Around the World," "Robert Louis Stevenson: His Poems," "Science in Our Lives," or "tomorrow.com."

To create a mood, often nothing more is needed than a one-word theme such as "Passages," "Romance," "Spooks," "Families," or "Happiness." This type of theme serves as a beginning to be thought about and built on in an imaginative way. Often it may be expedient to select material for the program about one word first, then develop a more specific theme afterward. Having a concentrated focus in advance may be too restrictive, especially when selecting literature to suit a particular reading level. It is not unusual to collect a kaleidoscope of five or six pieces and then find a common denominator that will serve as a theme.

Adapting Material

After selecting appropriate material surrounding a theme, the next step is adapting the literature. This means students will be adjusting or modifying the literature from its original state into a new form, the script. Obviously there will be differences between the material as written and the transformation, but it is prudent to make the new version as close to the author's intent as possible. This is not to say there is no room for creativity; many opportunities for rewriting and adding lines exist, as we will see later in this chapter.

Although a similar procedure is used to transpose nearly all types of literature, the specific application will differ depending on the selection. In short stories some of the narrative paragraphs may need to be converted into dialogue. Unless an entire book is used, an excerpt will require cutting and editing. Many visual elements in plays must be translated into spoken lines. Poems, usually left unaltered, still must be scripted for the most dramatic effect.

In group to adapt a script.

Prose

Most short stories are written to be read silently, but by determining who will speak the various lines and by cutting and rewriting some of the material, it is possible to reshape a selection into dramatic form. Let us look at Aesop's fable "The Travelers and the Purse," followed by its adaptation. In this example the adapted version adheres to the text exactly as the author wrote it. Two storytellers share the narrative lines, while the dialogue is spoken by the travelers.

The Travelers and the Purse
By Aesop

Two men were traveling in company along the road when one of them picked up a well-filled purse. "How lucky I am!" he said. "I have found a purse. Judging by its weight it must be full of gold."

"Do not say *I* have found a purse," said his companion. "Say rather *we* have found a purse and how lucky *we* are. Travelers ought to share alike the fortunes or misfortunes of the road."

"No, no," replied the other angrily. "*I* found it and *I* am going to keep it."

Just then they heard a shout of "Stop, thief!" and looking around, saw a mob of people armed with clubs coming down the road.

The man who had found the purse fell into a panic.

"We are lost if they find the purse on us," he cried.

"No, no," replied the other. "You would not say *we* before, so now stick to your *I*. "Say *I* am lost."

We cannot expect any one to share our misfortunes unless we are willing to share our good fortune also.[2]

Adaptation of "The Travelers and the Purse"

Storyteller I:	Two men were traveling in company along the road when one of them picked up a well-filled purse.
Traveler I:	"How lucky I am!" he said. "I have found a purse. Judging by its weight it must be full of gold."
Traveler II:	"Do not say *I* have found a purse," said his companion. "Say rather *we* have found a purse and how lucky *we* are. Travelers ought to share alike the fortunes or misfortunes of the road."
Traveler I:	"No, no," replied the other angrily. "*I* found it and *I* am going to keep it."
Storyteller II:	Just then they heard a shout of . . .
Storyteller I:	"Stop thief!"
Storyteller II:	and looking around, saw a mob of people armed with clubs coming down the road.
Storyteller I:	The man who found the purse fell into a panic.
Traveler I:	"We are lost if they find the purse on us," he cried.
Traveler II:	"No, no," replied the other, "You would not say *we* before, so now stick to your *I*. Say *I* am lost."
Storyteller II:	We cannot expect any one to share our misfortunes unless we are willing to share our good fortune also.

In a story with a limited number of characters or where characters are discussed in the narration but have no dialogue, they can be brought to life by writing them into the script. Adapting prose into play form becomes a highly creative writing experience during which students add updated, humorous lines to the dramatization or rewrite long narrative passages to hold the interest of the audience. If we were to adapt Hans Christian Andersen's "The Princess and the Pea," as we did the Aesop, without changing the original, the reading would be dull and lifeless. Instead, the adaptation keeps the story line intact, but the dialogue and other material is developed for characters otherwise entombed in the narrative passages of the text. Notice, too, how sound effects and choral readings may be included to punctuate certain occurrences.

The Real Princess
By Hans Christian Andersen

There was once a Prince who wanted to marry a Princess; but she must be a *real* princess. He traveled all over the world, in hopes of finding such a lady, but always there something wrong. Princesses he found in plenty, but whether they were *real* princesses he could not quite make out. There was always something that did not seem quite right. So he came home again, and was quite sad, for he wished so much to have a real princess for his wife.

One evening a terrible storm came on. It thundered and lightninged and the rain poured down from the sky in torrents; besides, it was dark as pitch. All at once there was heard a violent knocking at the door, and the old King, the prince's father, went out to open it himself.

It was a Princess who was standing outside the door. What with the rain and the wind, she was in a sad condition: the water trickled down from her hair, and her clothes clung to her body. She said she was a real Princess.

"Yes, we will soon find that out," thought the old Queen. But she said nothing, only went into the bedchamber, took all the bedding off, and put a pea on the flooring of the bedstead. Then she took twenty mattresses and laid them upon the pea, and then twenty eider-down beds upon the mattresses. On this the Princess had to lie all night. In the morning she was asked how she had slept.

"O, miserably!" said the Princess. "I scarcely closed my eyes all night long. Goodness knows what was in my bed. I lay upon something hard, so that I am black and blue all over. It is quite dreadful!"

Now they saw that she was a real princess, for through the twenty mattresses and the twenty eider-down beds she had felt the pea. No one but a real princess could be so delicate.

So the Prince took her for his wife, for now he knew that he had a true princess; and the pea was put in the museum, and it is there now, unless somebody has carried it off.[3]

Adaptation of "The Real Princess"

Sound Person:	(*Xylophone: three chimes.*)
Storyteller I:	There was once a prince and he wanted to marry a princess.
All:	But she must be a *real* princess.
Storyteller II:	So he traveled about, all through the world to find one, but there was always something wrong. There were plenty of princesses but whether they were *real* princesses he could not tell.
Prince:	There was always something that did not seem quite right.
Storyteller I:	So the Prince came home again, and was quite sad . . .
Prince:	I am very sad.
Storyteller II:	. . . for he wished so much to have a real princess.
Prince:	Do I want a princess!
Storyteller I:	One evening there was a terrible storm.
Sound Person:	(*Cymbal clash*)
Storyteller II:	There was thunder and lightning and the rain poured down in torrents.
All:	In torrents!
Storyteller I:	Indeed, it was a fearful night.
Storyteller II:	In the middle of the storm somebody knocked at the town gate.
Sound Person:	(*Hollow block knocking*)
Storyteller I:	The King himself went out to open it.
King:	Who goes there?
Storyteller II:	. . . shouted the king.
Storyteller I:	It was a princess who stood outside the gate.
Princess:	Yes, I am a princess but I'm in a terrible state from the rain and the rough weather.

Storyteller II: Mercy, how she looked! The water streamed down her hair and her clothes. It ran in at the points of her shoes, and out at the heels.

Princess: Wow, do I look a wreck! But believe me I am a real princess.

Queen: We shall soon find *that* out.

Storyteller I: . . . thought the old queen, but she said nothing.

Storyteller II: Then the queen went into the bedchamber and did a very strange thing.

All: What was that?

Storyteller I: She took all the bedding off the bed and then . . .

All: And then?

Storyteller II: She put a pea on the flooring of the bedstead.

All: A pea?

Queen: Yes, I laid an eensy, beensy, little pea on the bedstead.

Sound Person: *(Triangle: bing)*

Storyteller I: And then she took twenty mattresses.

All: Twenty?

Storyteller II: And twenty eider-down quilts.

All: Twenty?

Storyteller I: Indeed! And piled them all on top of the little pea.

Queen: This is where you are to sleep tonight, my dear.

Storyteller II: Said the suspicious queen.

Princess: That sure looks comfy after a night in the storm. Well, goodnight all.

Sound Person: *(Pause and then triangle: seven bells)*

Storyteller II: In the morning everyone asked:

All: How did you sleep, Princess?

Princess: Oh miserably! I scarcely closed my eyes all night long. Goodness knows what was in my bed. I seemed to be lying on something hard. My whole body is black and blue. It was dreadful!

All: Well!—Well!—Well!

Storyteller I: They saw at once that she must be a real princess when she felt the pea through twenty mattresses . . .

King & Queen: And twenty eider-down quilts!

Prince: No one but a real princess could be so delicate. I have found a *true* princess.

Storyteller II: So the prince asked her to be his wife.

Prince: Will you marry me?

Princess: Sure, Prince, after I get a good night's sleep.

Storyteller I:	And they lived happily ever after.
Storyteller II:	Oh, and about the pea. It was put into the Museum where it may still be seen.
Storyteller I:	If no one has stolen it.
All:	Now this is a true story.
Sound Person:	*(Xylophone: three chimes)*

As we can see, there are many ways of handling narration. Any number of "storytellers" may be employed to deliver the narrative portions of the story, or the characters may tell about themselves as well as speaking their dialogue lines. In addition reporters, animals, servants, gossips, and even something akin to a Greek chorus may be used to deliver narration. In fact, it is the use of narrative description that separates readers theatre from the usual stage production.

Rehearsing "The Princess and the Pea."

Poetry

Since the poet chooses words for their precise shades of meaning, it would not do for us to change them. If, because of time limitations, material must be cut, remove an entire stanza or verse rather than tamper with the words. Of course, a poem's form will change when scripted for readers theatre according to who says what.

Poems Containing Dialogue

A poem that contains dialogue can be treated much the same way as a short story. In "The Blind Men and the Elephant," lines are assigned in the obvious manner: Each person speaks his dialogue. Storytellers narrate. Following is the original poem and its adaptation.

The Blind Men and the Elephant
By John Godfrey Saxe

It was six men of Indostan
To learning much inclined,
Who went to see the Elephant
(Though all of them were blind),
That each by observation
Might satisfy his mind.
The First *approached the Elephant*
And happening to fall
Against his broad and sturdy side,
At once began to bawl:
"God bless me! but the Elephant
Is very like a wall!" Is very like a tree!"
The Second, *feeling of the tusk,*
Cried, "Ho! what have we here
So very round and smooth and sharp?
To me 'tis mighty clear
This wonder of an Elephant
Is very like a spear!"
The Third *approached the animal,*
And happening to take
The squirming trunk within his hands,
Thus boldly up and spake:
"I see," quoth he, "the Elephant
Is very like a snake!"
The Fourth *reached out an eager hand,*
And felt about the knee.
"What most this wondrous beast is like
Is mighty plain," quoth he
" 'Tis clear enough the Elephant
Is very like a tree!"
The Fifth *who chanced to touch the ear,*
Said: "E'en the blindest man
Can tell what this resembles most;
Deny the fact who can,
This marvel of an Elephant
Is very like a fan!"
The Sixth *no sooner had begun*
About the beast to grope

Than, seizing on the swinging tail
That fell within his scope
"I see," quoth he, "the Elephant
Is very like a rope!"
And so these men of Indostan
Disputed loud and long,
Each in his own opinion
Exceeding stiff and strong
Though each was partly in the right
And all were in the wrong!

Moral: So oft in theologic wars,
The disputants, I ween,
Rail on in utter ignorance
Of what each other mean,
And prate about an Elephant
Not one of them has seen![4]

Adaptation of "The Blind Men and the Elephant"

Storyteller I:	It was six men of Indostan to learning much inclined, Who went to see the Elephant (Though all of them were blind), That each by observation might satisfy his mind.
Storyteller II:	The *first* approached the Elephant and happening to fall Against his broad and sturdy side, at once began to bawl:
First:	"God bless me! but the Elephant is very like a wall!"
Storyteller I:	The *Second,* feeling of the tusk, cried,
Second:	"Ho! what have we here so very round and smooth and sharp? To me 'tis mighty clear this wonder of an elephant is very like a spear!"
Storyteller I:	The *Third* approached the animal and happening to take The squirming trunk within his hands, thus boldly up and spake:
Third:	"I see,"
Storyteller I:	quoth he,
Third:	"'Tis clear enough, the Elephant is very like a snake!"
Storyteller II:	The *Fourth* reached out an eager hand, and felt about the knee.
Fourth:	"What most this wondrous beast is like is mighty plain,"
Storyteller II:	quoth he
Fourth:	" 'Tis clear enough the Elephant is very like a tree!"

Storyteller I:	The *Fifth* who chanced to touch the ear, said:
Fifth:	"E'en the blindest man can tell what this resembles most; Deny the fact who can, this marvel of an Elephant is very like a fan!"
Storyteller II:	The *Sixth* no sooner had begun about the beast to grope Than, seizing on the swinging tail that fell within his scope
Sixth:	I see,"
Storyteller II:	quoth he,
Sixth:	"The elephant is very like a rope!"
Storyteller I:	And so these men of Indostan disputed loud and long, Each in his own opinion exceeding stiff and strong Though each was partly in the right and all were in the wrong!
Moral:	So oft in theologic wars, the disputants, I ween, Rail on in utter ignorance of what each other mean, And prate about an Elephant not one of them has seen!

Another way to script Saxe's poem is to have the characters share the narration with the Storytellers:

Storyteller II:	The *Third* approached the animal and happening to take The squirming trunk within his hands, thus boldly up and spake:
Third:	"I see," quoth he, "the Elephant is very like a snake!"

Poems Without Dialogue

Poetry without dialogue requires special handling. The best procedure to follow for creating a script with this kind of material is to add characterization. Asking the question, "Who could be saying these words and to whom?" makes it easy to visualize a character speaking. In "Somebody Said That It Couldn't Be Done" it is possible to invent two characters, a Reporter and a Doer.

Somebody Said That It Couldn't Be Done
Anonymous

Somebody said that it couldn't be done—
But he, with a grin, replied
He'd never be one to say it couldn't be done—
Leastways, not 'til he'd tried
So he buckled right in, with a trace of a grin;
By golly, he went right to it.
He tackled The Thing That Couldn't Be Done!
And he couldn't do it.[5]

Adaptation of "Somebody Said That It Couldn't Be Done"

Reporter:	Somebody said that it couldn't be done— But he, with a grin replied.
Doer:	He'd never be one to say it couldn't be done— Leastways not 'til he tried.
Reporter:	So he buckled right in, with a trace of a grin:
Doer:	By golly, he went right to it.
Reporter:	He tackled The Thing that Couldn't Be Done.
Doer:	And he couldn't do it.

In Shel Silverstein's poem entitled "US," two characters, "Me" and "Him," are the obvious readers.

US

By Shel Silverstein

> *Me and him*
> *Him and me,*
> *We're always together*
> *As you can see.*
> *I wish he'd leave*
> *So I'd be free*
> *I'm getting a little bit*
> *Tired of he,*
> *And he may be a bit*
> *Bored with me.*
> *On movies and ladies*
> *We cannot agree.*
> *I like to dance*
> *He loves to ski.*
> *He likes the mountains*
> *I love the sea*
> *I like hot chocolate*
> *He wants his tea.*
> *I want to sleep*
> *He has to pee.*
> *He's meaner and duller*
> *And fatter than me.*
> *But I guess there's worse things*

We could be—
Instead of two we could be three,
Me and him
Him and me.[6]

Adaptation of "US"

Me:	Me and him
Him:	Him and me, we're always together as you can see.
Me:	I wish he'd leave so I'd be free I'm getting a little bit tired of he,
Him:	And he may be a bit bored with me.
Me:	On movies and ladies we cannot agree.
Him:	I like to dance.
Me:	He likes to ski.
Him:	He likes the mountains
Me:	I like the sea.
Him:	I like hot chocolate.
Me:	He wants his tea.
Him:	I want to sleep
Me:	He has to pee.
Him:	He's meaner and duller and fatter than me.
Me:	But I guess there's worse things we could be
Both:	Instead of two we could be three,
Him:	Me and him
Me:	Him and me.

Where there is only one character speaking such as in the poem "Mother to Son," not only can lines be assigned to Mother, but shadows or several sides of the mother may be represented.

Mother to Son

By Langston Hughes

Well son, I'll tell you:
Life for me ain't been no crystal stair.
It's had tacks in it,
And splinters,
And boards torn up,
And places with no carpet on the floor—
Bare.
But all the time

I'se been a-climbin' on,
And reachin' landin's
And turnin' corners,
And sometimes goin' on in the dark
Where there ain't been no light.
So, boy, don't you turn back.
Don't you set down on the steps
'Cause you finds it kinder hard.
Don't you fall now—
For I'se still goin', honey,
I'se still climbin'
And life for me ain't been no crystal stair.[7]

Adaptation of "Mother to Son"

Mother: Well, son, I'll tell you: Life for me ain't been no crystal stair.

Shadow I: It's had tacks in it,

Shadow II: And splinters,

Shadow III: And boards torn up,

Shadow IV: And places with no carpet on the floor—

All: Bare.

Mother: But all the time I'se been a-climbin' on,

Shadow I: And reachin' landin's

Shadow II: And turnin' corners,

Shadow III: And sometimes goin' in the dark

Shadow IV: Where there ain't been no light.

Mother: So, boy, don't you turn back. Don't set down on the steps cause you find it kinder hard.

All: Don't you fall now—

Mother: For I'se still goin', honey, I'se still climbin'

And life for me ain't been no crystal stair.

Poems for Group Speaking

Some poetry is well suited to group speaking. Many interesting vocal effects can be achieved by utilizing choral reading or verse choirs. This kind of choral speaking utilizes the same tonal groupings as a singing chorus: high, medium, and low. Coupling choral reading with individual parts creates a script with great dramatic appeal. Carl Sandburg's "Jazz Fantasia" illustrates this well.

Jazz Fantasia
By Carl Sandburg

Drum on your drums, batter on your banjoes,
Sob on the long cool winding saxophones.
Go to it, O jazzmen.

Sling your knuckles on the bottoms of the happy
Tin pans, let your trombones ooze, and go husha-
husha-hush with the slippery sand-paper.

Moan like an autumn wind high in the lonesome tree-
tops, moan soft like you wanted somebody terrible,
cry like a racing car slipping away from a motorcycle
cop, bang-bang! you jazzmen, bang altogether drums,
traps, banjoes, horns, tin cans—make two people fight
on the top of a stairway and scratch each other's eyes
in a clinch tumbling down the stairs.

Can the rough stuff...now a Mississippi steamboat
pushes up the night river with a hoo-hoo-hoo-oo . . .
and the green lanterns calling to the high soft stars
. . . a red moon rides on the humps of the low river
hills . . . go to it, O Jazzmen.[8]

Adaptation of "Jazz Fantasia"

Chorus (medium voices):	Drum on your drums,
Chorus (high voices):	Batter on your banjoes,
Chorus (low voices):	Sob on the long cool winding saxophones.
All (loudly):	Go to it, O jazzmen.
Solo I:	Sling your knuckles on the bottom of the happy tin pans,
Solo II:	Let your trombones . . .
Chorus (low voices): (Drag it out)	Ooze,
Solo I:	And go . . .
Chorus (high voices):	Husha-husha-hush
Solo II:	With the slippery sand-paper.
Chorus (low voices):	Moan . . .

Solo I:	Like an autumn wind high in the lonesome treetops,
Chorus (medium voices):	Moan soft . . .
Solo II:	Like a racing car slipping away from a motorcycle cop,
All (loudly):	Bang-bang! you jazzmen,
Chorus (low voices):	Bang altogether drums,
	(Follow quickly one after the other increasing intensity.)
Chorus (high voices):	Traps,
Chorus (medium voices):	Banjoes,
Chorus (low voices):	Horns
All:	Tin cans—
Solo I:	Make two people fight on the top of a stairway . . .
Solo II:	And scratch each other's eyes in a clinch tumbling down the stairs.
Solo I:	Can the rough stuff. . . . now a Mississippi steamboat pushes up the night river with a . . .
Chorus (low voices):	Hoo-hoo-hoo-oo
Solo II:	And the green lanterns calling to the high soft stars
Solo I:	...a red moon rides on the humps of the low river hills
All: (Briskly)	Go to it, *(pause)* O jazzmen.

Another poem that can be adapted in a similar fashion is Eve Merriam's "Inside a Poem." It makes a splendid beginning to a readers theatre poetry program.

Inside a Poem
By Eve Merriam

It doesn't always have to rhyme,
but there's a repeat of a beat, somewhere
an inner chime that makes you want to
tap your feet or swerve in a curve;
a lilt, a leap, a lightning-split:—
thunderstruck the consonants jut,
while the vowels open wide as waves in the noon-blue sea.

You hear with your heels, your eyes feel
what they have never touched before:
fins on a bird, feathers on a deer;
taste all colors, inhale
memory and tomorrow and always the tang is today.[9]

Adaptation of "Inside a Poem"

Solo I:	It doesn't always have to rhyme,
Solo II:	But there's the repeat of a beat,
Chorus I: (rhythmically)	That makes you want to tap your feet.
Chorus II: (drawn out)	Or swerve in a curve;
All:	A lilt, a leap, a lightning-split:—
Solo I:	Thunderstruck (*pause*) the consonants jut,
Solo II: (exaggerated)	While the vowels open wide as waves in the noon-blue sea.
Chorus I:	You hear with your heels.
Chorus II:	Your eyes feel . . .
Solo I:	What they never touched before:
Chorus I:	Fins on a bird,
Chorus II:	Feathers on a deer;
All:	Taste all colors,
Solo I:	Inhale memory and tomorrow
Solo II:	And always the tang is (*pause*) today.

Plays

Plays selected for a readers theatre presentation should contain stories that do not rely too heavily on overt, physical action. The play is often easier to adapt than other forms of literature because it is already written in dramatic form. Nevertheless, it must be carefully rescripted for blocking as an oral reading.

Even if a play constitutes the complete readers theatre program, it will no doubt need cutting and rewriting to keep it within acceptable time limits. If only portions of the play are used, a narrator will be needed to provide the transitions from one segment to another. The characters, too, may be given additional lines to help bridge the cut portions. It is important to remember that we need not be tied to the original act and scene divisions nor be put off by the length of the play. Condensing portions of the play can be a highly creative activity through which children develop an awareness of the dramatic form.

In a scene from *The Fantasticks,* the character of El Gallo is a built-in narrator who easily supplies the needed transitions while other characters, with rewritten lines, provide additional missing links so that the plot is kept intact and the new sequence becomes an understandable, fluid whole. Following are segments of the play as originally written, followed by its adaptation.

The Fantasticks

By Harvey Schmidt and Tom Jones

Luisa:	The moon turns red on my birthday every year and it always will until somebody saves me and takes me back to my palace.
El Gallo:	That is a typical remark. The other symptoms vary. She thinks that she's a princess; That her name must be in French, Or sometimes Eurasian, Although she isn't sure what that is.
El Gallo:	Good. And now the boy, His story may be a wee bit briefer, Because it's pretty much the same.
Matt:	There is this girl.
El Gallo:	That is the essence.
Matt:	There is this girl.
El Gallo:	I warn you: it may be monotonous.
Matt:	There is this girl. I'm nearly twenty years old. I've studied biology, I've had an education. I've been inside a lab: Dissected violets. I know the way things are. I'm grown-up; stable; Willing to conform. I'm beyond such foolish notions, And yet—in spite of my knowledge— There is this girl.
Bell:	I'm her father. And believe me, it isn't easy. Perhaps that's why I love vegetables. So dependable. You plant a radish, and you know what you're about. You don't get a turnip or a cabbage, no. Plant a turnip, get a turnip; plant a cabbage, get a cabbage. While with children—I thought I had planted a turnip or at worst perhaps an avocado; something remotely useful. I'm a merchant—I sell buttons. What need do I have for a rose?—There she is. Missy, you must go inside.
Bell:	Hucklebee!
Huck:	Bellomy!
Bell:	Neighbor!

Huck:	Friend!
Bell:	How's the gout?
Huck:	I barely notice. And your asthma?
Bell: A trifle.	(*Coughs*) I endure it.
Huck:	Well, it's nearly settled.
Bell:	What is?.
Huck:	The marriage. They're nearly ready. I hid in the bushes to listen. Oh, it's something; they're out of their minds in love.
Bell:	Hurray.
Huck:	My son—he is fantastic!
Bell:	My daughter is fantastic, too. They're both of them mad.
Huck:	They are geese!
Bell:	It was a clever plan we had To build this wall.
Huck:	Yes. And to pretend to feud.
Bell:	Just think if they knew. That we wanted them wed.
Huck:	A pre-arranged marriage—
Bell:	They'd rather be dead! (*Music*)
Huck: Children!	
Bell:	Lovers!
Huck:	Fantasticks!
Bell:	Geese!
Huck:	How clever we are.
Bell:	How crafty to know.
Huck:	To manipulate children,
Bell:	You merely say "no."[10]

Adaptation of *The Fantasticks*

El Gallo:	Let me tell you a few things you may want to know before we begin the play. First of all the characters. A boy, a girl, two fathers, and a wall, which separates their properties. You see, the boy and the girl are neighbors.
Luisa:	I am the girl and the moon turns red on my birthday every year.
El Gallo:	That is a typical remark. The other symptoms vary. She thinks she's a princess. That her name must be in French. Or sometimes

Eurasian. Although she isn't sure what that is. In short, she's in love. Then, there's the boy.

Matt: I am the boy—and I live next door. I've studied biology. I've had an education. I know the way things are. I'm beyond foolish notions. And yet—there is this girl.

El Gallo: You see, he's in love too. Now the fathers.

Bell: I'm *her* father. And believe me it isn't easy. Perhaps that's why I love vegetables. So dependable. You plant a radish, and you know what you're about. You don't get a turnip or a cabbage, no. Plant a turnip, get a turnip; plant a cabbage get a cabbage. While with children . . .

Huck: Hi, Bellomy. Oh, I'm *his* father. My son is fantastic.

Bell: My daughter is fantastic, too.

Huck: They love one another.

Huck & Bell: And that's fantastic with us.

El Gallo: Well, maybe you don't see the problem yet. Everyone seems to be happy with the situation as it is, but listen . . .

Bell: Just think if they knew that we wanted them to wed.

Huck: A pre-arranged marriage. They'd rather be dead.

El Gallo: So there you have it. Neither the girl nor the boy must ever know their parents approve.

Bell: It was a clever plan we had to build this wall.

Huck: Yes and *pretend* to feud.

Bell: Just think if they knew that we wanted them to wed.

Huck: A pre-arranged marriage.

Bell: They'd rather be dead.

Huck: Children.

Bell: Lovers.

El Gallo: Fantasticks.

Huck: How clever we are.

Bell: How crafty to know.

Huck: To manipulate children,

Bell: You merely say "no."

Introductions, Transitions, and Conclusions

Once the theme has been decided upon and the material collected and adapted, the selections, for a compiled script must be knit together to form an intelligible unit with a clear beginning, middle, and ending. This is best accomplished by using an introduction, transitions, and a conclusion, all of which help to adjust listeners' expectations and add to the enjoyment of the literature.

Introductions

An introduction gets the audience ready to listen. It provides the exposition needed to clarify the material, present the theme, and set the scene. There are several ways this can be accomplished. The theme and program outline can be presented by a narrator:

> *Narrator:* It came to our attention that not too many people like poetry. They think poems are boring and sometimes they don't understand what they're all about. You are not these people, of course, but did you ever really go inside a poem where the words are?
> Today our readers theatre will take you on a journey through four very different kinds of poems. One, "The Pied Piper of Hamelin" by Robert Browning, tells an exciting story. A second, by Robert Frost, is about nature. It is entitled "Stopping by Woods on a Snowy Evening." Another is a funny poem called "US" by Shel Silverstein. And our title poem, by Eve Merriam, is all about poetry itself. Listen to *it* first—and then again at the end. Come with us "Inside a Poem."

In another form of introduction, characters may open a program in dialogue that reveals the theme and gives a hint of what is to come:

> *Character I:* I hate school.
>
> *Character II:* Me too especially English.
>
> *Character III:* Poetry . . . yuck!!!
>
> *Poem:* Sticks and stones may break my bones
> But names will never hurt me!
>
> *All Charcters:* Who are you?
>
> *Poem:* I am a poem without a doubt
> You three guys are missing out.
>
> *Character I:* You're a poem?
>
> *Character II:* What do you mean we're missing out?
>
> *Poem:* I said I'm a poem, a poet's creation
> I'm read and recited with due admiration
> I'm a riddle in rhyme, a story, a verse
> As a ballad I'm long, as a limerick I'm terse
> Give me a chance to show you my art
> Inside a poem where words have a heart.

Transitions

A sudden switch from one selection to another within a program can be confusing. Listeners need time to reflect on what they have heard and to get set for the next reading. A transition delivered by the narrator or, as above, by the characters, provides this bridge and also further develops the theme. For example, transitional narration from a program whose title is "How to be a Hero," might look like this:

> *Narrator:* Heroes don't win all the time. Sometimes they lose all the time. Observe our hero, Charlie Brown in "The Baseball Game."

Occasionally the transitions are themselves short readings that provide a lead-in to the next selection. In a readers theatre production a group of letters from several classes in a school describing what they like most at home, for example, can serve as the framework for the program. One or two letters, such as the following, can be read by the performers before each piece.

Performer: Dear Room 101.

If you want to know what I like best at home, it's when my dad cooks the meals. Then we really get to eat weird things!

Your school mate,
Alex Ander

This letter, used as a transition, is a natural introduction to a poem such as John Ciardi's "When Mommy Slept Late, Daddy Cooked Breakfast."

Conclusions

One goal of readers theatre is to create a cohesive whole, not to leave the audience feeling that several people stood and read literary selections. A written conclusion that rounds out the theme and moves the listeners to a further reflection on what they heard will help to unify the presentation, especially when the program consists of a collage of material. In addition, a conclusion pinpoints the exact ending so that the audience understands that the production is over.

Just as the introduction and the transitions should be kept simple and brief, so a conclusion is best when it is short and to the point. There is no need to go into long restatements of the readings. The major purpose of the program, after all, is to present the literature, and in most cases that material speaks for itself.

> *Narrator:* A poet once said: "Words are how what you think inside comes out." We hope our program let you in on what some poets were thinking about. Now that you've heard us you can see that poetry can be interesting and even fun, especially when you dig deep and go inside a poem where the words are.

The selection preceding the conclusion, the last on the program, should also help to close the presentation. Although it can be the climax, or the high point, a final piece should sound a serious, quiet note, guiding the listener out of the interpretive situation as naturally as he or she was eased into it. The introduction in the example above indicates that "Inside a Poem" by Eve Merriam will be read as a finale as well as an opener. Since young people delight in the familiar, what better way to end a program than with a repeat of a short selection that went before?

Finally, a conclusion is a good place to include ideas for follow-up activities:

> *Narrator:* If you liked our presentation about poetry, we would like to invite you to write a poem. Any kind will do. Send your selections to our classroom and we'll create a new readers theatre using many of them. Goodbye and have fun inside your poems.

Enhancing the Language Arts

Is it possible to teach creative writing? Can a teacher ignite the spark to generate imaginative written work? The answer is "maybe." At the very least we can free students to say something on paper without the fear of being "wrong." Ideas first, grammar and spelling later! Praise first, criticism later! Consider conducting a writing workshop in which every student gets a chance to occupy an "author's chair"[11] to read his or her work to the class. A supportive discussion with the audience will give rise to more creativity than pieces constructed for, and graded by, the teacher only.

Specifically, teachers can show students how to keep notes in a journal; how to use them to find a topic, create characters, recognize conflict, and employ dialogue and description. Questions and suggestions may point the way to a creative result: Who did you see on the bus today? What did they look like? What were they talking about? Did anything unusual happen? Can you make up a story about any of the characters you observed? Jot your thoughts down! Instead of giving students a topic, invite them to find their own. Perhaps the bus ride will net them one; if not, an idea may come when listening to music, shopping at the mall, or mowing the lawn. Encourage writing in the journal *daily*.

Students can relate their writing to a readers theatre script. They know that listeners (readers) are not interested in the mechanics of writing. An audience wants to know "what happens next." They want simple, clear expressions, with no extra words that cloud the story. This means writing like a playwright, telling the director and the actors what to do, where to go, and what to say. In fact, after discovering what makes a story "right" for readers theatre, young people are on the path to writing a good one themselves.

Students may also develop creative writing skills when adapting literature for a production. With guidance, as they struggle with the adapting process, they become responsive to the ways a story arouses interest and keeps the audience wanting more. Children will soon see that wit and humor have great appeal; that descriptions can be shortened to "show" rather than "tell." Inevitably they will come to understand that words can be turned into pictures and that they have the power to do this in original work.

Poetry, too, will gain respect when students write a poem themselves. It is not surprising to note that babies respond to rhythm right from the start. They react naturally to anything that has a beat, a pattern. Young people seem to lose interest in this phenomenon as they grow older, except perhaps for the *boom-boom* of their CDs as they listen to music. But we can revive this wonderful attribute by having students read poetry aloud, as we do in readers theatre, and by encouraging them to write original poems. No, as Eve Merriam says, "It doesn't always have to rhyme." Free verse offers the writer opportunities to put meaningful words on paper that have magical qualities springing up without warning and without rhyme, even inspired by those CDs. "Rap" is a kind of poetry, after all.

Again, as in preparation for prose writing, journals should be carried everywhere. Ideas, gathered from real-life experiences and jotted down in a notebook, can stir the aspiring poet to action. The student will discover that a poem need not carry a complex, symbolic message. It can be a simple telling of a happening or a rhyme that conjures up a mood. Students can start by looking at ordinary words, then exchanging them for powerful, emotion-laden pellets. They can substitute "smashed" for "broke," "blunder" for "mistake," "inky" for "black," "colossal" for "large," "outrageous" for "different." After a while this exercise can be fun while producing an enlarged vocabulary and words to populate a poem. Who knows, the next readers theatre production may be a complete original work.

Let's Review

Scripts may be developed from a single work of prose, poetry, or drama, but they may also combine all the genres. Very often these compiled scripts are the most interesting. A compiled script should have a broad central theme that affords the widest latitude for selecting material. Sometimes a title of one of the selections within the script serves as its theme. Scripts that tell a story about a figure from the past or about material of a specific subject, such as science or history, need more specific themes. But even a one-word theme, such as "Spooks," is often all that's needed to begin the process of selecting appropriate literature.

Adapting material for readers theatre involves modifying the literature from its original state to a form suitable for presentation. A similar procedure is used to transpose all types of literature, but the specific adaptation depends on the selection. Full-length books generally require cutting and editing. The visual elements in plays need to be translated into spoken lines. Poems should be left unaltered where possible.

Some prose may be adapted by using the text exactly as the author wrote it. Other stories must be reshaped by cutting or rewriting some of the material. Storytellers or narrators are employed to read the narrative portions of prose, while dialogue is spoken by the characters as they appear in the text.

Poetry should be kept intact. If time is a factor it is better to remove an entire stanza or verse rather than tamper with the words. But a poem's form will change when scripted for readers theatre according to who says what. Poetry without dialogue can be used by adding characterization. For example, in Langston Hughes's poem, "Mother to Son," two *Shadows* representing the mother can be used to read lines alternately with her. Some poems lend themselves to group or choral speaking.

Plays are easier to adapt than other forms of literature because they are already written in dramatic form. But they still must be rescripted for oral reading. If only a portion of a play is used, a narrator can provide the needed transitions.

Once a theme has been decided upon and the material collected and adapted, the script must be knit together with an introduction, transitions, and a conclusion. An introduction outlines the theme and program to come. A narrator can read the introduction or it can be presented by using the characters, who introduce the program in dialogue. Transitions are prepared to provide bridges between selections. These can be read by a narrator or may be short readings that deliver the lead-in to the next selection. A conclusion ties up the program by rounding out the theme. It serves to unify the presentation, especially when the program consists of a collage of material. Finally, a conclusion pinpoints the exact ending of the production.

Creative writing activities can take place when students are working with adapting and compiling material for a readers theatre. Educators may ask students to keep a daily journal for recording ideas and inspirations gleaned from their everyday observations. Students may translate these impressions into original prose and poetry, which may eventually be used as a readers theatre script.

Notes

1. Leslie Irene Coger and Melvin R. White, *Readers Theatre Handbook*, 3rd ed. rev. (Glenview, IL: Scott, Foresman, 1982), 12.

2. *The Aesop for Children* (Chicago: Rand McNally, 1919), 24.

3. Hans Christian Andersen, *Hans Andersen's Fairy Tales,* illus. W. Heath Robinson (London: The Folio Society, 1995), 214.

4. John Godfrey Saxe, "The Blind Men and the Elephant," in *The Oxford Illustrated Book of American Children's Poems,* ed. Donald Hall (New York: Oxford University Press, 1999), 24–25.

5. William Cole, ed., *Pick Me Up: A Book of Short Poems* (New York: Macmillan, 1972), 30

6. Shel Silverstein, *"Where the Sidewalk Ends* (New York: HarperCollins, 1974), 36.

7. Langston Hughes, *The Collected Poems of Langston Hughes,* ed. Arnold Rampersad (New York: Alfred A. Knopf, 1994), 30.

8. Carl Sandburg, *Smoke and Steel* (New York: Harcourt, Inc, 1920, 1948), 63.

9. Eve Merriam, *It Doesn't Always Have to Rhyme* (New York: Atheneum, 1964), 3.

10. Harvey Schmidt and Tom Jones, *The Fantasticks* (New York: Avon Books, 1968).

11. Arlene Silberman, *Growing Up Writing (*New York: Random House, 1989), 107.

Chapter 5

CLASSROOM PROCEDURES

NARRATOR 1:	What was the King's problem? We shall see for here he comes now. All rise!
KING:	Good morning.
ALL:	Good morning. Long live the king!
KING:	I know you must be wondering why I called you all together.
ALL:	We are wondering.
KING:	Well, it's my daughter.
JESTER:	Oh, King is she ill? I will cheer her up with a joke. Did you hear the one . . .
FINANCE MAN:	Is it her allowance? Our treasury can spare another coin. The stuff at the mall has become so expensive.
PUBLICIST:	If she doesn't like her picture in the Castle Courier, we can touch it up.
MUSIC MAN:	Can it be that music she listens to all day? She must be sick of rap, give her a little doo wop . . .
ALL:	NO DOO WOP!!!!!
KING:	None of these problems are what is troubling me.
NARRATOR 1:	Just what is it about the King's daughter that is troubling him?

(*Readers theatre continues . . .*)

Working in the Classroom

Readers theatre allows students to have a major hand in forming their own drama from start to finish. Unlike the conventional school play for which children are handed scripts, here they select their own material, adapt it for presentation, and become the characters in the literature.

Imaginative classroom procedures to accomplish such a goal inspire even the most reluctant learners to participate. With a little effort, it is possible to create a readers theatre production worthy of a larger audience.

Teacher helps with script writing.

Preparing for Adaptation

The most satisfying way to arrive at the concept of presenting a dramatic program is to allow it to flow naturally from a unit of study, a trip taken, a report given, or any other shared class activity. Suggesting the readers theatre format as a means of illuminating that experience is a logical next step.

The process of introducing the technique will vary with the abilities and backgrounds of our students. Following are suggestions for a classroom discussion designed to activate interest in a readers theatre project and to develop an understanding of adapting and staging literary material.

Getting Started

Asking students to relate some of their play-going and performing experiences provides a springboard for learning about readers theatre. Hold a class discussion about the theatre:

Teacher: Most of us have seen a play or even performed in one at one time or another. Can anyone tell us about an experience you had with the theatre?

Student: I went to the theatre with my grandmother on my birthday. We saw *The Music Man*. It was awesome!

Student: Oh, I saw that. They did it at the high school.

Teacher: Yes, that's a wonderful show. It's a musical.

Student: I was in a play once. I played an Indian in *The Last Train Out*.

Teacher: For those of us who haven't been to the theatre or haven't been in a play, can you tell us about it?

Student: A play is actually like real life, except people pretend to be real.

Student: They talk to each other like they are thinking up their words at that very moment, but they're not.

Teacher: Yes, the actors actually have studied a script. They rehearse and rehearse and after awhile the play appears to be as real as life. What else in a play makes it seem real?

Student: There are costumes and scenery that looks like the place where the characters are.

Student: There's furniture and other props around that people use in real life.

Teacher: What about the audience? Where are they?

Student: They're sitting in their seats in the dark.

Student: There are lights on the stage, not in the audience, so the actors cannot see the audience.

Teacher: Right. In the theatre it's as if there are four walls to the stage instead of just three. This makes the audience feel as though they are looking on without the characters' knowledge.

Student: Yes, it's like the audience isn't there.

Teacher: Exactly. For most people, theatre means actors on a raised stage with lights, scenery, and costumes, and the audience is invisible. But there is another kind of theatrical event that can take place almost anywhere, even in front of a classroom. Can anyone think of it? It is something like a play we can do in a classroom.

Student: Act out stories?

Teacher: Yes, by reading aloud in a dramatic style, we can turn a story into a theatre event. This kind of theatre is called readers theatre. Readers theatre is something like a play because the readers portray the characters in the story, but like story telling, much of the action, the scenery, and the costumes have to be imagined by the audience. For this reason, readers theatre is often called theatre of the imagination. And the audience is very much involved.

A Sample to See and Read

For readers theatre activity to be meaningful to young students, it is important that they see and read a sample story and its dramatization. We can begin with a simple tale, Aesop's "The Travelers and the Purse." (For story and adaptation, see Chapter 4.) Distribute the material to the class. After reading the story together, try the adapted version in round-robin, reading from seats. Discuss the story and the script:

Teacher: What makes the two versions different from one another.

Student: One is in story form and one is in play form.

Teacher: Yes, the script was adapted from the story. What does the word *adapt* mean? Look it up.

Student: I found it! For adapt, the dictionary says, "To make suitable; to fit, or suit; to adjust."

Teacher: Okay, so how does the definition apply here?

Student: The original story was adjusted and made suitable to be a script.

Teacher: Good, we now have a dramatic version of the story. Can you tell me what qualities of the story are preserved in the script?

Student: There are descriptions of people and the things they do like in the story.

Teacher: That's right. Such passages are called "narrative" paragraphs. Who reads these narratives in the script?

Student: Storytellers.

Teacher: Yes, in this instance they are called "storytellers," They can also be called narrators. What other differences between story and script do we see?

Student: The characters seem much more real in the script than the story.

Teacher: Of course. By speaking his or her dialogue lines, a reader brings a character to life.

Choose the Story

The time has come to plan an adaptation together with the class. A very short, easy-to-read tale is best for this purpose. As an example we can use Aesop's "The North Wind and the Sun."

The North Wind and the Sun
By Aesop

The North Wind and the Sun had a quarrel about which of them was the stronger. While they were disputing with much heat and bluster, a Traveler passed along the road wrapped in a cloak.

"Let us agree," said the Sun, "that he is the stronger who can strip that Traveler of his cloak."

"Very well," growled the North Wind, and at once sent a cold, howling blast against the Traveler.

With the first gust of wind the ends of the cloak whipped about the Traveler's body. But he immediately wrapped it closely around him, and the harder the Wind blew, the tighter he held it to him. The North Wind tore angrily at the cloak, but all his efforts were in vain.

Then the Sun began to shine. At first his beams were gentle, and in the pleasant warmth after the bitter cold of the North Wind, the Traveler unfastened his cloak and let it hang loosely from his shoulders. The Sun's rays grew warmer and warmer. The man took off his cap and mopped his brow. At last he became so heated that he pulled off his cloak, and, to escape the blazing sunshine, threw himself down in the welcome shade of a tree by the roadside.

Gentleness and kind persuasion win where force and bluster fail.[1]

Adapt the Story

Distribute a copy of the story to the class. Tape large poster paper to the chalkboard on which to record the adaptation. List the title of the original work, the time it takes place, the setting, and the characters on the poster. Discuss the adaptation:

Teacher: How shall we turn the story into a script?

Student: Let us give the dialogue lines to the characters who say them in the original story.

Teacher: Give me an example.

Student: Well the sun says, "Let us agree that he is the stronger who can strip that Traveler of his cloak."

Teacher: Good. And what about the narrative that sets the scene and describes the situation?

Student: We can have a storyteller or a narrator read those lines. He can start the story off by saying, "The North Wind and the Sun had a quarrel about which of them was the stronger."

Teacher: Fine, but as you can see, there is a great deal of narrative.

Student: We can have two narrators.

Student: We can cut some of the narration out.

Teacher: Can we change some of the descriptive passages to dialogue lines?

Student: Sure. Instead of having the narrator say the two were quarreling, we can have them quarrel.

Student: Yes, let's make up lines for the characters, so there will be less long stuff for the narrator.

Teacher: Good. But can we take another approach? Can we give each character some dialogue and also have the characters narrate the events and describe their own actions?

Student: No, people don't really talk like that.

Teacher: But remember, readers theatre is story telling too.

Student: How can we speak *about* a character and still *be* that character at the same time?

Teacher: Let us try it.

Student: Okay, the North Wind can say, "Very well," growled the North Wind, and at once sent a cold, howling blast against the Traveler.

Student: Or else he can say, "Very well," growled the North Wind, "I will send a cold, howling blast against the Traveler."

Teacher: Good. That's the idea.

Write the names of the characters, including the narrators, in bold letters in the margin of the poster script. As decisions are made about who says what, write the lines assigned to each character next to the appropriate name.

Encourage the students to update their piece. Suggest adding humor through exaggeration and repetition of phrases. Even the use of a slang expression in an unlikely place adds to the fun of writing and performing.

Teacher: Do you think we can add a funny line or two to the fable? It's rather short and humorless.

Student: The traveler has no dialogue. Can we give him a funny line to say?

Student: Yeah. When the wind blows he can say, "Martha was right, I should have worn my long underwear."

Student: And when the sun shines on him, he can say, "Come on man, cool it, cool it!"

Teacher: Great! If we want to, we can make the story a little longer by adding other characters to the script.

Student: We can add animals and flowers who make comments along the way.

Work through the entire story in this fashion, helping all the students to participate in the writing until the script is complete. Type it in and print it out for performance.

Enhancing the Language Arts

In the course of preparing a readers theatre production the students will need to become familiar with some of the specialized expressions indigenous to the theatre. Consistent with our goal of increasing vocabulary, the understanding and use of theatrical terms adds a dimension of "theatre reality" to the project and creates a unique addition to the students' language repertoire. To this end the following terms are defined:

Acts: The principal divisions of a play
Adaptation: A story, poem, or play rewritten to suit the new situation
Ad lib: Lines not appearing in the script, invented by the readers
Audition: A tryout to determine the best actor for the part
Blocking: Determining the positions of readers with a scene on stage
Business: Bits of action performed by the readers
Cast: The group of performers in the production
Casting: Selecting readers for their parts
Center stage: The middle area of the stage
Characterization: The reader's interpretation of a character
Counter: To shift position on stage for a balanced stage picture
Cross: To go from one stage area to another
Cue: A verbal or nonverbal signal to say or do something
Dialogue: Conversation between characters on stage
Director: The person who supervises the entire production
Downstage: The area of the stage closest to the audience (front)
Entrance: An indication of a reader's arrival on stage
Exit: (Latin for "he goes out") An indication of a reader's leaving the stage
Extras: Subordinate characters with nothing specific to say or do
Farce: Exaggerated dramatic situation for a humorous effect
Freeze: To remain in a fixed position without moving
Left stage: The position on the stage on the reader's left as he or she faces the audience
Offstage focus: Looking up at a fixed spot out in the audience when reading
On-stage focus: Looking up at the other characters when reading
Pantomime: Suggesting a story or an idea through facial and body movements only
Plot: The story line of a script
Properties: (props) Objects or items needed in the performance
Rehearsal: Practice sessions to perfect the performance
Right stage: The position of the stage on the reader's right as he or she faces the audience
Scene: A division of an act
Script: The book containing lines the players read
Upstage: The area of the stage furthest from the audience (back)
Upstaging: A maneuver to draw the audience's attention to oneself
Wings: The space at the sides of the stage where players wait out of sight of the audience

Preparing for Performance: Physical Elements

"The kids in the production seemed so professional. They knew what to do, where to go and how to get us all involved." This comment after a readers theatre presentation was the result of simple preparatory work on the part of the teacher and her students. Aside from selecting and analyzing the literature, students will enjoy learning about the areas of the stage, blocking the script, characterization, stage business, entrances and exits, and eye focusing.

Areas of the Stage

Rehearsals become more productive when students can take directions easily. The nine areas of the stage can be learned without difficulty and facilitate direction. These demarcations apply wherever a performance takes place. The front of a classroom, the center of the library, the end of a lunchroom or a gymnasium, as well as the auditorium stage provide the designated space for readers theatre.

After selecting a stage area, have the students divide it into nine equal parts using colored chalk or washable paint. Stand in the center space:

Teacher: What can we call this area of the stage?

Student: Middle

Teacher: It is the middle, but in the theatre another word for middle is used. Can you think of it?

Student: Center?

Teacher: Yes, this part of the stage is called "Center Stage." Please mark a big "C" in this box. *(Face the class, hold out your right arm.)*

Teacher: Which arm am I holding out?

Student: The right.

Teacher: Correct. Then the square on the right of center is called "Right Center." Mark "RC" in that square please.

(Follow the same procedure to locate "Left Center.")

Teacher: Notice that when we refer to "right" and "left" we are always referring to the actor's right and left.

Student: But the people in the audience are facing the other way. They may get mixed up.

Teacher: No, because the audience does not use the stage. They do not have to take stage direction.

Before naming the remaining areas, explain that years ago stages were "raked," which means they were on an incline, higher at the back than the front. This was done so that audiences could see everyone on the stage. Thus, the square in front of center is called "Downstage Center" and the one behind is called "Upstage Center." Using the same method as before, describe and mark the other locations. (See Figure 5.1.)

Engage the students in a game involving stage locations. Ask a volunteer to give directions and another to follow the directions, such as "John move Up Left." Add other students until all have had a chance to walk to and name the locations.

UR (Upstage Right)	UC (Upstage Center)	UL (Upstage Left)
RC (Right Center)	C (Center)	LC (Left Center)
DR (Downstage Right)	DC (Downstage Center)	DL (Downstage Left)

Figure 5.1. Nine acting areas of the stage.

Blocking the Script

Blocking is working out the readers' positions on stage. Blocking is not to be confused with a character's individual movements: waving, smiling, head scratching. These movements are called *business.* Blocking refers to the *spatial changes* of the characters: standing, sitting, crossing. If we block our characters imaginatively we create variety. If characters know who is where, and where to go, a readers theatre program becomes professional. Fran Tanner suggests using a chess board and chess pieces to represent the readers as a technique for helping students visualize their movements on stage.[2] Suggestive staging allows students to be "on" or "off" without formal entrances or exits. A few indicative movements are sometimes all that is needed for the audience to envision the setting and to conceptualize incidents as they are read by the actors.

To illustrate the importance of blocking, select a cast of readers for the story "The North Wind and the Sun." Have them stand in a line on the stage area. Ask them to read all or part of the script. Afterward, discuss what you have learned:

Teacher: When characters are on stage they create a kind of stage picture. What do you think of this stage picture?

Student: The readers should not stand in a straight line.
Teacher: How can we make the picture more interesting?
Student: The Wind and the Sun can stand on stools because they are supposed to be higher up.
Student: The Traveler can start out in the center and then walk across the stage later.
Student: The two Flowers can kneel Down Left.
Student: And the narrator should be Down Right.
Teacher: Let's try out some of these suggestions.

Explain that planning these positions and other stage movements that add interest to a presentation is called "blocking" the performance. Often a director will prepare a blocking chart before rehearsing a script (see Figure 5.2). This makes it easier to tell each player where to go and when to move. Of course, the blocking can be changed as the production takes shape. Even when we block as we rehearse, it is still important to record the positions decided upon. A blocking chart preserves stage directions for forthcoming sessions.

Stool X Sun		Stool X Wind
	X Traveler	
Narrator X Music Stand		Two Flowers X X

AUDIENCE

Figure 5.2. Initial blocking for Aesop's "The North Wind and the Sun."

Characterization

The time has arrived to speak about the characters in a script. Analysis of the lines in the script provide clues to important information about the people who must be brought to life if a readers theatre presentation is to be believable. What do the characters think about themselves? What do they think of the other people with whom they interact? Are they honest, silly, lazy, good-natured, grumpy? How do they act and react to the situations involved in the story? To discover the answers to these questions, students must examine the script. How the reader uses the information to put his or her imagination, voice, and body to work is called *characterization*. Even our short fable provides clues to the characters' attributes and deserves discussion:

Teacher: We have decided to include six characters in our script—the North Wind, the Sun, the Traveler, two Flowers, and a Narrator. What are they like?

Student: Well, the North Wind is a big blowhard. Ha, ha!

Student: Yeah, he's conceited.

Student: He thinks he knows it all.

Teacher: How did you reach these conclusions?

Student: It's obvious. The story says he growls and he tore angrily at the Traveler's cloak.

Student: You can tell by those words what he's like. Then you can imagine the rest.

Teacher: Good thinking! What about the Sun?

Student: Oh, she's a doll.

Teacher: What makes you think the Sun is a female?

Student: She seems gentle and warm.

Student: . . . and feminine.

Teacher: Interesting. What about our invented characters—the flowers? How will they be portrayed?

Student: They're just bystanders.

Student: Sure, but they're going to comment on the action.

Teacher: Yes, and therefore they are characters, too.

Students are able to grasp the basic ideas of analyzing the personalities who inhabit a script. Imagining what the characters are like and how they feel gives the reader a clearer impression of how to represent them. Students also understand that certain components in a story can be included in non-traditional ways. That is, we may give voice to comments, moods, descriptions, and opinions found there and incorporate them in the script. Once these constituents are assigned dialogue, they too become characters in a readers theatre script and are worthy of study.

Stage Business

What the reader does on stage with his or her eye movements, facial gestures, hands, and body is called *stage business*. Movements employed in a readers theatre production differ from those used in a conventional play. Readers create an illusion of action rather than actually engaging in the physical motions described in the text. If these limited actions are accomplished with credibility, the full picture is completed in the imagination of the audience.

Returning to "The North Wind and the Sun," we can ask students to experiment with stage business that conveys the character's intent:

Teacher: How can our traveler show that he is being blown about by the wind and that he will not take his coat off?

Student: He can sway like he's being pushed around by the wind.

Student: He can wrap his coat tightly around him.

Teacher: Swaying is a good idea. But if he is holding a script it will be difficult to wrap his coat around him.

Student: Let him use one hand to kind of hug himself.

Student: I know, he can just pull his head into his turtle neck.

Teacher: These are good suggestions. What happens when the sun shines? The script calls for him to remove his coat.

Student: He can fan himself with his script.

Student: He can sweep his hand across his chest and then throw his arm way out and pantomime dropping his coat.

Teacher: Great ideas. Fanning himself and then using an exaggerated motion of dropping his coat will definitely work as stage business. Let's try it.

Yes, there is "theatre" in readers theatre. The audience expects to see more on stage than a group of people reading in front of music stands. We want the listeners to imagine many things, but we want to help them with this process by illuminating the text with motions and gestures. For example, in "The Fisherman and His Wife," a fairy tale by the Brothers Grimm, the script calls for the characters to go to bed. Isabel, the wife, and her husband need only close their eyes and allow their heads to fall toward each other in an exaggerated manner. While the narrator explains that the two characters fall asleep, the audience sees a suggestion of the action. Similarly, when the fisherman takes leave of his wife, he merely faces away from her. Isabel, then, utilizes the freeze position, standing still in place to indicate she is out of the action.

Entrances and Exits

Entrances and exits of the characters as they move in and out of a scene are also more restricted than in the traditional play. One way to indicate which readers are actually in the sequence is to have the characters who are outside of it turn their backs to the audience. An alternative is to have those who are not in the scene lower their heads and maintain the freeze position until the time comes for them to enter. Another choice is for characters in the scene to stand, while nonparticipants sit. In the example above the action shifts back and forth rather quickly between flounder and fisherman and wife and fisherman. Any one of the described actions—sitting and standing, freeze positions, or turning away—works effectively to indicate the rapid scene changes.

Eye Focus

While readers need not memorize lines for a performance, after several rehearsals they learn their parts well enough to look up from their scripts. The use of facial expression helps convey the meaning of the literature to the audience. Especially important is eye focus. Where does the reader look? At the other character(s)? At the audience? Over the heads of the audience? Leslie Coger and Melvin White speak about three types of focus: on-stage focus, offstage focus, and a combination of on-stage and offstage focus.[3]

On-stage focus, usually employed in the conventional play, means that readers look at each other when they speak and react. If dialogue is addressed to a particular character, the reader focuses on that character. Tanner suggests that on-stage focus be "used with care as it takes the scene out of the audience's imagination and places it on stage."[4]

Offstage focus refers to the technique of looking at the audience directly or envisioning the scene in some imaginary location, often just over the heads of the audience. This is not to say the players stare at a particular spot on the back wall, but rather they are seeing the action, picturing the characters doing something, out in the middle of the audience. For example, without looking at the fish, the fisherman imagines him struggling on the line and, of all things, talking to him. He creates the scene while looking off the stage and reacting to an imaginary fish. The listeners clearly see the fisherman's vivid reactions and engage in the fantasy encounter along with him. (See Figure 5.3.)

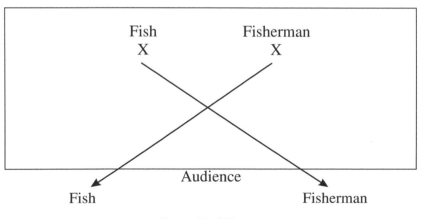

Figure 5.3. Offstage focus.

Often, a combination of on-stage and offstage focus works best. Narrators and storytellers who are reading descriptive passages will usually look offstage, sometimes directly at the audience. Although for the most part the characters in the story use offstage focus, they also can be directed to use on-stage focus for dramatic effect and to highlight a particular occurrence. Suspense and variety are added to the performance when the readers deliberately switch there eye focus. It is important to be consistent, however, so that players and audience alike understand their roles in the performance and feel themselves a part of the creative process.

A First Try

One of the most wonderful things about readers theatre activity is that students can feel the thrill of performing immediately upon arriving at the front of the room. So even before interpretation skills are discussed, or voice and diction exercises are engaged in (see Chapter 6), children can try reading their adapted scripts "on stage." Exchanging views about how to proceed is a good idea:

Teacher: We learned a lot about the stage and how to block the script, and what the characters should do and where they should focus their eyes. Would you like to try our story "The North Wind and the Sun?"

Students: Yes.

Teacher: Fine. Since everyone had a hand in adapting the tale, it would be good if each of you had a part in it.

Student: Yeah, but there are only six parts.

Teacher: What can we do to give everyone a chance to be involved?

Student: I know, let's divide up the class into groups and . . .

Student: Awesome!! We can have five casts. Then we can all do our version of the script.

Teacher: What a wonderful idea! Each group can perform the story the way they think it should be done. Then we can discuss those elements of the productions we want to keep in our final presentation.

Student: Who will direct us?

Student: I think each group should appoint its own director.

Teacher: Looks like you're on your way.

All that remains is to divide the class into small workshop groups, each responsible for its own enactment. After the experimental performances, discuss the various ideas that were generated by the readers, reviewing blocking, stage business, and eye focus.

Production Aids

When the literature has been adapted and the readings practiced, students want to know how to use their scripts on stage, what to wear during the performance, and how sound effects and music can be used. Although readers theatre makes fewer demands on students than the conventional play, there are specific fundamentals indigenous to this art form to be discovered and discussed.

Use of Scripts

Scripts are generally held by the players during a readers theatre performance. Since these scripts are seen by the audience, uniformity in size and color is desirable. An art lesson can be incorporated into the preparations for the production. Using oaktag, cardboard, or other firm material, students will enjoy making their own script bindings and covering them with a simple fabric, wallpaper, or construction paper. Keep in mind that it is easier to handle a small script that does not obscure the reader's face. Half the average paper, 5½-by-8½ inches, is a good script size. It can then be held in one hand with the other hand free for gesturing.

Scripts should be double spaced, leaving large margins all around, and duplicated uniformly for all participants. Characters' names should stand out from the dialogue. When ready, the readers may circle the name of the characters they are portraying and highlight their lines. It is best not to type stage directions, even in parentheses, since children may make the mistake of reading them aloud. To prevent turning pages needlessly, clip pages together when interpreters are not in the scene.

As mentioned previously, after several rehearsals many students have memorized their lines. This gives them the opportunity to use their eyes to establish the imagined scene. No matter what, readers' eyes should not be glued to the script. The most professional results are achieved when interpreters glance at the script occasionally, looking up and out whenever possible. If the script is positioned on a lectern the reader has little to do with it except to turn the pages. If, however, the script is held, students can be instructed to place it in one hand, angled slightly away from the body, and to think of it as an extension of their arms.

Sometimes a script may be used as a property. It can become a book, a fan, a steering wheel, a newspaper, or any other object mentioned in the story. For the book report scene in "You're a Good Man, Charlie Brown" (see Chapter 10), readers can use their scripts as notebooks in which to write their reports. To create a special effect, a reader may be instructed to put the script down on a table or chair for a prescribed period of time in the production, picking it up again when directed to do so. Creative use of scripts keeps the audience interested and serves as a reminder that readers theatre is a shared literary experience that differs intrinsically from the traditional play.

Costumes, Sets, and Properties

There is no end to the costumes, sets, and properties that can be used in a stage presentation. A production complete in every detail has the advantage of being realistic. One of the values of readers theatre is that much of the fuss involved in a full fledged, costumed play may be omitted without sacrificing the literature or the audience's enjoyment. In fact, when readers discover that the credibility of the characters depends on little more than their interpretive skills, they strive to perfect their delivery.

Just as a minimal amount of stage movement serves to illustrate the action depicted in the text, so simple, neutral clothing is advisable for the performance. Students may decide to dress alike in plain T-shirts and dark pants or skirts. Keeping in mind that this is theatre of the imagination, just one distinguishing feature of a costume is all that is needed to suggest a character's identity. A white mobcap with a wide ruffle does for Margaret in "The Three Wishes." When Charlie Brown sports a baseball cap, or when several brightly colored scarves encircle the forehead of the enchanted flounder, the audience easily recognizes the character and imaginatively fills in the details. When a reader plays more than one part, a quick hat change tells all. As in the other aspects of the production, students can be involved in creating clever headgear. Tin foil and glitter still make a fine king's crown. Attics and thrift shops can be scoured for suitable hats and decorative items for the production.

Because there are usually several scene changes during a production, light set pieces are recommended. High and low stools are easy to move around. They can represent horses, cars, trains, and much more. Students may sit on them, stand on them, and even lie down on them. Music stands or lecterns hold scripts for narrators, storytellers, and other characters who remain in one place. The stands themselves can be used as props when appropriate. Decorating them as trees in a forest, tables, automobiles, and the like adds interest. Using them as a depository for hats, scarves, and props gives them a double reason for being on stage.

When the readers are positioned on different levels rather than standing on a flat surface, an interesting, dimensional effect is created on stage. In the opening scene of "You're a Good Man, Charlie Brown," Charlie Brown may be seated on a high stool, center, Snoopy on a low stool next to him, and the other characters grouped around the two. In Maurice Sendak's *Where the Wild Things Are*, the narrator may stand at a lectern on one side of the stage, Max down center, with the Wild Things perched on crates, stools, and step ladders behind him. The effect is a jungle-like dramatic stage picture that adds variety and excitement to the production.

Audiences are quick to imagine objects mentioned in the script, especially if a gesture or appropriate stage business accompanies the reading. When Sybil raises her hand to toast the fairies in "The Three Wishes," no glass is needed. And when Margaret, in the same story, bent over, swings her head to and fro like an elephant swinging its trunk, the audience has no trouble visualizing the string of sausages said to be hanging from her nose. Now and then, however, a property is used. Nothing less than a security blanket will do for Linus in the Charlie Brown script.

Preparing hats and props for the performance.

Sound and Music

The use of aural effects can add drama to a readers theatre script. If there are students in the class who play instruments, use them to augment selected portions of the script with musical interludes. Appropriate background music may be incorporated behind narration or poetry. Music can be played before the show begins and after it ends. It can be included to indicate the passage of time or a change of scene. A trumpet announces the arrival of a king. A flute provides the musical accompaniment to a parade or the entrance of a fairy. Drums set a jungle scene. Acoustic guitars create a romantic mood. Although we do not want this embellishment to steal the show, the judicious use of music adds to the production.

Exciting effects can be achieved by using percussion instruments. A triangle, a hollow block, a small xylophone, or a cymbal punctuate and highlight dramatic moments in a script. Gongs and bells indicate the beginnings and endings of scenes in a full-length story or segments in a compiled script. In "The Three Wishes," a cymbal clash proclaims the granting of each wish. In Thurber's "The Little Girl and the Wolf," striking the hollow block marks the demise of the wolf. Even kazoos and combs wrapped in wax paper are fun to use at playful moments.

Vocal sound effects are always appropriate in readers theatre. These can be spoken in chorus, and often help an audience visualize a scene. Barnyard sounds, ocean waves, city noises, crowds, and machinery all can be approximated by the readers to add variety to the script. Sound effects make interesting additions to the performance, but they should not be overused or become more important than the readings.

Where to Stage the Program

Almost any space can become a stage for readers theatre: the front of a classroom, an in-the-round area, a media resource center, a lunchroom section, an auditorium, a library. The latter, with shelves of books serving as a backdrop, is the ideal location for a performance. The books and selections used in the presentation can be prominently displayed. The invitation to read them afterward is clear. Other scenery is unnecessary since the very idea of this art form is for the readers to call up an imaginary world that resides inside all of us. Keeping the playing space neutral allows this phenomenon to take place.

Traditional Readers Theatre

Although we have discussed adding physical action, costumes, sets, and properties as well as music and sound effects to the performance, let us not forget that traditional readers theatre did not incorporate any of these. The more formal aspect of this activity was to provide an illumination of a text by having it read aloud. This is a good thing to bear in mind with beginning and remedial readers. By following the old tradition, performers can remain stationary, seated on stools or boxes with scripts in hand or on lecterns; there is no need to memorize their lines, and they are free to read aloud to others using only their oral interpretive skills. This can be an easy and fruitful way to start a readers theatre program with children who are shy or have reading difficulties.

Enhancing the Language Arts

"I'll be the teacher, you be the student," said eight-year old Debbie.
"I don't want to be a student, I'd make a good astronaut," boasted Bobbie, also eight. "But I'll come to your class and tell the kids how to walk in space."

Kids are natural actors. They delight in pretending to be someone else. This native characteristic provides the motivation for teaching students how to think—the most challenging of the language arts. When young people are asked how they would turn a story into a script, or what the characters in the literature are like, or how they would block the movements on stage, or what business the characters should engage in, and other questions about the production of readers theatre, they eagerly strive to provide intelligent answers. They are inspired to remember experiences and translate them into decisions about the presentation.

This innate interest in dramatic activity presents a rare opportunity to encourage students to use their ability to make reasoned decisions. By suggesting that they relate their ideas about the production and by probing into the reasons for their conclusions, we can help children recognize their capacity to make choices. We can explain that every choice they make is potentially in conflict with its alternative. If a decision is made to place a character "down center," we have eliminated placing him or her "up right." Why? If we say a man should bend over when he speaks, we have decided against his standing straight. Why? In fact, it will be interesting for young people to learn that many of our actions are based in conflict. Robert Frost explains this poetically in "The Road Not Taken."

Most children, and even some adults, do not realize that they are engaging in the reasoning process all day, every day. Each time we decide to do something, we have probably thought it out. Maybe our thinking was faulty or perhaps we did not spend enough time on the process, or possibly our past experiences did not supply us with the information needed to make the right decision, but we went through the procedure nevertheless. With probing questions about characterization, blocking, settings, costumes, music, and the like, we can demonstrate the "why" and "how" of solving problems. It is no easy task to teach one to make good judgments, but awareness of the thinking process and the capacity a student has to make sensible choices are a beginning.

Let's Review

Classroom procedures include preparing for an adaptation, learning about the physical elements of the performance, and incorporating production aids into the project.

Preparing for an adaptation includes holding a class discussion about the theatre, preparing a sample script using a short story, and eventually adapting it together with the students.

In the course of developing a readers theatre production, students should become familiar with the specialized expressions associated with the theatre. The understanding and use of theatrical terms adds another dimension to the project.

The physical elements of the performance entail the study of the nine areas of the stage, blocking the script, characterization, stage business, entrances and exits, and eye focus. Finally, trying out a script for the first time gives students a chance to practice what they learned.

Incorporating production aids, which will serve to polish the performance, includes learning about the preparation and use of scripts, costumes, sets, properties, sound, music, and the space to serve as a stage for the presentation.

Innate interest in dramatic activity provides fertile ground for teaching young people about reasoning. When students make choices about the production, educators are in a position to explain and demonstrate "why" and "how" we solve problems.

Notes

1. *The Aesop for Children* (Chicago: Rand McNally, 1919), 91.

2. Fran Averett Tanner, *Readers Theatre Fundamentals,* 2nd ed. (Topeka, KS: Clark Publishing, 1993), 117.

3. Leslie Irene Coger and Melvin R. White, *Readers Theatre Handbook*, 3rd ed. rev. (Glenview, IL: Scott, Foresman, 1982), 100.

4. Tanner, *Readers Theatre Fundamentals,* 114.

Chapter 6

PREPARING FOR PERFORMANCE

NARRATOR 1:	Listeners, as you may already know, the King told his Cabinet that his problem concerns his daughter
NARRATOR 2:	How could a princess who has everything including a king for a father possibly want more?
KING:	Ah, but that's just it. She wants nothing.
ALL:	Nothing?
KING:	Nothing!!
JESTER:	Surely she wants humor . . .
FINANCE MAN:	. . . and money
PUBLICIST:	. . . and publicity
MINSTREL:	. . . and music, a little doo wop maybe?
ALL:	Cool it with the doo wop!!!
KING:	The problem is . . .
ALL:	Yes?
KING:	My daughter does not want to inherit the kingdom. She refuses to rule!!
ALL:	She will not rule?
JESTER:	Oy! A flaming liberal!!!
NARRATOR 2:	Imagine that! The princess doesn't want the monarchy. What now???

(Readers theatre continues . . .)

Warming-Up

Voice, diction, and interpretive reading activities help students develop skills useful in readers theatre and in their daily lives as well. Warming-up sessions, including exercises in vocal projection, pronunciation, muscle toning, and theater techniques, introduced before each rehearsal, are beneficial and fun to do.

Like any team getting ready for the game, students are anxious to prepare to do their best work. As they improvise bodily actions and practice lines from the script, they will naturally improve in speech and fluidity of movement. In addition, the exercises described in this chapter will help readers create a more polished performance.

Vocal Projection

Start the discussion about projection by example. Speak to the class in a soft, almost inaudible voice. For instance, give a command that cannot be fully heard. When students respond, explain how important it is to have a message delivered to the very last row of the classroom or even as far as row "z" in an auditorium. This may seem difficult to accomplish, but with an understanding of our vocal mechanisms and how they work, everyone can develop an efficient, controlled voice.

Loudness is not gained by shouting. Shouting irritates listeners and worse, irritates the reader's vocal cords. What then makes the voice heard by every member of an audience? One answer is proper breathing. Yes, we all breathe to live and never think about this function as it relates to our speech. Breathing for life is a reflex action whereby we inhale breath and then quickly release it after a short pause. When we speak, we do so on the outgoing breath. Most of us are unaware of the process and often fail to take in enough breath to meet the demands of the material being spoken. Generally this is the result of shallow breathing caused by poor abdominal expansion.. To counteract this failing and correct breathing faults we can provide exercises that will help students achieve effective projection when reading aloud.

Exercises for Improving Breathing

When it is important for our readers to be heard at a distance, or when long phrases are read, more breath is needed than in everyday conversation. The goal of all breathing exercises is first to learn *how* to breathe properly so as to expand and improve lung capacity and second to learn to *relax* so as to control the breath supply.

Abdominal Breathing

Stand up. Place one hand on your chest and the other on your abdomen (under your rib cage). Sharply inhale. The hand on your chest should remain relatively still, while the hand on your abdomen should move out with the expansion of the abdominal muscles. Lightly and slowly exhale. Repeat until your are able to maintain the proper movement of the abdomen: out during inhalation, in during exhalation.

Relaxation Exercises

1. *Inhale, exhale*: Stand up. Place your hands flat on your abdomen (under your rib cage). Inhale and exhale slowly, each to the silent count of four. When breathing in (as above) feel your abdomen and lower chest expand like a balloon being filled with air. When breathing out, notice your abdomen and chest collapsing as if the air was let out of the balloon. (There must be very little shoulder lifting, and the abdomen must not be sucked in during inhalation.) Repeat several times.

2. *Yawn:* Open your mouth wide as if yawning. Take a deep breath. Hold for five seconds. Exhale. Relax your throat muscles. Repeat several times.

3. *Stretch and yawn:* Stand up. Stretch, with your arms reaching to the ceiling. Feel the tension. Hold for five seconds. Relax and produce an easy yawn. Repeat several times.

4. *Rag doll:* Stand up. Drop your head forward. Let your body drop over from the waist. Allow your arms to dangle. Swing slowly back and forth three or four times. Return your waist, then your head to a standing position slowly. Repeat several times.

Vocalizing Exercises

1. *Head roll:* Stand up. Keep your feet flat. Roll your head completely around your body slowly. When your head reaches your right shoulder say "easy." Drop your head back slowly, breathe out, and say "ah-h-h." When your head reaches your left shoulder say "lazy." Drop your head forward on your chest slowly, breathe out, and say "ah-h-h." Repeat "easy—ah-h-h," "lazy—ah-h-h" with relaxed head roll several times. (This exercise is good to do before every reading.)

2. *Vowels:* Stand up. Keep your feet flat. Inhale. Exhale slowly, intoning "a" as in lay. Hold it as long as possible with ease. Inhale. Exhale slowly, intoning "e" as in me. Hold it as long as possible. Continue the exercise with all the vowels.

3. *Gliding:* Stand up. Keep your feet flat. Inhale. Exhale, gliding from "oo" as in moon to "e" as in me and finally to "aw" as in law. (Try this exercise with one-half of the class on either side of the room. The first group intones the call "oo-e-aw." The second group answers with the same call.) Repeat several times with other sounds. Maintain relaxed tones.

4. *Numbers:* Stand up. Keep your feet flat. Inhale. Count slowly on a single exhaled breath, 1-2-3-4-5-6-7-8-9-10. Inhale. Count slowly on the exhale, 11-12-13-14-15-16-17-18-19-20. Notice that the first grouping is produced easier on a single breath than the second because of additional syllables.

5. *Exploding:* Stand up. Keep your feet flat. Inhale. On the exhaled breath explode the word "hoo." Inhale. On the exhaled breath explode the word "hay" Continue the exercise with other "h" sounds such as "how", "hee," and "hah." (This exercise is fun to do with a divided class, each group answering the other with their explosive sounds.)

6. *Conversation:* Do this in pairs. Two characters, Joan and John, sit opposite each other with their knees almost touching. They hold the following conversation:

    Joan: Where are you going?

    John: I am going to school.

    Joan: I am going to school too.

    John: May I go with you?

    Joan: Why certainly!

    The two characters then move farther apart and repeat the performance. Finally, they are on opposite sides of the room. They must not shout at each other. The use of extra breath from the abdomen will produce the words more intensely. (This exercise works well out of doors.)

7. *Breathe and speak:* Take a deep breath (from the abdomen). Read the following selection on the exhaled breath as far as you can before you must inhale again. Read quickly but be certain to produce all the sounds and to make the meaning clear. Maintain a tense abdomen as you speak:

Rats!
They fought the dogs and killed the cats
And bit the babies in the cradles,
And ate the cheeses out of the vats,
And licked the soup from the cooks' own ladles,
Split open the kegs of salted sprats,
Made nests inside men's Sunday hats,
And even spoiled the women's chats
By drowning their speaking
With shrieking and squeaking
In fifty different sharps and flats.

—From "The Pied Piper of Hamelin," by Robert Browning

Diction

A discussion about diction can take place by asking the class to say the five-syllable word "articulation." Ask them to say it again and this time to try to tell what parts of the mouth are involved in the saying of the word. Discuss the meaning of the word. *Articulation* means the way the sounds of a word are shaped by a person's lips, teeth, and tongue. Say the word "articulation" in an exaggerated fashion to demonstrate how lips, teeth, and tongue are involved. Have the students do the same. "Ar-tic-u-la-tion." Ask the students to isolate each sound and explain how it is made. Try other words.

Diction refers to the correctness and clearness of word pronunciation. To develop good diction it is essential to pay attention to the articulation of the words we say, making sure to shape the words properly with the teeth, lips, and tongue. Projection, too, is aided by good diction. The more power that must be used to make oneself heard, the more exact the articulation must be. (The Joan and John exercise above demonstrates the connection between diction and projection.) The following exercises work on improving diction.

Exercises for Improving Diction

1. *Speaking distinctly:* In pairs, speak the following lines distinctly:

    A. I live in an ice house.

    B. I live in a nice house.

    A. I go to summer school.

    B. I think the summer's cool.

    A. I see your two eyes.

    B. I know you are too wise.

    A. It is five minutes to eight.

    B. You have five minutes to wait.

    A. Give me some ice.

    B. Give me some mice.

    A. His acts are fun.

    B. His ax is sharp.

A. Eat Red's pies.

B. Look out for red spies.[1]

It takes time and thought to say each sentence correctly. Repeat the exercise, changing partners.

2. *Differing sounds*: Work on these pairs of words to be certain there is a difference between them:

pin-pen	kin-ken	tin-ten	him-hem
sit-set	big-beg	Min-men	Minnie-many[2]

3. *Substitutions*: All italicized letters should be pronounced "e" as in "eh":

g*e*t	*a*ny	Ch*e*mistry
ag*ai*n	*e*ngineer	T*e*nnessee

To practice ear training, which is important for accuracy of word pronunciation, try making wrong sounds deliberately, such as "git" for "get," "inny" for "any," "agin" for "again." Make sure students hear the difference.[3]

4. The following words are all said with "i" as in "ee":

king	ring	sing	rinse
think	since	drink	milk

Again, for ear training, try making wrong sounds such as "keng" for "king," or "seng" for "sing."[4]

5. *Vowels and diphthongs:* The following sentences have problem vowels and diphthongs for which there is a temptation to add other sounds. Try them.

a. How now brown cow, browsing loudly in the mow?

b. Sam sat in the class and waited for the man to stand.

c. Ben sent a hen.

d. The guide tried to get us to walk the mile-wide isle.[5]

6. *Recite aloud:* Use a mirror when reciting the following poem. See your cheeks puff out as you say the "wh" words:

> *See the mermaid on the whale,*
> *"Whoa!" she cries, "Don't whisk your tail!"*
> *"Whoa!" she cries, "It makes me slip.*
> *Must I whack it with my whip?"*
> *Said the whale with a mournful whine,*
> *"Your tail whisks as well as mine;*
> *Tails were made to whisk and flop,*
> *Whacking will not make them stop."*

> —Anonymous

7. *Ending sounds:* Watch the problem "ng" sound at the ends of words. The careless substitution of "n" in its place is especially common in the following six words:

doing *not* doin'	coming *not* comin'
fishing *not* fishin'	walking *not* walkin'
going *not* goin'	talking *not* talkin'

8. *Reciting aloud:* Recite the following stanza aloud to practice the "ng" sounds:

> *There was a rustling that seemed like a bustling*
> *Of merry crowds justling at pitching and hustling;*
> *Small feet were pattering, wooden shoes clattering,*
> *Little hands clapping and little tongues chattering,*
> *And, like fowls in a farm-yard when barley is scattering,*
> *Out came the children running.*

—From "The Pied Piper of Hamelin," by Robert Browning

Responding on Cue

In the theatre, a "cue" is a signal to say or do something planned in advance. If the script calls for a character to open a window when Adam says the line, "Whew, I am hot," the words, "I am hot" are the cue to open the window. Cues tell an actor when to speak or move. Usually cues are the last three words of a fellow reader's speech. Movement or facial expressions can also serve as cues that signal one to speak or move. Characters in a dramatized story must sound as much like genuine people as possible. The dialogue and the action must not lag. Readers who "pick up" their cues promptly without unnatural pauses create fast-paced theatre and sustain audience interest.

Responding Exercises

Invite two students to the front of the room. Ask them to carry on a conversation about school. After a brief dialogue has taken place, stop them and ask the class what they observed about two people talking together. Point out how one person's sentence prompted the other person to say something. For example: Student A: "School is boring." Student B: "Yeah, I think so too." Student B was responding to a kind of a signal from Student A. Ask what else can be observed about two people having a conversation. Explain that when two people speak to one another they keep up a certain pace. One person generally waits until the other finishes a sentence, but does not hesitate before responding.

The following exercises will help to demonstrate how cues elicit reactions:

1. Instruct the class to respond to the following cues:

    Instructor: "Clapping is a good exercise."

    Response: (*Everyone claps.*)

    Instructor: "The King is dead!"

    Response: "Long live the King!"

    Instructor: "Sit down quietly."

    Response: (*All sit.*) "Sh-h-h-h."[6]

2. Pair off the class into twos. Give each couple an exercise they will do twice, once to give a cue, once to respond to a cue:

    Brian: "Reach for the sky!"

James: (*Reaching.*) "Okay, but I'll never make it."

Snoopy: "Charlie Brown, you never feed me."

Charlie Brown: (*Hand to forehead.*) "Good grief!"

Continue these exercises using conversations from the readings.

Developing Empathy

Empathy, in its simplest form, is sharing and understanding the feelings of another. In *Act Now!*, Nellie McCaslin writes, "Actors need to understand human feelings in order to know why people behave as they do. One of the best ways to understand other people is to 'get into their shoes'."[7] She suggests that a good way to begin to understand the actions of others is to remember some of our own feelings in particular situations. How did we feel when we were angry, happy, afraid, or excited? Reviving these feelings will aid in portraying the characters in our scripts.

Reaction Exercises

1. As a class, react to the following situations:

   a. Your mother says you can have a party and invite all your friends.

   b. You are grounded tonight.

   c. Someone has stolen your bicycle.

   d. The teacher is talking about something you find boring.

   e. Your dog was hit by a car.

   f. You received an A+ on your composition.

2. Pair off. Following are short story lines, one for each couple. Meet privately to work up the sequence. Present it to the class. Reverse roles.

   a. (*In a hurry to catch the bus, Tom meets Mr. Jeans, his father's friend*):

   Mr. Jeans: Hi Tom, how are you?

   Tom: Fine, Mr. Jeans, but . . .

   Mr. Jeans: Is Dad all right? I heard he had a cold?

   Tom: He's okay now, Mr. Jeans, I'm . . .

   Mr. Jeans: Could you give him this note, Tom, I'm going out of town and won't get a chance to call him.

   Tom: Sure, but . . .

   (*Tom sees the bus leave without him; he reacts.*)

   b. (*Two friends are discussing pets*):

   Jane: I always wanted a dog but my mother says we can't afford to buy one.

   Deb: I have a poodle.

   Jane: Oh, how I would love to have a poodle.

   Deb: My dog is about to have a litter; you can have your pick.

   (*Jane reacts.*)

c. (*Two people in a car*):

> Bob: You're driving too fast.
>
> Dan: Don't be silly, I'm only doing forty.
>
> Bob: But you're a new driver. Go more slowly!
>
> Dan: Chicken! Just for that I'll go fifty.

(Bob reacts.)

d. (*Radio announcer and fan*):

> Announcer: It's two to nothing, favor the Loners at the bottom of the ninth. Here comes Butch Jones for the Rokers.
>
> Fan: Come on Butch!
>
> Announcer: Strike three! Butch Jones is out and so are the Rokers.

(Fan reacts.)

e. (*Principal on loud speaker and Amy*):

> Principal: And now students, the announcement you've been waiting for—the winner of the poster contest.
>
> Amy: I never win anything!
>
> Principal: Amy Smith!

(Amy reacts.)

After the exercises, discuss the emotions each character experienced. Explain how these emotional responses can help students discover how to empathize with their characters in a script and in that way portray them more realistically.

Oral Interpretation

It is essential that our students recognize the difference between acting and interpretation of literature. Acting is a staged event entailing scenery, lights, costumes, and a collection of props. The actor, fully made up and costumed, moves about the stage as he or she interacts with the other characters in the play. He or she speaks only the dialogue of the character being played. The audience is expected to believe that the actor *is* that character. The interpreter, on the other hand, creates a meaningful *rendition* of the literature, often with script in hand. The readers theatre interpreter, like the actor, has scripted dialogue, but must often breathe life into narrative and expository material as well. He or she does not travel about the stage as much as the actor does but uses gestures and limited bodily movements to add meaning to the readings. The audience is asked to imagine much of the action. They are called on to see "the play" in their minds eye. Student interpreters help them do this primarily by employing oral interpretation skills. It is important, therefore, that our readers practice oral interpretation exercises to develop the ability to communicate the meaning of the literature in a dramatic and expressive manner.

Interpretation Exercises

1. Ask students to say the sentence "Let's go to school" as if

    a. They like school.

    b. They hate school.

    c. They want to go school but the person they're speaking to does not.

2. Have them say the sentence "She took my pencil" as if

    a. They did not want her to take it.

    b. They do not care that she took it.

    c. They were glad she took the pencil instead of another classmate's pencil.

3. Ask students to say the sentence "The boys kicked the old man in the leg and ran off howling with laughter" as if

    a. They think this is really funny.

    b. They think this is sad.

    c. They think this is cruel.

4. Have students say the sentence "Jane loved her dog better than anyone in the world" as if

    a. They think this is ridiculous.

    b. They think Jane is wonderful.

5. Ask them to say the sentence "My teacher is great" as if

    a. They really think so.

    b. They do not like their teacher.

    c. They think their teacher is better than another student's teacher.

6. *Read aloud with expression:* Have students read the following passages, silently at first, and then aloud with expression, making certain the meanings are clear:

    a. "It was Monday morning and Tom Sawyer was miserable. He was always miserable on Monday mornings because it meant he had to go to school. Tom began to scheme. There had to be a way, some way, to avoid going to school. He could be sick and stay home. But as much as he tried, Tom could not find the least little thing wrong with himself. (From *The Adventures of Tom Sawyer* by Mark Twain)

    b. "Towards evening the ugly duckling came to a little miserable peasant's hut. This hut was so dilapidated that it did not itself know on which side it should fall; and that's why it remained standing. The storm whistled round the duckling in such a way that the poor creature was obliged to sit down, to stand against it; and the wind blew worse and worse. Then the duckling noticed that one of the hinges of the door had given way. The door hung so slanting that the duckling could slip through the crack into the room; and that is what it did. (From *The Ugly Duckling* by Hans Christian Andersen)

Instruct students to read the above passages (and others) silently. Ask them to create mental pictures of the scenes they will be describing. Explain that the goal of the interpretation is to have listeners experience similar images. When it is time for them to read aloud, advise them to speak slowly and distinctly so as to give the audience time to receive the message and imagine the scene.

Using the Tape Recorder

One of the most effective means of helping students improve their diction and interpretive skills is for educators to use a tape recorder. Hearing themselves on tape, young people become aware, often for the first time, of their speech and voice problems. Once weaknesses become apparent they can be worked on and corrected. At the same time, when students listen to their recordings of interpretive exercises it becomes easier for them to discover the specific nuances of expression needed to achieve the desired result.

Toning the Body for an Energized Performance

We ask our readers to express themselves orally, but we cannot divorce the voice from the body. A synthesis of mental attitude and physical responsiveness produces a convincing readers theatre interpreter. Before the reader says a single word, his or her body reveals much about him or her and the literature he or she is about to deliver. When each part of the body is limber, in a state of balance, the student interpreter feels ready to bring his or her character to life. Again, like athletes who warm up to keep their muscles toned, our readers need to tone up their bodies, as well as their voices, to produce an animated performance. For this reason exercises to encourage good posture, physical poise, and muscle tone are recommended.

Exercises for Posture

1. *Balance*: Stand tall with your body fully aligned; feet shoulder-width apart flat on the floor. Feel your shoulders balanced easily on top of your spine. Feel your head squarely over your shoulders, shoulders over torso, torso over legs, and legs over feet. Feel relaxed and centered. In this position, gradually tense your feet, legs, torso, shoulders, and head. Hold onto the tenseness to the silent count of five, then slowly release your feet, legs, torso, shoulders, and head. Repeat several times.

2. *Say and perform*: Perform the actions (italicized) as you say the following:

    a. I am *pushing the baby in her carriage.*

    b. I am *trying to lift this heavy trunk.*

    c. I am *carrying this big bag of groceries.*

    d. I am *pulling you on your sled.*

    e. I am *jumping up and down with joy.*

    After the students complete the "perform and say" exercises, ask them to repeat them, this time only *suggesting* the actions rather than actually performing them. Explain how the suggestive, limited movements appropriate for readers theatre can express the varied meanings in the literature.

3. *Muscle tone*: Stand up with your feet flat on the floor.

    a. Raise your eyebrows. Hold for a silent count of five. Relax. Repeat several times.

    b. Smile with your lips closed. Pull the smile tightly toward your ears. Hold for a silent count of five. Relax. Repeat several times.

    c. Stretch your arms up to the ceiling. Pull each arm in turn as if reaching for rungs on a ladder.

    d. Stretch your arms out to the sides. Pull both over your head. Stretch. Clap your hands over your head. Return your arms out to the sides. Repeat several times.

    e. (Space permitting). Jump and leap while singing an appropriate nursery rhyme jingle (or any other well-known song).

After the students perform the body exercises, ask them to read some of the selections above or portions of the story they are working on. Energy levels should carry over to the readings.

Enhancing the Language Arts

There is no question that the complexities of modern life depend heavily on our ability to communicate effectively. To meet this challenge our students require instruction in speech and oral communication. This includes learning how to transmit a message accurately and understandably, pronounce words correctly and distinctly, and project their voices appropriately and energetically. Yet although communication plays an important role in all of our lives, there are no prescribed procedures for teaching children the skills needed to produce oral expressions adequately. The National Communication Association's standards state: "Understanding and skill in communication must be a vital part of K through 12 education. There is a growing awareness of the relationship between student success in grades K through 12 and communications skills. . . . Students should no more be deprived of intentional, organized education in speaking, listening, and media literacy than they are deprived of instruction in reading, writing, mathematics, or science."[8] How, then, should educators incorporate such instruction into their curricula?

The readers theatre program allows for concentration on oral reading, speaking, and listening skills. As we prepare readers to perform we can be sensitive to our students' speech problems. Are they unusually fearful to speak in front of others? Do they have trouble articulating their ideas? Do they fail to pronounce words properly and clearly and thereby distort their messages? Can they be heard by receivers of the communication? Do they understand the communication of others? Are they actively listening?

Improving Speech and Speaking Skills

The first rule about changing communication deficiencies is for students to become *aware* of their problems. By utilizing voice and diction exercises we can unearth articulatory and projection faults of which children may not be cognizant. Using the tape recorder, we can help them overcome persistent flaws that occur in their daily speech. By including class time for "talking" to one another; telling stories and jokes, describing current events, interviewing each other, delivering short speeches, debating, and performing in our dramatized literature, we give young people an opportunity to construct clear and concise communicative transactions. No "and ers"! No "like you knows!"

Reticent speakers, too, can be helped by gradually bringing them into oral communication situations. They can begin in one-to-one private conversations with other students, perhaps preparing interviews. Then they can be assigned to a workshop group where they will be asked to seek and deliver specific information. This can entail going to the library and reporting back to the group about the stories they found for readers theatre. Rehearsing the material over and over with others in their small groups gives them the needed impetus to take part in a class presentation. After the performance reticent speakers may feel ready to engage in short impromptu speeches about their experiences. Desensitizing the speaking situation in small increments allows for building confidence in a nonthreatening atmosphere.. The more frequently students speak in informal and formal situations, the less fearful and more competent they become. Because the readers theatre program includes everyone, the reticent speaker is provided with the ideal circumstance of belonging and performing within a group.

Improving Listening Skills

One of the benefits of becoming aware of one's communication effectiveness is that students grow to be better listeners. Listening skills tend to increase as we pay attention to the various aspects of speech. Educators can direct young people to become *active* listeners. Like any other skill, good listening comes from practice. It is easy to let our attention wander since we think much faster than a speaker can talk. We have plenty of time to be distracted by our private thoughts. This means we must work on having young people concentrate on what they hear. One way to accomplish this is to tell students to listen for specific ideas. When we direct listeners to answer the familiar journalistic questions—*who, what, where, when, how,* or *why*—they learn to focus on the main points of a communication and become more active listeners. Other listening opportunities occur when preparing and performing in a readers theatre program around which a unit on the art of effective listening can be constructed.

Preparing a Full-Length Program

Now that the class has worked together and has become familiar with the process of adapting, staging, and warming up for readers theatre, we are ready to prepare a full-length presentation. There are many ways to parcel out the work involved in such a production. Students who enjoy writing may be given the task of adapting the material. Others may be cast as readers, and still others may assist with the directing and staging of the production. One of the best procedures to follow, especially when working with a compiled script, is to divide the class into small workshop groups, each responsible for one selection from the total presentation. In this way every student has a hand in adapting, directing, and performing a complete entity. Add to this the necessary transitional material, which we may write together with our students, and a complete readers theatre is ready for performance.

Workshop Groups

When making up workshop groups for a compiled script, consider the reading level of each student. Every group should contain a healthy mix of reading abilities as well as other talents. Better readers will automatically help those who are slower since all want the project to succeed.

After deciding on a theme, the students may be asked to choose their own material or the class can select the segments for each group. The best idea is to hold the workshops in the library where books are available and librarians are there for guidance. But no matter where the groups get together, the literature should meet the criteria for a successful readers theatre experience (see Chapters 2 and 3).

Send each group to a different corner of the room to choose a selection and to prepare the script. Time and materials should be available for discussing and adapting the material. The instructor or librarian must be on hand at all times for consultations with individual groups (see Chapter 4). Bear in mind that one double-spaced, typed page takes about two minutes to read on stage.

Those students who have difficulty reading or who are reluctant to participate for one reason or another will be encouraged to join in the activity by working on a story already selected and adapted. This gives them a head start on the process and develops the self-confidence they need to be part of the project. There are many readers theatre scripts ready for use in the classroom. See the Bibliography in this volume for books that contain scripts for all reading levels.

Getting help with the script.

Casting and Directing

When the scripts are prepared, the groups are ready for casting. Who will play what role, who will direct the performance, and who will help with the staging depends very much on the degree of perfection sought. If you are preparing a classroom presentation, you may want to allow the students to do everything with little supervision. On the other hand, if you are seeking a "finished" program, you will want to be more involved with the casting and the directing.

If this is to be an all-student production, instruct the groups to decide on a director, who will then help assign the roles after everyone who wishes to read does so. Suggest that decisions be made with the approval of all members.

If directing and casting are to be left up to the instructor, tryouts should take place within each group. A permissive and creative attitude allows for student suggestions and fosters a noncompetitive atmosphere. Try to engender the excitement of discovery and delight inherent in preparing a program for an audience. Whichever procedure is followed, it is important that all students be completely familiar with the entire script and have a chance to input their ideas.

First Rehearsals

The recommended way to begin rehearsing is for the members of each group to sit at their table and read their assigned lines for meaning. That is, they should read with a minimum of expression to get the gist of what the characters are saying and to whom they are speaking.[9] Questions asked of the readers about the way each understands his or her character, including the part of the narrator, will help them determine how best to play their parts. Eventually, with some direction, students will find the appropriate expressions needed to bring their characters to life. At the same time an interplay among the characters emerges as students begin to understand the "back and forth" element of dialogue.

Student director gives advice.

Blocking Rehearsals

When the readers are ready to put the script on stage, they will need to plan where the characters will stand or sit, if and when they will move around, and where they will focus. As discussed previously, drawing up a plan before students move to the platform is the best idea. Keep it simple, with appropriately placed stools, ladders, crates, etc., to create interesting levels. Students will experience a sense of security when they know their exact placement and the required movements.

Final Rehearsals

Once on stage, rehearsals become more meaningful. Now the readers must become aware of the audience. Vocal projection, using the script properly, determining the advantages of on-stage or offstage focus, and interacting with other characters, acting and reacting, all become important factors at this time. Students are best advised to read slowly, looking out and up from their scripts. When readers are out of the scene or not speaking, they must be given direction as to what behavior is appropriate.

Instructing students as to what to expect during the performance is a good idea. Interruptions from wiggling, squealing children in the audience should be anticipated. It is not unusual for a child in the audience, empathizing with a character on stage, to call out. Unexpected laughter may also surprise the readers. In such circumstances students should learn to "ride over" interruptions and to remain in character throughout. They must not wait too long for laughter to subside, nor should they laugh at themselves or fellow readers. *Playing up* to the audience can be overcome with careful pre-performance preparation.

The king practices his lines.

Using the Videotape Machine

The language of the body, face, and eyes plays an important part in a readers theatre production. Videotaping students performing the exercises and the rehearsals will create an awareness of the role the body plays in sending messages to an audience without fully acting out the motions described in the text. No matter how often one might tell the readers that their extraneous body movements are distracting, or that their posture needs improvement, they do not fully understand until they actually see themselves on tape.

Taping rehearsal sessions and then the final performance is not only an invaluable means of demonstrating deficiencies but is also an effective way of preserving a showcase for those unable to be present for the show and for the benefit of future classes. It should be done whenever possible.

Postscript Regarding Copyright Laws

Laws exist that protect the writers of creative literary material. These copyright laws are not always clear about what is allowed to be performed in a classroom or auditorium. Usually "fair use" exceptions permit teachers and librarians to stage presentations developed or adapted from copyrighted materials for educational and instructional purposes. In any event, it is prudent to inquire of the publishers what their policies on classroom and auditorium performances are. When calling or writing to the permissions department of a publisher, make certain to mention that no admission fee is being charged and that the material is used for instructional purposes. When admission fees are charged, however, royalty fees may come into play. Inquire about this aspect *before* preparing a script for performance.

Let's Review

Warming-up exercises for improving vocal projection, diction, and theatre techniques are beneficial for a more polished performance of readers theatre.

Breathing exercises help students to relax and control the breath supply important for vocal projection. Diction exercises focus on articulating sounds distinctly. Theatre techniques include responding on cue, developing empathy, and the expressive interpretation of lines.

To respond on cue, students should become familiar with the signals that precede their actions and reactions. Characters in a dramatized story must sound as much like genuine people as possible. Empathy also contributes to this ability when readers share and understand the feelings of others.

It is important for readers to recognize the difference between acting and interpreting. The actor expects the audience to believe he or she *is* the character portrayed. The interpreter, on the other hand, creates a meaningful *rendition* of the literature, often with a script in hand. Oral interpretation exercises are designed so that students can become more expressive interpreters. In addition, since the body reveals much about the reader even before he or she speaks, exercises to tone the body and foster good posture and physical poise are encouraged to energize the performance.

Educators are advised to offer instruction in speech and oral communication. Time should be set aside to allow students to engage in the various exercises that will help develop effective communication skills. In addition to these drills, students should be engaged in story and joke telling, delivery of short speeches, debating, and interviewing. Reluctant speakers can gain more confidence when small, incremental opportunities to speak are presented to them.

Preparing a full length readers theatre program involves parceling out the work to the class. One of the best procedures to follow is to divide the class into small workshop groups, each responsible for one selection of a compiled script. The library is the ideal place for this activity.

Casting, directing, and rehearsing for the performance can be managed by the students with some supervision, or if a more finished program is sought, the instructor can be more involved. Whichever method is used, the students should become familiar with the entire script and have a chance to input ideas and suggestions.

It is recommended that at first rehearsals students should read for meaning with a minimum of expression. Blocking rehearsals involves planning where the characters will be situated on stage and where and when they will move. Final rehearsals demand more meaningful, expressive readings. Students now become aware of the audience. Vocal projection, use of scripts, eye focus, and interactions with other characters all come into play at this time. Anticipating audience reactions should be noted, and readers must be advised to ignore distractions and stay in character throughout.

Videotaping oral interpretation exercises, rehearsals, and final performances is recommended for students to become aware of their deficiencies and for the edification of future readers theatre classes.

It is prudent for teachers and librarians who plan to present published material for an audience to ask the publisher of that material about its permission policies.

Notes

1. John P. Moncur and Harrison M. Karr, *Developing Your Speaking Voice,* 2nd ed. (New York: Harper & Row, 1972), 171.

2. Donald H. Ecroyd, *Speech in the Classroom,* 2nd ed. (Englewood Cliffs, NJ: Prentice-Hall, 1969), 43.

3. Ibid.

4. Ibid.

5. Ibid., 45.

6. Maxine McSweeney, *Creative Children's Theatre* (New York: A. A. Barnes, 1974), 123.

7. Nellie McCaslin, *Act Now!* (New York: S. G. Phillips, 1975), 23–24.

8. *The Speaking, Listening, and Media Literacy Standards and Competency Statements for K–12 Education* (Washington, DC: National Communication Association, 1998), 1–2.

9. Leslie Irene Coger and Melvin R. White, *Readers Theatre Handbook*, 3rd ed. rev. (Glenview, IL: Scott, Foresman, 1982), 146.

Chapter 7

THE PERFORMANCE AND AFTERWARD

NARRATOR 1:	Of all things, the princess does not want to inherit the kingdom!!!!
KING:	That is my dilemma. My daughter refuses to become a ruler. I am at a loss as to what to do.
FINANCE MAN:	Is there no other relative who can take on the job?
KING:	I have only one other relation.
ALL:	Who is that?
KING:	My nephew Arnold.
ALL:	Well?
KING:	Arnold's an accountant in New York. He would never leave such a good job.
PUBLICIST:	I know what to do! Why not let the people of the kingdom decide?
JESTER:	The people? What do the people know? You saw what happened to those guys in America when they tried to elect a president.
MINSTREL:	You're right. There's got to be a better way.
ALL:	What shall we do?
NARRATOR 2:	Well, audience, it seems that our characters cannot solve the problem as to who will inherit the monarchy.
NARRATOR 1:	Can you come up with an answer?
NARRATOR 2:	If you have an ending to the story please let us know. Send your ideas to our classroom.
NARRATOR 1:	If we choose your entry, we will use it in our production and you will get to be writer in residence for our next readers theatre.
MINSTREL:	Yeah, and don't forget to include a little doo wop . . .
ALL:	**No doo wop!!!!**

EPILOGUE: Hi!
I'm the epilogue. You may remember me. I used to be the prologue.
But now that our story is coming to a close, I have a new role.
Please let us hear from you soon. Until then . . .

ALL: Goodbye.

(The End)

The Big Moment Arrives

Finally, the performance is at hand. Students are excited and a little nervous. The most important thing a director can do now is to reassure the readers that they will do well. The performers want to know that no matter what happens they will succeed in entertaining the audience. Confidence is instilled when children are told that nervousness is natural and even helpful since it serves to heighten the energy needed for the performance. To relieve tensions prior to the performance, use a few of the warm-up exercises that include stretching and relaxing. Deep-breathing exercises are also appropriate.

Performing student script, The Witch and the Jesters.

On Stage, Everyone!

Before performing for a large audience, consider taking the show "on the road." Moving the performance from classroom to classroom is a way of presenting the readings in a warm, friendly atmosphere. Here spectators are physically close to the readers and feel a part of the events taking place on stage. The close proximity also makes it possible to invite audience participation, which delights young observers. In Maurice Sendak's *Where the Wild Things Are,* Max shouts, "Let the wild rumpus start!" It is a surprise and thrill for the audience when the Wild Things run about showing their terrible teeth and claws and pulling two or three spectators on stage to join the players. "The Bridge," a short, short story, calls for each character to say only one line. Audience members, after seeing it performed by our readers, know it well enough to be able to try it themselves. The result is fun and gratifying for all.

Once the readers perform in the classroom setting, it is much easier to move to a larger room, such as the library or auditorium. Now that they are experienced, the students feel secure and satisfied that they can evoke the planned responses from an audience. In all instances, make certain that the performers know the physical limits of the stage area wherever they may be. Mapping out the specific space in which the action takes place will make it easier to designate *offstage* areas where students who are not on stage may *sit* until they are needed.

"Let the wild rumpus start!" from *Where the Wild Things Are.*

It's All Over But the Shouting

The director nods. The xylophone pings for the last time. Applause breaks the spell. The students on stage bow. Readers theatre is over. Spectators babble with delight about the event. "That queen should have her head cut off." "If I had three wishes I would have wished for a motorized scooter and some good video games." "I loved the part where the donkey fell in the water." Without too much analysis, it is easy to see that everyone enjoyed the experience. For our purposes, however, the project does not end with the final performance. As educators we can capitalize on the excitement and motivation generated by the event by creating follow-up activities to foster additional writing, reading, and speaking benefits. We can also evaluate the readers theatre outcomes and determine their contribution to our language arts curriculum.

Audience members enjoying the performance.

Audience members enjoying the performance.

Follow-Up Activities

Motivation engendered by a readers theatre performance can be sustained after the program has taken place. Following are suggestions that may serve as points of departure for other creative projects.

Discussion and Public Speaking

After participating in readers theatre students want to talk about the experience. This is a good time to hold a class discussion about the success of the program. Conversing together after a shared event gives each person an opportunity for self-expression. Untold advantages accrue from expressing thoughts and feelings and listening to those of others.

Students should be invited to prepare individual talks to deliver to the class or other classes about the part of the program in which they participated. They may wish to describe the technique for selecting the literature, preparing the script, directing the characters, interpreting a role, and performing for an audience.

An exercise that can precede a collaborative creative writing effort is to suggest that students make up dialogue around a theme as they talk together in small groups. The recorded results can be used in the next readers theatre production.

Improvisational or creative dramatics, a relative of readers theatre, can be introduced as a quick way of enacting a story, poem, or play. Younger children enjoy this activity as they try out character voices and actions.

Mock television interviews involving the readers, writers, and directors of the script inspire spontaneous, effective oral communication. These give students an opportunity to ask and respond to questions about the readers theatre program. Similarly, a "Meet the Press" panel can be formed with pupils acting as reporters and guests engaged in give and take about the readers theatre event.

Writing

To encourage critical writing skills, ask students to write a review of the performance for local newspapers. The review should include the way the production was prepared and some firsthand observations of what took place on stage.

Now that students have adapted a story into play form, they may be ready to write an original scene with a two- or three-person dialogue. Afterward the pupils can invite members of the class to enact these sequences. Writers should be encouraged to improve their scripts as they listen to their work being read aloud.

Composition ideas, which are often difficult to find, grow out of the readers theatre experience. Writing on such topics as "How I Felt Being a Character in a Story" or "Performing in Readers Theatre is an Unusual Happening" gives students a chance to be creative while expressing their reactions to the event.

Writing fan letters to the readers is a fun assignment for observers of the performance (see Figure 7.1). The letters can include what the children liked in the production and what favorite story they want to see enacted in a future readers theatre.

April 27, 2001

Dear Readers,

I just loved your cute acts. They were really funny. I especially enjoyed your readings of Life Spand and The Bridge. Both were filled with lots of humor and bunches of giggles. All the plays were acted out superbly. All the readers showed lots of enthusiasm for their characters.

I really appreciate the stories you selected and would love to see more of them performed. My teacher says we can try to put on our own readers theater performance in our classroom. We can't wait to get our turn in the limelight.

Your fan,
Emma Sade-Ramer

P.S. Best line: Newsreporter, "Wow!, what a story!"

2/16/2001

Dear Class 209,

I really enjoyed your performance very much. I thought the morals of the stories were really great. My favorite act was The Miller, The Son, and the Donkey. I really think Norman should take up donkey-acting as a profession. He was great. I really thank you for letting me see this performance.

Sincerely yours,
Scott Greenspan

Figure 7.1. Fan letters from appreciative student audience members.

Listening

It is well known that the principle behind learning to listen is that listening should have a purpose. Toward this goal, participants and audience members alike can be told to listen for the "big moments" in the script, to locate the climax of the story, or to find the choices that confront one or more of the characters. Students should then be asked to write or tell about what they heard.

Reading

Now that students are aware of what it takes to find appropriate literature for a readers theatre, they are motivated to be on the alert for suitable material as they read for pleasure. A good way to store ideas for future productions is to keep a readers theatre file in the classroom and the library. After reading a possible selection for dramatization, the pupil fills out a card that describes the story line and the characters portrayed. (See Figure 7.2). Finally, finished scripts can be filed in the library to serve as records of success, as practice pieces, and as examples.

```
                    Pupil Name:
Name of Selection:
Author:
Type: (story, poem, play)
Characters:
Story Line:
```

Figure 7.2. Readers theatre file card.

Let's Give It Again!

The thrill of performance often motivates students to want another chance to present the program. Extra performances mean new audiences must be recruited, but this is usually not difficult. Other classes in the school, neighboring schools, PTA groups, and the local public library will welcome the program. Our students benefit from additional performances as they learn to adapt to different situations, gain greater self-confidence, and find subtle meanings in the literature they had not recognized before. Like a troupe of players with a show "on the road," pupils work in harmony with one another, recreating the excitement of performing in each new circumstance.

Evaluation

Books about measuring educational achievement suggest direct observational techniques such as rating scales and checklists as appropriate methods for evaluating student accomplishment of specific objectives of a unit of work.[1] The following rating scales and checklists are convenient devices for assessing the readers theatre experience. The first scale (Figure 7.3, pages 110–111) records general impressions regarding changes in pupil attitudes, motivations, and skills as a result of the project. The second (Figure 7.4, page 112), to be filled out for each child, asks more specific questions about pupil response and progress made in reading, writing, speaking, and listening. The scales are supplemented by an abbreviated checklist that is useful in assessing the creative involvement of the students in the project. Finally, for those who are interested in judging the quality of the readers theatre script, staging, and performance, a more detailed checklist is offered. All are reproducible handouts.

Because creative behavior often indicates a willingness to learn new ideas and skills, the instructor may use the first checklist[2] as a gauge for evaluating a student's responsiveness to readers theatre activity. This evaluation is valuable for estimating the effect such activity has on the enhancement of the language arts in the classroom. If affirmative responses outweigh negative responses, it is logical to assume that the student has benefited from the readers theatre project in light of the standards set down by the International Reading Association and the National Council of Teachers of English. (See the standards listed in Chapter 1.)

The second checklist is helpful to review before and after readers theatre is staged. Before the readers take the stage the instructor can help students make necessary changes and revisions to perfect the final performance. Afterward the instructor may wish to use the evaluation for future readers theatre activity.

Checklist for Evaluating Creative Behavior

____ 1. Intense absorption in listening, observing, and doing

____ 2. Intense animation

____ 3. Use of analogies in speech and writing

____ 4. Tendency to burst out to complete teacher's sentence

____ 5. Eagerness to tell others about discoveries

____ 6. Follow-up at home or in community of ideas generated at school

____ 7. Manifestations of curiosity

____ 8. Spontaneous use of experimentation and discovery approaches

____ 9. Imaginative play

____ 10. Excitement in voice about discoveries

____ 11. Habit of guessing outcomes and checking accuracy

____ 12. Low distractability

____ 13. Tendency to lose awareness of time

____ 14. Continued creative work after "time is up" (bell or deadline)

____ 15. Penetrating observations and questions

Checklist for Evaluating the Readers Theatre Script, Staging, and Performance

Script

_____ 1. Does the material meet the criteria set down for a good readers theatre script?

_____ 2. Are the transitions prepared so the program flows intelligibly? Does the program have a beginning, middle, and end, giving it the unity of a complete and finished production?

_____ 3. Are the lines divided up meaningfully? Is there an understanding of who is saying what and why?

Staging

_____ 1. Are the readers arranged to create an interesting stage picture?

_____ 2. Do students know how and when to enter and exit? Are these entrances and exits clear to the audience?

_____ 3. If stools, ladders, etc., are used, can they be moved on and off with dispatch?

_____ 4. Do students focus so that the audience understands where the described action is supposed to take place?

_____ 5. Are movements clear? Do they illuminate the text?

_____ 6. If sound effects are used, do they serve the purpose intended? Can they be heard clearly?

_____ 7. Are all the hats that are used easy to put on and take off? Do they stay on and in place throughout the performance?

_____ 8. Are the scripts in good shape? Are pages fastened in securely?

Performance

_____ 1. Is the script performed smoothly without breakdowns and interruptions?

_____ 2. Is the speech of the readers clear and distinct?

_____ 3. Do students show an understanding of what they are reading?

_____ 4. Do the readers avoid word-by-word delivery?

_____ 5. Are interpretive skills employed to their fullest?

_____ 6. Do the readers create believable characters and good mental images?

_____ 7. Do the readers listen to each other and react meaningfully?

_____ 8. Do the readers handle scripts and props unobtrusively and efficiently?

_____ 9. Does the performance come to a recognizable end?

_____ 10. Do the readers know how to bow and where to go at the close of the production?

Rating Scale of Changes Resulting from the Readers Theatre Project

Directions: Place an "x" in the appropriate space below each question. In the space for comments, include anything that helps clarify your rating.

1. Did those children who usually react negatively to a learning situation respond more readily to readers theatre activity?

     no change __   some change __   substantial change__

Comment: _____

2. Were shy and withdrawn students more willing to participate in the readers theatre experience than in other performance-oriented activities?

     no change __   some change __   substantial change __

Comment: _____

3. Were students noticeably more motivated to read material connected with readers theatre activity than with other available reading?

     no change __   some change __   substantial change __

Comment: _____

4. Were students more willing to write scripts than other writing assignments?

     no change __   some change __   substantial change __

Comment: _____

5. Were students more willing to engage in oral reading exercises relating to the performance of readers theatre than in the usual drills?

     no change __   some change __   substantial change __

Comment: _____

Figure 7.3. Rating scale of changes resulting from the readers theatre project (*continued on next page*).

6. Were the students more respectful of each other's opinions in the decision-making process connected with the readers theatre performance than at other times?

   no change ___   some change ___   substantial change ___

   Comment: _____

7. Were students more motivated to produce creative ideas for the readers theatre project than on other occasions?

   no change ___   some change ___   substantial change ___

   Comment: _____

8. Did the students show greater comprehension and appreciation for the literature selected for the readers theatre project than in other reading situations?

   no change ___   some change ___   substantial change ___

   Comment: _____

9. Did the students enjoy working on the readers theatre project more than on other projects in the language arts curriculum?

   no change ___   some change ___   substantial change ___

   Comment: _____

10. Did the students show greater interest in doing another readers theatre production than they usually exhibit for other projects?

    no change ___   some change ___   substantial change ___

    Comment: _____

Figure 7.3. Rating scale of changes resulting from the readers theatre project (*continued*).

Rating Scale of Student Response in the Readers Theatre Project

Directions: Rate each item on the basis of 4 points for outstanding quality or performance, 3 points for better than average, 2 points for average, 1 point for inferior, and 0 for unsatisfactory. Circle the appropriate number to indicate your rating, and enter the total of these numbers at the bottom of the sheet.

1. How would you rate this student's enthusiasm for the project?　0　1　2　3　4

   a. The student read only one story for the script.　0　1　2　3　4

   b. The student read two or three stories for the script.　0　1　2　3　4

   c. The student surveyed a broad variety of stories for the script.　0　1　2　3　4

   d. The student surveyed a broad variety of stories and discussed　0　1　2　3　4
      options critically.

2. To what extent did this student seem eager to seek out and　0　1　2　3　4
   read material for possible use in the project?

3. To what extent did this student seem eager to read a part　0　1　2　3　4
   in the group script?

4. To what extent did this student contribute ideas for the　0　1　2　3　4
   creation and staging of the script?

5. How would you rate this student's receptiveness to ideas　0　1　2　3　4
   generated by his or her classmates?

6. How would you judge this student's interest in listening to　0　1　2　3　4
   the readings delivered by his or her fellow classmates?

7. How would you evaluate this student's comprehension of　0　1　2　3　4
   the literature used in the project?

8. To what extent did this student appreciate the literature used　0　1　2　3　4
   in the project?

9. To what extent did this student respond to the voice,　0　1　2　3　4
   diction, and interpretive reading exercises?

10. To what extent did this student exhibit improvement in his　0　1　2　3　4
   or her oral reading skill?

Total of circled numbers: _____

Figure 7.4. Rating scale of student response in the readers theatre project.

Let's Reviews

Before the performance, the director should reassure the readers that they will do well no matter what happens. Warm-up exercises will help to relieve tensions at this time. In preparation for a larger audience, it is a good idea to move the performance from classroom to classroom. The close proximity makes it possible to invite audience members to participate. After the performance, educators can capitalize on the motivation generated by the event by creating follow-up activities. Speaking activities include discussion of the event, individual talks, small group participation, improvisational or creative dramatics, and mock television interviews. Writing activities include writing reviews of the event for local newspapers, creating original dialogue to be enacted in the future, writing compositions containing student reactions to the event, and writing fan letters to the readers.

Listening should have a purpose. Participants and audience members can be told to listen for the "big moments" in the script, the climax of the story, or to find the choices that confront the characters.

Reading activities include finding suitable material for future performances as students read for pleasure. A readers theatre file is a good way to store ideas and scripts.

Students benefit by giving additional performances of the script. They adapt to different situations, gain self-confidence, and find subtle meanings in the literature they had not recognized before.

Direct observational techniques such as rating scales and checklists are appropriate methods for evaluating student accomplishments. A scale that records general impressions regarding pupil attitudes, motivations, and skills as a result of the project can be employed by the educator. A second scale, filled out for each child, asks more specific questions about pupil responses and progress made in reading, writing, speaking, and listening. Checklists are useful for those interested in assessing the creative involvement of the students and for judging the quality of the readers theatre script, staging, and performance.

Notes

1. See Norman E Gronlund and Robert L. Linn, *Measurement and Evaluation in Teaching,* 6th ed. (New York: Macmillan, 1990), 375–398; Betty Wallace and William Graves, *Poisoned Apple* (New York: St. Martin's Press, 1995), 96–97.

2. Adapted from a list of 230 signs of creative classroom behavior compiled by 200 students in E. Paul Torrance's class, "Creative Ways of Teaching." E. Paul Torrance, "Creative Abilities of Elementary School Children," in *Teaching for Creative Endeavor,* ed. William B. Michael (Bloomington: Indiana University Press, 1968), 20–21.

Selected References for Part 1

This list includes adaptable works mentioned in the text.

Asemon, Janet, and Isaac Asemon. *How to Enjoy Writing.* New York: Walker, 1987.

Barnes-Murphy, Frances, retold. *The Fables of Aesop.* Illus. Rowan Barnes-Murphy. New York: Lothrop, Lee & Shepard, 1994.

Bunting, Eve. *Smoky Night.* New York: Harcourt Brace Jovanovich, 1994.

Carbone, Elisa. *Starting School with an Enemy.* New York: Alfred A. Knopf, 1998.

Childress, Alice. *When the Rattlesnake Sounds.* New York: Coward, McCann & Geoghagan, 1975.

Christopher, Matt. *The Comeback Challenge.* New York: Little, Brown, 1996.

Cleary, Beverly. *Dear Mr. Henshaw.* New York: William Morrow, 1983.

Clements, Andrew. *The Jacket. New York:* Simon & Schuster, 2002

———. *The Janitor's Boy.* New York: Simon & Schuster, 2000.

Cooper, Susan. *The Bogart.* New York: Aladdin Paperbacks, 1993.

Daleos, Kalli. *If You're Not Here, Please Raise Your Hand: Poems About School.* New York: Simon & Schuster, 1990.

Danziger, Paula. *The Divorce Express.* New York: Delacorte Press, 1982.

Dasent, Sir George Webbe, trans. *East O' the Sun and West O' the Moon.* Illus. P. J. Lynch. Cambridge, MA: Candlewick Press, 1991.

Davis, Ossie. *Escape to Freedom: A Play About Young Frederick Douglass,.* rev. ed., ed. Beverly Robin Tresny and Eileen C. Palmer. Metuchen, NJ: Scarecrow Press, 1986.

———. *Langston: A Play.* New York: Delacorte Press, 1982.

Dubrovin, Vivian. *Write Your Own Story.* New York: Franklin Watts, 1984.

Forest, Heather. *Wisdom Tales from Around the World.* Little Rock, AR: August House, 1996.

Francis, Robert. *Come Out in the Sun.* Amherst: University of Mass. Press, 1965.

———. *The Orb Weaver.* Middletown, Conn.: Wesleyan University Press, 1960.

Freedman, Florence B. *It Happened in Chelm.* New York: Sapolsky Publishers, 1990.

French, Vivian. *Why the Sea Is Salt.* Illus. Patrice Aggs. Cambridge, MA: Candlewick Press, 1993.

Frost, Robert. *You Come Too.* New York: Holt, Rinehart & Winston, 1959.

Gay, Kathlyn. *They Don't Wash Their Socks.* New York: Walker, 1990.

Glenn, Mel. *Back to Class.* New York: Clarion Books, 1982.

———. *Class Dismissed.* New York: Clarion Books, 1982.

————. *Class Dismissed II.* New York: Clarion Books, 1982.

————. *My Friend's Got This Problem, Mr. Candler.* New York: Clarion Books, 1991.

Grimes, Nikki. *A Dime a Dozen.* New York: Dial Books for Young Readers, 1997.

Guthrie, Donna, Nancy Bentley, Katy Keck Arnstein. *The Young Author's Do-It-Yourself Book.* Brookfield, CT: Millbrook Press, 1994.

Hall, Donald, ed. *The Oxford Illustrated Book of Children's Poems.* New York: Oxford University Press, 1999.

Hesse, Karren. *Letters from Rifka.* New York: Puffin Books, 1993.

————. *Out of the Dust.* New York: Scholastic, 1997.

Jennings, Coleman A. *Theatre for Young Audiences.* New York: St. Martin's Press, 1998.

Jones, Terry. *Fantastic Stories.* New York: Viking, 1993.

Kimmel, Eric A. *Ten Suns.* Illus. Yongsheng Xuan. New York: Holiday House, 1998.

Lansky, Bruce, compiled by. *Kids Pack the Funniest Poems.* New York: Meadowbrook, 1991.

Leedy, Loreen. *Messages in the Mailbox.* New York: Holiday House, 1991.

Lionni, Leo. *Fish is Fish.* New York: Alfred A. Knopf, 1970.

Lowry, Lois. *The Giver.* New York: Bantam Doubleday Dell Books for Young Readers, 1993.

Mahy, Margaret. *The Seven Chinese Brothers.* Illus. Jean and Mon-sien Tseng. New York: Scholastic, 1990.

Martin, Rafe. *Mysterious Tales of Japan.* Illus. Tatsuro Kinchi. New York: G. P. Putnam's Sons, 1996.

McCaffrey, Anne. *Dragonsong.* New York: Atheneum, 1976.

McKissack, Patricia C. *The Dark-Thirty.* New York: Alfred A. Knopf, 1992.

Merriam, Eve. *Chortles.* New York: Morrow Junior Books, 1989.

Mischel, Florence D. *How to Write a Letter.* New York: Franklin Watts, 1988.

O'Brien, Robert C. *Mrs. Frisby and the Rats of Nimh.* New York: Aladdin Paperbacks, 1971.

Otfinoski, Steve. *Putting it in Writing.* New York: Scholastic, 1993.

Parish, Peggy. *Amelia Bedelia.* New York: HarperCollins, 1963.

Patterson, Katherine. *Jacob Have I Loved.* New York: Thomas Y. Crowell, 1980.

Paxton, Tom. *Birds of a Feather and Other Aesop's Fables.* Illus. Robert Rayensky. New York: Morrow Junior Books, 1993.

Perkins, Patricia Barrett, foreword. *Aesop's Fables.* Illus. Charles Santore. New York: Jelly Bean Press, 1988.

Phillips, Louis. *Haunted House Jokes.* New York: Viking, 1987.

Poe, Edgar Allan, Brad Bayert, ed. *Poetry for Young People: Edgar Allan Poe.* New York: Sterling, 1995.

Polacco, Patricia. *Luba and the Wren.* New York: Philomel, 1999.

―――. *Thank You Mr. Falker*. New York: Philomel, 1998.

Prelutsky, Jack. *The New Kid on the Block*. New York: Greenivillon Books, 1984.

―――. *Something Big Has Been Here*. New York: Greenivillon Books, 1990.

Prelutsky, Jack, ed. *The 20th Century Children's Poetry Treasury*. New York: Alfred A. Knopf, 1999.

Prelutsky, Jack, selected by. *The Random House Book of Poetry for Children*. New York: Random House, 1983.

Roberts, Wilo Davis. *The Girl with the Silver Eyes*. New York: Atheneum, 1980.

Rylant, Cynthia. *A Blue-Eyed Daisy*. New York: Simon & Schuster, 1985.

―――. *A Couple of Kooks and Other Stories About Love*. New York: Orchard, 1990.

―――. Henry and Mudge (Series). New York: Aladdin, 1987.

―――. *Soda Jerk*. New York: Orchard, 1990.

Sacher, Louis. *Holes*. New York: Farrar, Straus & Giroux, 1998.

―――. *Sideways Stories from Wayside School*. New York: Lothrop, Lee & Shepard,1989.

―――. *Wayside School Gets a Little Stranger*. New York: Lothrop, Lee & Shepard,1989.

―――. *Wayside School Is Falling Down*. New York: Lothrop, Lee & Shepard, 1989.

San Souci, Robert D. *A Weave of Words*. Illus. Raúl Colón. New York: Orchard Books, 1998.

Sandburg, Carl. *Poetry for Young People: Carl Sandburg*. New York: Sterling, 1995.

Say, Allen. *Stranger in the Mirror*. Boston: Houghton Mifflin, 1995.

Schwartz, Alvin. *And the Green Grass Grew All Around: Folk Poetry for Everyone*. New York: HarperCollins, 1992.

Scieszka, Jon. *Squids Will Be Squids*. New York: Viking Penguin,1998.

Sendak, Maurice. *Where the Wild Things Are*. New York: Harper & Row, 1988.

Silverman, Erica. *Raisel's Riddle*. New York: Farrar, Straus & Giroux, 1999.

Sobol, Donald. Encyclopedia Brown (Series). New York: Scholastic, Bantam Nelson or Delacorte, 1963.

Soto, Gary. *Baseball in April*. New York: Harcourt Brace Jovanovich, 1990.

Spinelli, Jerry. *The Wringer*. New York: HarperCollins, 1997.

Stanek, Lou Willett. *Thinking Like a Writer*. New York: Random House, 1994.

Sword, Elizabeth Hauge, and Victoria Fournoy McCarthy. *A Child's Anthology of Poetry*. Hopewell, NJ: Eco Press, 1995.

Swortzell, Lowell, ed. *All the World's a Stage*. New York: Delacorte Press, 1972.

Thayer, Ernest L. *Casey at the Bat*. New York: Godine, 1988.

Trelease, Jim. *The Read-Aloud Handbook*. New York: Penguin, 1995.

Weiss, Harvey. *How to be a Hero*. New York: Parents Magazine Press, 1968.

Wells, Rosemary. *Streets of Gold*. New York: Dial Press, 1999.

Wilde, Oscar. *The Fairy Tales of Oscar Wilde.* Illus. Michael Hague. New York: Henry Holt, 1993.

Wise, William. *Perfect Pancakes, If You Please.* New York: Dial Press, 1997.

Wolff, Virginia Euwer. *Make Lemonade.* New York: Henry Holt, 1993.

Woodruff, Elvira. *The Memory Coat.* New York: Scholastic, 1999.

Wyse, Lois, and Molly Rose Goldman. *How to Take Your Grandmother to the Museum.* New York: Workman Publications, 1998.

PART 2

Model Readers Theatre and Sample Scripts

Rehearsing "The Bully"

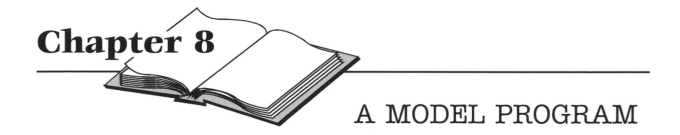

Chapter 8

A MODEL PROGRAM

The model readers theatre program presented in this chapter was directed by the author with the cooperation of the classroom teacher at the Number Six School, Woodmere, New York. A fifth-grade class composed of students on all reading levels was selected to participate. This project was accomplished in ten one-hour sessions, plus the performance. The sessions took place on ten consecutive days. A description of each day's activity is offered below. Many of the preparatory exercises mentioned as part of a day's activities are described in "Compiling and Adapting Material" (Chapter 4), "Classroom Procedures" (Chapter 5), and "Preparing for Performance" (Chapter 6).

Day One

The principal arranged for us to come early in the morning so that the children would be alert and receptive to new ideas. The plan was to engage the pupils in two discussions. The first would center on plays and the children's theatrical experience. This would lead us into an explanation of readers theatre. The second discussion would be about the fable, "The Miller, His Son, and the Donkey." We would present the story to the class and have them read it silently. Afterward we would talk together about the author, the plot, and how we might adapt it for readers theatre.

Here is what happened:

READERS THEATRE LEADER (RTL):	What do you think of when you hear the word "theatre?"
GERRI:	Actors and actresses.
DANNY:	Costumes.
TRACY:	Scenery.
RICHARD:	Curtains and spotlights.
STEVEN:	Scripts and a director.
RTL:	Very good. You seem to know something about plays and the theatre. Can you tell me about some of the plays you have seen?
WENDY:	I saw *Annie* on Broadway. It was a musical with a lot of singing and dancing and acting.
JACKIE:	I was in a play last year. It was a Chinese play called *The Prince.* I played the nurse.
LYNNE:	And I painted some of the scenery and pulled the curtain.

RTL: Well, you know a lot about what goes into producing a play. Can anyone name another type of theatre, other than a play?

KENNY: I once went to an opera. There were singers instead of actors. The singers sang the story.

ROBERTA: There's ballet where everyone dances.

GERRI: There are puppet shows and magic shows.

RTL: Yes, there are many situations involving performers and an audience. There is even a kind of theatre where the players read to their audience. This is called readers theatre.

LIZ: You mean the actors hold books on stage and just read them aloud to the people?

RTL: Well, something like that except the readers don't just read their stories in an ordinary way, they read as if they were the characters in the stories.

MELANIE: I know, it's like a storyteller who reads with a lot of expression. My library has a storyteller like that. She pretends to be all the characters in the stories she reads.

RTL: Yes, readers theatre is like story telling, but instead of one storyteller there are several. Each reader pretends to be one or more of the characters in the story, so it is something like a play, too.

NORMAN: Do the actors read from stories or plays?

RTL: They can read everything: stories, poems, and plays. But even if they read a play, they hold their scripts on stage and only suggest the action. We'll talk more about the differences between readers theatre and a conventional play tomorrow.

A readers theatre leader holds a session.

The children were told that for the next ten days they would be preparing a readers theatre program for presentation to the school. To learn the process they would first work on adapting and performing a sample story. Copies of this sample, "The Miller, His Son, and the Donkey," were then distributed to each child to read silently. After a discussion about the author and a review of the theme and the plot of the story, the students began the adaptation by setting the scene and determining the characters:

RTL:	Let's start writing our script by setting the scene. Where do you think this fable takes place?
DANNY:	I think it takes place a long time ago because no one sells donkeys in a market these days.
MELANIE:	It could be today. Maybe in some small town in Arizona or somewhere. They still sell donkeys like that.
DOMINICK:	It's hard to say because the whole thing is a fable. I guess it could be anytime.
RTL:	Shall we say "anytime" then as the time of the story?
ALL:	**Okay.**
RTL:	Where does the story take place?
JANE:	In a little village.
LIZ:	It's not in a village because they are on a road somewhere.
RICHARD:	Yeah, so why don't we just say on a road somewhere going to market?
RTL:	That sounds right. Now, can you tell me who are the characters in the story?
STEVEN:	A miller and his son.
TRACY:	Also the donkey.
SCOTT:	But the donkey doesn't talk.
RTL:	Let's include the donkey. Perhaps you'll want to write a line or two for it to say.
RICHARD:	Well, for that matter, the son doesn't say anything in the story either. We can give him a couple of lines, too.
RTL:	Yes, when we adapt a story for our kind of theatre, we are free to write in dialogue where we need it. Now, what other characters are found in the fable?
ROBERTA:	The farmer, a peddler, and a woman.
JIMMY:	Also, some townspeople.
RTL:	Good. Is there anyone else you want to include?
STEVE:	Yes, a storyteller.
RTL:	I'm glad you mentioned that. We also call the storyteller a narrator. Tell me, what part of the fable will he or she read?

STEVE: Well, there are parts in the story where no one is speaking but there is important stuff to know. We can have the narrator read those parts.

RTL: Good. The narrator is an important character. He or she sets the scene and gives descriptions of action that the other characters in the story can't enact.

On large poster script taped to an easel in front of the room, we noted decisions about the time, place, and characters in the fable. Some of the students copied this information into their notebooks.

Comments

Room 209, as the class was called, was an average class of twenty-eight students. The more outgoing pupils participated in the opening discussion, while others were more reticent at first. One child, Ram, who we learned was generally uninterested in any class work, sat with his head down.

Once the children were told that they would be preparing for a school production, they were motivated to read the fable presented in class. They became eager to answer the questions that led to transposing the story into a script. The goal of a performance in only two short weeks heightened the responses of even the most passive members of the class. Pupils were especially encouraged to understand that their contributions played an important part in the finished program.

We were pleased to see the magic of a readers theatre project begin to take hold on Room 209. By the end of the first session almost everyone was involved in the deliberations and looking forward to the days ahead.

Day Two

On the second day we planned to compare readers theatre, item by item, with the conventional play and list the differences on the chalkboard. We would then introduce the nine acting areas of the stage by chalking them on the classroom floor. This would help the children learn how to give and take stage directions. Finally, we would continue with the adaptation of "The Miller, His Son, and the Donkey," begun the day before.

Here is what happened:

RTL: Can you describe some of the differences between the conventional play and readers theatre?

RICHARD: In regular theatre you have to memorize your lines. In readers theatre you just read them.

RTL: Any other differences?

ROSE: In readers theatre you don't need scenery, a curtain, or an intermission.

KENNY: There is less action in readers theatre.

STEVE: But the readers can do things that show the audience what is happening, can't they?

RTL: Of course. There isn't the kind of action found in a conventional play, so it is an important part of readers theatre to suggest some of the action.

TRACY: Well, if there isn't a lot of action or moving around, how does the audience know where the story takes place or when some time has passed?

RTL: Does anyone know the answer to that?

LORI: The narrator reads where the story takes place and all the other stuff the audience needs to know.

RTL: Very good. Are there any other differences between readers theatre and plays that you can think of?

RAM: In a play you have to try to speak like the characters would really sound. In readers theatre you can speak in your regular voice.

RICHARD: I don't think that's right. I think you have to try to act like the character even if you're reading it from a book or something. That part is just like acting in a play.

RTL: Yes. When you listen to a story being read aloud, you are much more interested in it if the reader does a little bit of acting.

We chalked the nine stage acting areas on the floor and discussed them. The students were told that during the next session they would be playing some games to help them learn the stage locations.

The story was distributed. Pupils were asked to read the opening paragraph silently and decide on the first lines of the script. As before, the material was written on poster paper on the easel. Again, many of the students copied the script in their notebooks:

RTL: How shall we begin? What should be the opening lines of our script, and which character will read them?

WENDY: The narrator should speak first.

RTL: Good. We need him to set the scene.

STEVE: He should say, "One day, there was a miller . . ."

RICHARD: No, there should be more adjectives. Let him say, "One sunny day . . ." instead of "one day."

RTL: All right. Can you continue?

RICHARD: "One sunny day a miller and his son set off for the marketplace."

RAM: Then the miller can say, "Let's not ride the donkey so he will be fresh when we sell him."

RTL: That's a good line. Now let's establish that the donkey was with them and that they were going to the market to sell it. What shall we do about that?

JANE: Why don't we use the line that's written in the story? It says "They were going to sell their old donkey."

RTL: And who will say that line?

JIMMY: The narrator.

RTL: Fine! What next?

DANNY:	Give the son a line. He doesn't say anything.
RAM:	Let him say, "Father, shall we ride the donkey today?"
RTL:	Very good. Incidentally, we want to give the donkey some lines. Can anyone think up something?
LYNNE:	Let it bray.
RTL:	Anything else? Can we make it funny?
DOMINICK:	When the father gets on it the donkey can say "Give me a break."
RAM:	Or how about, "Oh, my aching back!"
CALVIN:	When both the miller and his son get on it, the donkey should yell, "Give me a Prozac!"
RTL:	Those are great lines. Let's use them. You're doing fine.

Comments

Outlining the differences between the conventional play and readers theatre served to develop a fuller understanding of the new technique. The discussion gave the students another opportunity to speak about plays and theater, a subject that obviously interested many of them.

Drawing the acting areas of the stage on the floor produced a good response from all. Everyone wanted to learn the locations. There was great excitement about the stage games promised for the following day.

Motivation continued to be high when we shifted to adapting the fable. We noticed that the brighter students still seemed to contribute the most, but several of the others made very amusing suggestions for good lines before the second session ended. Even Ram began to take a genuine interest in the proceedings. He was further encouraged by the warm reception given his comments.

Day Three

We scheduled stage-location games for the third day and prepared copies of a sketch showing the nine acting areas of the stage. At the bottom of the page we included some stage terms and definitions that we planned to go over in class. We would then complete the adaptation of our fable.

Here is what happened: The sketches were distributed and reviewed. The pupils played stage-location games. A discussion of terms followed:

RTL:	When we block our script, what will we be doing with it?
DAWN:	(*After reading the definition.*) We will be telling the characters where we want them to be in the scene.
RTL:	Good. Now Roberta, if the director told you to counter, what would you do?
ROBERTA:	I would move out of the way.
RTL:	Right. Lori, if I told you to stand above the desk on stage, where would you go?
LORI:	I would go upstage behind the desk.

RTL:	You are all very good learners. What can we do in readers theatre to show that characters are not on stage?
JIMMY:	To show they were off stage they could turn their backs.
RTL:	Yes. Is there another way to show this? Scott?
SCOTT:	They could duck down.
CALVIN:	They could sit down in the audience.
NORMAN:	The characters could walk off to the side.
RTL:	Those are all fine suggestions that we will try when we block our script.

After the discussion, copies of the fable were distributed once again. The adaptation continued:

RTL:	There seems to be a great deal of narration beginning with the line, "The miller and his son both got down." Is there a way we can cut some of it?
GERRI:	Yes, we can change it into lines for the characters to speak.
RTL:	Okay Gerri, take a line from the narrator and give it to one of the characters.
GERRI:	Instead of the narrator saying that they tied the donkey's feet up, the miller can say, "Let us tie up the donkey's four feet and put the pole on our shoulders."
RTL:	Good thinking! Now what do you think the donkey would say about being carried upside down tied to a pole?
MELANIE:	"I'll get you for this!"
LIZ:	"I'm getting sea sick."
RTL:	That's a funny line. Now, let's look at the next part of the story where it says that the townspeople came running from all sides. Who should read those lines?
RICHARD:	It seems like the narrator must say those lines.
RTL:	Why?
RICHARD:	Because it's description. He's describing how the people felt about what they saw.
RTL:	That's true, but can't we have the people saying those lines themselves?
STEVE:	Can we have everybody saying them together?
RTL:	Why not? Let's have some choral reading in this script. Why don't we try it to see how it sounds.
ALL.	**"From all sides the people came running. Never had they seen such a sight."**

The children completed the adaptation. It was to be processed and ready for reading by the next session.

Comments

By the time the stage-location games were over, we were certain most pupils could move about the stage on command. The technical terms included on the handout sheet were understood as well.

The most elusive concept for the students was that of suggested action rather than realistically portrayed action. What would we do when the script called for tying up the donkey's four legs, turning it upside down, and carrying it on a pole? Some pupils suggested we use a cardboard or stuffed donkey and actually show the procedure. We explained that with a simple movement to indicate the action, such as standing sideways with the donkey in the middle, the audience would see the occurrence in their mind's eye.

Work on the adaptation was concluded with many exceptionally creative suggestions for the script. The children were pleased with the results and appeared anxious to do the reading scheduled for the following day.

Day Four

Armed with copies of the completed readers theatre script, "The Miller, His Son, and the Donkey," we planned to spend most of the fourth session reading and rehearsing it. We prepared several vocal exercises for the rehearsal to encourage good projection. To keep motivation high, we would again announce that if all went well, we would be ready at the end of our tenth session to present a full-fledged production to an audience. Everyone in the class would be involved.

Here is what happened: We announced the date of the future production. The children, as a group and then in pairs, worked through the vocal projection exercises. A copy of the finished adaptation was passed out to each student. The children were requested to read it through silently. A brief discussion of the script followed:

RTL: You did a very good job of adapting the fable into script form. Are there any changes you would like to make?

ROSE: How can the townspeople say, "Some people pitied the miller and his son," when they *are* the "some people?"

RTL: Readers theatre often allows us to be both the storyteller and the characters in the story at the same time. As we said before, readers theatre is story telling in a very dramatic way.

RICHARD: I think we should leave out a lot of those "he said" and "she said" words.

RTL: Let's try it with and without these words when we read the script aloud. Then we'll decide.

Three casts were selected, which would give everyone in the class a chance to read. Each cast, in turn, read the script aloud from their seats two times. The first readings were uninterrupted. During the second readings some interpretive-reading suggestions were made:

RTL: (*To the farmer.*) As a farmer you have always used the donkey as a beast of burden carrying heavy loads. Now you see this incredible scene. The two tired, hot people are trudging alongside a donkey who is carrying nothing at all. How do you feel?

STEVE: I can't believe it.

RTL: Very good. Try to read the lines that way.

STEVE: "What fools you are ! A donkey is to ride isn't it? Then why do you walk?"

RTL: Fine! Now, Miller, do you think you would do what the farmer tells you right away?

RICHARD: I guess I would think about it a minute.

RTL: Of course. Why not pause before you speak?

RICHARD: (*Pausing.*) "Climb up on the donkey, Son."

RTL: (*To the donkey.*) Suppose two heavy people got on your back. How would you feel?

NORMAN: Loaded down. Ugh.

RTL: Right. Then try reading as if you had a heavy load on your back.

NORMAN: "Double trouble. Give me Prozac."

RTL: Good. Now tell me, when a word is to be stressed, what can you do to indicate that on your script?

LYNNE: Underline it.

RTL: Right. How can we show we want a pause in the sentence?

LORI: Put a dash or a line where the reader must wait.

RTL: Yes. Use a slash line like this ["/"] for a short pause and a double slash like this ["//"] for a long pause. For example, ". . . and there was the donkey going to market // *upside down.*"

ROBERT: Since I am the narrator, how should I read my lines?

RTL: Well, if you wanted the audience to imagine the donkey kicking, you have to help them to imagine it by reading expressively.

ROBERT: You mean when I read the words "struggle" and "wiggle" I should read them in a struggly and wiggly way?

RTL: Exactly.

The readings and interpretation direction continued until everyone had a chance to participate.

Comments

The children remained excited about the prospect of creating and staging a complete production for an audience. They responded well to the vocal exercise.

There was complete cooperation during the reading rehearsals. Ram now wanted to be part of the project and was a willing participant.

We were careful to select the good readers for the first round of rehearsals so that struggling readers would be familiar with the lines when their turn came. This idea worked out very well.

We gave the students interpretive reading directions. They liked working on their parts and enjoyed the special attention they received.

Day Five

For the first part of the fifth session, we planned to continue working on theatre skills. Our discussion would cover "on-stage" and "offstage" focus. Following this, we would block the sample script, "The Miller, His Son, and the Donkey." We mapped out the positions and movements of each character on a series of sketches and made enough copies of these for the class. After the children had studied the sketches, each cast, in turn, would be asked to read the script in position on stage. We hoped to coordinate the script reading with the prescribed stage movements by the end of this work period.

Here is what happened: A discussion about focus took place. Blocking charts were then passed out to each child:

RTL:	Can you find your character in the sketches?
ALL:	**Yes.**
RTL:	All right, where do the miller, the son, and the donkey stand when the story begins?
RICHARD:	Center stage.
RTL:	Good. Where does the narrator stand?
WENDY:	Down right.
RTL:	Correct. If you look on the sketch you will see a half box in front of the narrator. Can anyone tell me what that represents?
DANNY:	A music stand to put the script on.
RTL:	Yes. And what are those two circles supposed to be?
LYNNE:	Two stools, a high one and a low one.
RTL:	Right. Now when the farmer is not in the scene, where does he go?
TRACY:	Up left.
RTL:	Good. Notice the little arrows. They point to where the character is facing. Why does the farmer face up stage and not the audience?
TRACY:	The farmer faces up stage to show the audience that he is not in the scene.
RTL:	Very good.

The blocking was completed. Each cast rehearsed on the classroom stage chalked on the floor.

Comments

We were pleased to see the children become more familiar with the readers theatre technique. The concept of on-stage and offstage focus was quickly understood in the framework of an upcoming production.

Once all the blocking symbols were explained, the children found the sketches easy to follow. We were certain they would have no trouble preparing such a plan when called on to block a story of their own.

Blocking our fable went smoothly. All of the pupils had an opportunity to read their lines and walk through their parts. By the time the third cast rehearsed, the readers all knew their positions on stage and where and when to move.

Day Six

For the first part of session six we planned more speech warming-up exercises. This time our concentration would be on diction. We would divide the class into workshop groups. Each workshop would receive its story to prepare for the final readers theatre production. Toward this end we brought along five folk tales that, together with "The Miller, His Son, and the Donkey," would make up the program we chose to call "Folk Stories from Around the World." (See Chapter 9.)

Each workshop would be composed of students with mixed reading abilities. The number of pupils would match the number of characters needed for a given story. To make it easier for some of the slower learners to prepare for the production, we would give them the sample fable we worked on in class to perform.

We would inform the class that in four days we hoped to give an "out-of-town" performance (a preview for another class). If this went well, we would schedule a performance for most of the school to see.

Here is what happened: After practicing diction exercises, plans for the production were made and a date set for an out-of-town performance. The selected stories were distributed and one, "The Stone-Cutter," was discussed:

RTL:	What special thing do you notice when you read this tale?
JACKIE:	There is only one dialogue line in the whole story.
RTL:	That's right. How will you prepare this story for readers theatre?
SCOTT:	We can make up some dialogue lines from the narrative sections the way we did in "The Miller."
RTL:	That's one good way to involve more characters. In there another?
ROBERTA:	We can leave the story the way it is, but whenever a character is mentioned, that character can read those lines.
RTL:	Very good. Can you give the class an example of what you mean?
ROBERTA:	We can make a character called Nobo who can say the lines about himself the way the townspeople did in the fable.
RTL:	Tell us which line Nobo would read.
ROBERTA:	The story opens with, "Nobo was a lowly stonecutter," and it goes on about him. Well, Nobo can read those lines.
RTL:	Fine. Can someone continue?
ROSE:	In one of the paragraphs it says, "One day a prince went by." The Prince will read these lines about himself.
RTL:	Excellent. What a wonderful way of doing this poetic story. I think it's going to be a very interesting selection.

The class was divided up into workshop groups. Each met in a different section of the room to begin work on its assigned story. The teacher walked around the room helping the children with their adaptations.

Comments

The diction exercises helped the children improve their delivery of the lines.

The students became increasingly excited about the upcoming performance. Most were motivated and curious enough to read all the distributed stories as well as their own.

The groups went to work on their projects with enthusiasm. The room was alive with animated talk as pupils exchanged ideas about how their story was to be adapted. We walked around to offer help, but were surprised to find how little was needed.

Day Seven

The subject of "cues" would be our theatre lesson for the seventh session. We would use several exercises to illustrate how to effectively respond on cue. The workshop groups would meet again to complete their adaptations and begin the blocking.

Here is what happened: After the discussion about cues, the children were asked about their progress:

RTL: Has any group completed its adaptation as yet?

DAWN: Yes, we finished "The Clever Judge."

NORMAN: And we did "The Little Girl and the Wolf."

RTL: Would you each tell us a little about what you decided to do?

DAWN: In group one we took it paragraph by paragraph. We decided who was talking and assigned the lines to that person.

RICHARD: Then we cut out all the "he saids" in the story and we gave the non-dialogue lines to a narrator.

DAWN: Except we cut some of the narrator's lines in the beginning because they were too long.

NORMAN: In group two we didn't cut out anything in our script. We even left in lines like ". . . said the little girl," and ". . . the wolf said." We have the characters saying those lines themselves.

JANE: We cut some stuff out of "The Stone-Cutter." And we wrote in a whole bunch of characters. Now we have more characters than kids to play them.

RTL: What will you do?

JANE: Some of us are going to have to read more than one character. But that's all right. We're going to change our hats so that the audience will know who's speaking.

RTL: A good idea! You're all doing very well. As soon as you complete the adaptations, we'll go on to the blocking.

The groups met to work on their adaptations and their blocking sketches. The teacher gave assistance where needed.

Comments

We were delighted to find several of the groups already finished with their adaptations when the session began. It appears they were so anxious to work on the scripts that they did so in their free time. With some help from us, they then completed their blocking sketches and were ready for rehearsal. The students were very pleased with the work they accomplished and could not wait to see their scripts "in print" (processed and photocopied), promised for the following day.

We presented exercises for responding on cue. We involved the students in game-like techniques that both captured their imagination and added to their knowledge of theatre skills.

Day Eight

We came prepared with the finished processed scripts. Part of session eight would include making simple, oaktag script covers. We would also give instructions on how and where to hold the scripts during the performance. The groups would then proceed with blocking and reading rehearsals. For homework we would ask each pupil to write a line or two of introduction for the group's story. These we would discuss on the following day.

Here is what happened: The scripts were passed around and examined by the class. Students constructed colorful covers. Then the problems of handling the scripts during the production were discussed:

RTL: Suppose I were a reader on stage. How would you advise me to hold the script. Like this? *(In front of face.)*

ALL: **No.**

RTL: Why not?

SCOTT: Because we can't see your face.

LIZ: And we can't hear you too well.

RTL: Where shall I hold it then?

LORI: You should hold it down from your face about to the middle of your chest.

RTL: Like this? *(Holding script down with both hands.)*

TRACY: Yes, but not with two hands.

RTL: Why not?

TRACY: Because you might need a hand free to make a motion in the story.

RTL: Can you give me an example of such a motion?

TRACY: Well, in "The Four Silly Brothers," the man is supposed to hit the brothers on the head. He'll need a hand to make believe he's doing it.

LORI: In our script, "The Clever Judge," the judge must hand the plaintiff a ring. He should have one hand free to do it.

RTL: You're right. We should hold the script in one hand. Now, can anyone tell me the difference between a stage motion and real-life motion?

JANE: I think a stage motion should be bigger than a real-life motion.

RTL: Why is that?

JANE: So that everyone, even those sitting in the back, will be able to see what it is.

LIZ: Yes, especially because in readers theatre we're only going to be using suggestions of the action. We want to get the audience to understand what we're doing.

RTL: Very good. Let's practice some motions indicated in the stories as we hold the scripts in one hand.

The students worked on some of the actions and motions together as a class. Afterward, in groups, with blocking sketches in hand, they rehearsed positions and movements as they read the lines of their scripts. The teacher helped in these efforts.

For homework, pupils were asked to prepare short introductions to their stories. They were also told to bring in any old hats they might have at home.

Comments

The students expressed pride in seeing their work neatly processed and distributed to the class. The covered scripts looked very professional, and everyone felt glad to have one in hand at last. No one seemed to have any trouble with our explanations of where and how to hold the scripts during a performance.

At first the blocking rehearsals produced a great deal of lively activity. In time, however, a director either emerged or was appointed by each group and everything began to stabilize. We were certain one or two more "run throughs" would result in a satisfactory performance.

Day Nine

During the ninth session we would rehearse the six stories in the library. This was where the final performance was to take place. Before that, however, we would allow time for group preparation of introductions. Final decisions would be made about hats for the presentation. For later on in the day, we arranged to present the performance to a sixth-grade class who consented to be our "out-of-town" audience.

Here is what happened: The pupils met in groups to pool ideas about introducing their stories. No introduction was to be more than three sentences long. The teacher walked around to offer help with these lines. All of the final selections were read aloud. One member of each group, usually the narrator in the story, was assigned the material for the performance. The students then discussed the hats they brought in and decisions were made about who would wear what. (Some of the more fanciful hats were constructed by the children during art periods.)

The class moved to the library where the first full rehearsal was held. This was directed by the teacher. Since the lunchroom area was rather large, the children chalked the stage size out on the floor. This defined the playing space and corresponded to the area they were accustomed to in the classroom.

Each group was told when and where to enter the stage. They were also shown where to sit when their sequence was not on. Figure 8.1 shows the seating arrangement and the stage area.

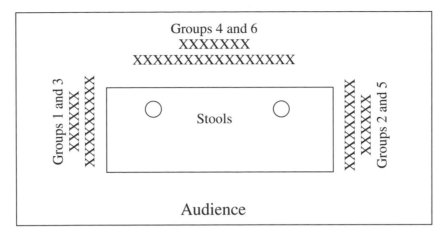

Figure 8.1. Seating arrangement.

Later that day, the out-of-town trial performance was presented for the sixth-grade class. The observers were asked to evaluate three things:

1. Were the lines read clearly and distinctly?

2. Did the readers look up from their scripts enough to make contact with each other and with audience members?

3. Were the action and the movements of the readers meaningful?

After the program the observers analyzed the performance while the readers noted their reactions:

RTL: How did you like this readers theatre?

PUPIL: The stories were really interesting and all the readers spoke clearly and distinctly.

RTL: This trial performance is to help us to learn how to improve our production. Do you wish to suggest any changes?

PUPIL: I think it was great, except the readers read too fast. If they would slow down they would sound more like the characters they're supposed to be.

PUPIL: Yes. They sound like they want to get through with it real fast.

RTL: Are there any other suggestions?

PUPIL: I want them to look away from their scripts more. Sometimes you can't see their faces.

RTL: Very good comments. What about the action and the movements of the readers? Did you understand what was taking place at all times?

PUPIL: Yes. All the action was good. I could even tell that the sun was burning the flowers in "The Stone-Cutter."

PUPIL: And I could tell when Nobo became the mountain by the way he stood.

PUPIL: Also it was easy to imagine people sitting on the donkey's back when they sat on the two stools right behind it. That was good.

PUPIL: I liked that the characters turned their backs on the audience when they weren't in the scene. It's amazing how you didn't need any curtains or anything to know this.

RTL: Thank you for helping us. You are very good critics.

Comments

The students worked efficiently in their small groups preparing introductions for the stories. Time forced us to limit this creative writing activity to fifteen minutes.

Once on stage, everyone was eager to make the program work. We noted, happily, that everyone in the class was now completely involved in the project.

The pupils followed directions very well. In a short time they had mastered the necessary stage language. We observed that some of the readers did not trust themselves to look up from their scripts to make contact with fellow players. This problem was alleviated by designating certain words in the script as signal words. On seeing these cues, a reader would read ahead silently and finish the line looking up. We would review this technique on the following day.

A potential problem was absenteeism. Who would play the parts of absent students? We soon learned that almost any child in the class could step into another's role with little trouble. Having read and heard the other stories during the preparations, pupils were familiar with all the lines and quickly learned the related movements.

The trial performance before the sixth-grade class was a worthwhile experience. Many of the program's loose ends came together as readers readily accepted the praise and criticisms of their peers. The repeated advice to "slow down" and "look up" had a beneficial effect on the players. Everyone seemed ready for the final performance the next day.

Day Ten

The performance was scheduled for the period following the tenth session. We prepared for it with three major activities. First, we would have the students read the scripts once more from their seats. By separating the reading from the action, pupils would be more conscious of their lines. They would be encouraged to read more slowly and feel secure enough to look up often. Second, we would discuss some of the problems players might encounter during the performance, such as interruptions from audience members and mishaps with hats and scripts. Third, we prepared a set of physical exercises designed to relieve tensions and stage jitters.

Following the session, Grade Five, Room 209, would file into the library. There the audience of fourth, fifth, and sixth graders would be waiting. The readers theatre production, "Folk Stories from Around the World," would be presented.

Here is what happened: The students read the script aloud from their seats. They were instructed to recite their lines very slowly, pausing often to take deep breaths. They were also urged to look up as often as possible, using the designated signal words as cues. Following the rehearsal, a discussion about possible performance problems was held:

Fifth-grade class ready for performance.

RTL: Can anyone tell me what you should do if someone in the audience calls out to you, or interrupts you in some other way while you are reading in performance?

LORI: I think we shouldn't pay any attention to them and go in with the reading.

RTL: Yes, a professional will ignore outbursts from the audience. But what if people laugh at the funny lines?

RICHARD: We should wait until the laughter dies down and then go on.

RTL: That's right. It is important to stay in character at all times so that the audience sees you as the person you are playing. Okay, what should you do if, by chance, your hat falls off your head or your script falls down?

STEVE: We shouldn't let it bother us and try to pick it up when we can.

RTL: Should you apologize or laugh?

JANE: No, as you said, we should stay in character and do the best we can.

RTL: Very good. If your hat falls off, you may want to leave it on the floor and continue reading without it. Pick it up at a time when you are not noticed so much. Of course, to avoid this problem altogether, your hat should be fastened on securely.

ROSE: What should we do if we make a mistake or lose our place?

RTL: Can someone answer that?

RAM: We must go on and not make a big deal about it.

CALVIN: Can't someone whisper the line to the person who forgets?

JACKIE: That's too noticeable. I think the person should just go on.

RTL: Yes. It's good to go on and forget about a missed line. The trick is to try not to make a face or otherwise show the audience that a mistake has been made.

SCOTT: Should we wear our hats while we are in our seats waiting to go on?

RTL: What do you think about that?

SCOTT: I think we shouldn't let anyone see us with our hats on until we go on stage.

RTL: I think that's a good idea. It will be more surprising and interesting for the audience if they see you for the first time in character on stage. Another reason for this is that the spectators should not be distracted from the performance taking place. In your seats around the stage you are very visible to the audience. It is best for you to remain quiet and unnoticed.

After the discussion, pupils engaged in physical exercises.

When the session ended, the class went to the library, where they took their seats around the stage area. All hats and scripts were placed under their chairs until needed. Before the performance began, the principal made the following announcement to the audience:

PRINCIPAL: Two weeks ago, students in Room 209 began preparation for a readers theatre. After working on one story together with the director, each group transposed, cast, blocked, and directed its own story. The result is the readers theatre you will see today. This is not a conventional play, but a series of dramatized readings. The program is called, "Folk Stories from Around the World."

The spectators were then told that after the performance each of them would be asked to write a letter to one of the characters. The letter would describe the writer's impressions of the character as he or she appeared in the story.

The room quieted down when the teacher sounded a bell and the readers theatre script, "Folk Stories from Around the World," became a reality.

Comments

The last reading rehearsal was the best yet. It was obvious that the children felt completely at home with their lines. At last, many of the characters seemed to come to life.

The discussion about possible mishaps during the performance relieved pupils' anxiety about what to do in case of an emergency on stage. Although much of this information was given to the readers during the ten sessions, these last minute specifics helped to allay their fears.

Physical exercise was an important preparatory activity. The students appeared much less tense and nervous after the brief workout. By eleven o'clock, the time of the performance, everyone in Room 209 was in good spirits, physically and mentally ready to do their best.

The readers theatre production was a success by all standards. The library was transformed into a theatre. Students learned to read with meaningful expression. They moved professionally about the stage. Interacting with their classmates, they created a bond among themselves, the audience, and the literature that no one of them would soon forget.

Chapter 9

MODEL PROGRAM SCRIPT: FOLK STORIES FROM AROUND THE WORLD

Folk Stories from Around The World[1]

Adapted by the Fifth Grade Class, Number Six School, Woodmere,
New York as part of the Model Readers Theatre Program

Cast of Characters

- **"The Storyteller"**

    Narrator 1, 2

    King

    Farmer

- **"The Miller, His Son, and the Donkey"**

Narrator	Peddler
Son	Woman 1, 2
Miller	Blacksmith
Farmer	Wife
Donkey	Townspeople 1, 2

- **"The Stone-Cutter"**

Narrator	Prince
Nobo	Sun
Spirit	Cloud
Rich Man	Mountain
Stone-cutter	

- **"The Four Silly Brothers"**

    Narrator 1, 2

    Matthew

    Mark

    Luke

    John

    Man

• **"The Clever Judge"**

    Narrator 1, 2

    Judge

    Plaintiff

    Defendant

• **"The Little Girl and the Wolf"**

    Narrator

    Girl

    Wolf

Production Notes

Each group in the Model Readers Theatre Program prepared its own segment of this compiled script. Each segment is introduced by a Narrator or Narrators, who always stand stage left behind lecterns or music stands. Hats include a crown for the King, straw hats for the Miller, the Son, the Farmer, the Blacksmith, and the Peddler. The donkey wears a headband with two ears attached. The Women and Townspeople wear vintage hats or head scarves. Brightly colored, flowing scarves of various lengths are tied around the foreheads of Nobo, the Rich Man, the Prince, the Spirit, the Sun, the Cloud, and the Mountain. The Spirit places a new head piece on Nobo each time a wish is granted. Baseball caps for the Four Silly Brothers are worn sideways and backwards. The Judge wears a British-style white wig, and the two characters who appear before him wear fedoras with signs in the hatbands saying "Plaintiff" and "Defendant." The Wolf sports two big ears on a headband, and the Girl, carrying a basket, wears a red head scarf. Three stools of different heights are on stage for use in the stories that require them. For example, the King sits on a high stool while the farmer sits on a low one. A small ladder is also available for "The Stone-Cutter" sequence, which Nobo mounts step by step until he becomes a Mountain. Musical interludes between stories, either taped or live, connect the segments and add to the program.

The Storyteller

NARRATOR 1:   A hundred years ago an African storyteller said that when one has traveled along a road he can sit down and wait for a story to overtake him. He said a story is like the wind. It comes from a far place and it can pass behind the back of a mountain. Here now is Room 209 to present a readers theatre called "Folk Stories from Around the World." We hope you will travel with us on our journey and allow our tales to overtake you. Our first presentation is about stories. Listen as we learn of a clever farmer who outwitted a king in the Ethiopian folk tale entitled "The Storyteller."

NARRATOR 2: Once, there was a king in the land of Shoa who loved nothing so much as listening to stories. Every moment of his spare time was spent listening to the tales told by the storytellers of the country, but a time came when there were no stories left that he hadn't heard. His hunger for stories came to be known in the neighboring kingdoms, and wandering singers and storytellers came to Shoa to be rewarded for whatever new tales they could bring. But the more tales the king heard the fewer were left that he had not heard.

NARRATOR 1: And so, finally, in desperation he let it be known throughout the land that whatever storyteller could make him cry, "Enough! No more!" would receive a great piece of land and the title of Ras, or prince. Many men, inspired by the thought of such wealth and honors, came to tell him stories, but always he sat and listened eagerly without ever protesting that he had heard too much.

NARRATOR 2: One day a farmer came and offered to tell stories until the king was so full of them that he would cry out in protest. The king smiled.

KING: The best storytellers in Ethiopia have come and gone without telling me enough. And now you come in your simple innocence to win the land and the title of Ras. Well, begin, you may try.

NARRATOR 1: And so the farmer settled himself comfortably on a rug and began.

FARMER: Once there was a peasant who sowed wheat. He mowed it when it was grown, threshed it, and put all the precious grain in his granary. It was a rich harvest, one of the best he had ever had. But, this is the irony of the tale. In his granary there was a tiny flaw. A hole big enough to pass a straw through. And when the grain was all stored an ant came and went through the hole and found the wheat. He carried away a single grain of it to his anthill to eat.

KING: Ah-ha! This is one of the stories that I have never heard.

FARMER: The next day, another ant came and carried away a grain.

KING. Ah-ha!

FARMER: The next day still another ant came and carried away a grain.

KING: Yes, yes, I understand. Let us get on with the story.

FARMER: The next day another ant came, and carried away another grain. And the next day another ant came and carried away another grain.

KING: Let us not dally with the details, the story is the thing.

FARMER: The next day another ant came.

KING: Please, please.

FARMER: But there are so many ants in this story. And the next day another ant came for a grain of wheat, and . . .

KING: No, no it must not be!

FARMER: Ah, but it is the crux of the story. And the next day another ant came and took away a grain . . .

KING: But I understand all this. Let us pass over it and get on with the plot.

FARMER: And the next day another ant came and took his grain. And the next day . . .

KING: Stop. I want no more of it!

FARMER. The story must be told in the proper way. Besides, the granary is still nearly full of wheat and it must be emptied. That is the story. And the next day . . .

KING: No, no enough, enough!

FARMER: And the next day another ant . . .

KING: Enough, enough, you may have the land and the title of Ras!

NARRATOR 2: So the farmer became a prince and owned a great parcel of land. This is what people mean when they say:

KING AND FARMER. **ONE GRAIN AT A TIME BRINGS GOOD FORTUNE.**

(All exit Right.)

(Musical interlude)

The Miller, His Son, and the Donkey

NARRATOR: "The Miller, His Son, and the Donkey" is a fable by the Greek slave, Aesop. It is a simple tale that has a moral at the end. One sunny day a miller and his son set off to the marketplace to sell their old donkey.

SON: Father, shall we ride the donkey today?

MILLER: No son, we won't ride him for it's a hot day. We want him to look fresh when we sell him.

NARRATOR: All three walked slowly down the road. Soon they met a farmer.

FARMER: What fools you are! A donkey is to ride isn't it? Then why do you walk?

NARRATOR: The miller didn't like that.

MILLER: Climb up on the donkey, son.

DONKEY: Why didn't that joker keep his mouth shut? *(Bray.)*

NARRATOR:	Pretty soon they met a peddler pushing a cart.
PEDDLER:	Aren't you ashamed of yourself young man? Your legs are young and strong. You should let your father ride.
NARRATOR:	The miller wasn't a bit tired but he said:
MILLER:	Get down, son.
NARRATOR:	And they changed places.
DONKEY:	Oi vay!
NARRATOR.	They had not gone far when they passed some women going to the market.
WOMAN 1:	What kind of man are you?
WOMAN 2:	Look at this! A big strong fellow like you riding while his poor little boy has to walk.
NARRATOR:	The miller didn't know what to do.
MILLER:	I'm confused.
NARRATOR:	But at last he said,
MILLER:	Son, get up behind me.
DONKEY:	Double trouble! Give me a Prozac!
NARRATOR:	Then a blacksmith and his wife happened by.
BLACKSMITH:	Look at that poor donkey! The poor creature can hardly walk. I call it cruel to overload a dumb animal that way.
WIFE:	I agree. Those two look more fit to carry the donkey than he is to carry them.
NARRATOR:	So the miller and his son both got down. The father stepped off the road and cut a long pole.
MILLER:	Let us tie up the donkey's four feet and put the pole on our shoulders.
NARRATOR:	And there was the donkey going to marketplace upside down.
DONKEY:	What a way to go! I'm seasick.
NARRATOR:	From all sides the people came running. Never had they seen such a sight.
TOWNSPEOPLE 1:	Some people pitied the miller and his son.
TOWNSPEOPLE 2:	Some pitied the donkey.
ALL:	*(Pointing.)* Ha! Ha! Ha! Ha! Ha!
NARRATOR:	Meantime, the donkey was very unhappy.
DONKEY:	Boy, am I unhappy.
NARRATOR:	He didn't like being carried.
DONKEY:	And upside down at that.
NARRATOR:	And he was upset by all the noise.

DONKEY: Boy, is it noisy.

NARRATOR: He started to struggle and wiggle. Just as they stepped on Market Bridge, he got one of his feet loose and kicked hard at the boy.

SON: Ouch! Cut that out!

NARRATOR: He dropped his end of the pole. The next minute, the donkey had rolled off the bridge into the water. And before anyone could fish him out, he drowned.

DONKEY: How do you expect me to swim with three feet tied to the pole?

MILLER: I tried to please everybody.

SON: But you pleased nobody.

MILLER: And now my old donkey is lost.

NARRATOR: Moral:

ALL: **IF YOU TRY TO PLEASE ALL . . .**

NARRATOR: YOU WILL PLEASE NONE.

(All exit Left.)

(Musical interlude)

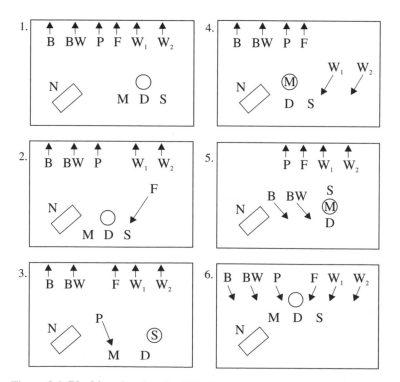

Figure 9.1. Blocking sketches for "The Miller, His Son, and the Donkey."

M = Miller, D = Donkey, S = Son, B = Blacksmith, BW = Blacksmith's Wife, P = Peddler, F = Farmer, N = Narrator, O = Stool, W = Woman 1 and 2, ↑ = face direction

The Stone-Cutter

NARRATOR:	The Stone-Cutter is a beautiful Japanese story about Nobo, a poor stone-cutter who was not satisfied with his lot. The tale tells what happens to him when he wished for too much.
NOBO:	Once upon a time there lived a stone-cutter named Nobo who worked every day cutting large slabs of stone out of the great mountain.
SPIRIT:	The spirit, who lived in the mountain, admired the stone-cutter because he worked hard and never complained.
NOBO:	Nobo was a happy man until one day when he delivered a stone to a rich man's house.
RICH MAN:	There the lowly stone-cutter saw all sorts of beautiful things he had never seen before. His eyes grew large as he stared longingly upon the gilded furniture, the splendid rugs, and the sparkling chandeliers.
NOBO:	"Oh, if only I could be a rich man and sleep in a bed with silken curtains and golden tassels. How happy I should be," said Nobo.
SPIRIT:	Suddenly, the voice of the spirit who lived in the mountain could be heard, "Your wish has been granted, a rich man you shall be."
NOBO:	And a rich man he became! Nobo was thrilled to find himself in a stately home with splendid furniture and a bed just like the one he wanted. But as a rich man he had little to do except gaze out the window.
PRINCE:	Then one day, while he looked out his window, he spied a carriage drawn by servants dressed in scarlet and gold. In the carriage sat a prince and over his head a golden umbrella was held to protect him from the sun's rays.
NOBO:	"Oh if I were only a prince," said Nobo, " I could ride in such a carriage and have a golden umbrella held over my head. Then I would be happy."
SPIRIT:	Again the voice of the spirit who lived in the mountain could be heard, "Your wish has been granted, a prince you shall be."
NOBO:	And a prince he became! He rode around in a fine carriage. Servants dressed in scarlet and gold bore him along.
SUN:	But as he rode he noticed that no matter how much water was poured on the gardens, the rays of the sun scorched the grass and the flowers. And in spite of the golden umbrella held over his head, the sun's rays caused his face to burn.

NOBO: "The sun is mightier than I am," said Nobo. "If only I were the sun I would have great power."

SPIRIT: Once again the voice of the spirit of the mountain was heard, "Your wish has been granted, the sun shall you be.

NOBO: And the sun he became! Nobo was proud. He shot his beams everywhere, above to the heavens and below to the earth.

CLOUD: But in a short time he saw that a cloud covered his face. He was powerless to shine his rays.

NOBO: "The cloud holds my rays captive," said Nobo, "it is mightier than the sun. Oh, how I wish I were a cloud, more powerful than any.

SPIRIT: Still again the voice of the spirit of the mountain was heard, "Your wish has been granted, the cloud shall you be."

NOBO: And the cloud he became! He lay between the sun and the earth. To his joy the earth grew green again and flowers blossomed from the rain he supplied.

MOUNTAIN: But that was not enough for him. For days and weeks he poured down rain till the rivers overflowed their banks and towns and villages were destroyed. Only the great mountain remained unmoved.

NOBO: "Could it be that the mountain is mightier than I?" asked Nobo. "Oh if only I were the mountain how happy I should be."

SPIRIT: And the spirit of the mountain answered, "Your wish is granted, the mountain shall you be."

NOBO: And the mountain he became! Proudly he stood glorying in his power. Neither the heat of the sun nor the force of the rain could move him. "This is better than all," said Nobo. "Now I shall be happy. I need never call on the spirit again."

SPIRIT: So, the spirit of the mountain went away never to come again.

NOBO: But one day Nobo heard a strange noise at his feet.

ANOTHER
STONE-CUTTER. It was a lowly stone-cutter chiseling into his surface.

NOBO: Nobo was frightened. A trembling feeling ran through him. The spirit was gone. There was nothing more.

(The entire cast enters and bows. Then the Narrator appears.)

NARRATOR: Now listeners, if you do not like this ending we can supply another. Let us take the story back to where Nobo says:

NOBO: And the mountain he became! Proudly he stood glorying in his power. Neither the heat of the sun nor the force of the rain could move him. "This is better than all," said Nobo, "now I shall be happy." But one day he heard a strange noise at his feet.

ANOTHER STONE-CUTTER: It was a lowly stone-cutter chiseling into his surface.

NOBO: "Could it be that a mere man of earth is mightier than a mountain?" said Nobo. "Oh if only I were a man!"

SPIRIT: And the spirit of the mountain answered: "Your wish is heard. A man once more you shall be!"

NOBO: And a man he was. He toiled again at his trade of stone-cutting. His bed was hard and his food scanty, but he learned to be satisfied. He did not long to be someone else. He was happy at last.

SPIRIT: And he heard the voice of the mountain spirit no longer.

(All exit Right.)

(Musical interlude)

"The Stone-Cutter."

The Four Silly Brothers

NARRATOR 1:	We are all foolish and stupid sometimes, but "The Four Silly Brothers" in this English folk tale are very silly indeed.
NARRATOR 2:	Once there were four brothers: Matthew, Mark, Luke, and John. One day, as they returned home from work, they talked and sang and remembered what a fine day it had been. Suddenly the eldest brother, Matthew, stopped and said,
MATTHEW:	Are we all here?
ALL:	**Of course.**
MATTHEW:	Are you sure? I'd better count to make sure. One, two, three, there, I told you someone was missing. We are four brothers yet I can count only three. Someone is still in the fields.
NARRATOR 1:	The next brother, Mark, said,
MARK:	Wait a minute, let me count. One, two, three. Oh dear! One of us is lost. We must find our lost brother.
NARRATOR 2:	As they rushed off in a great panic, the third brother, Luke, who was good at counting sheep and generally very clever, stopped them.
LUKE:	I'll count. One, two, three . . . Oh quick! Let's go and find our lost brother before night falls.
NARRATOR 1:	Off they went, searching and calling for their lost brother until the sun started to go down. John, the youngest brother, was beside himself with grief.
JOHN:	Let me count again before we have to go and tell the sad news to our parents. One, two, three . . . only three.
NARRATOR 2:	The four brothers were standing in the road, wailing and bemoaning the loss of their brother, when a gentleman came along.
MAN:	What's all this?
ALL:	**We've lost our brother.**
JOHN:	There were four of us this morning, but now there are only three.
MAN:	Three? How do you work that out?
MATTHEW:	Look.
NARRATOR 1:	And he counted his brothers.
MATTHEW:	One, two, three.
NARRATOR 2:	The gentleman smiled as he saw the foolish brothers were not including themselves as they counted.
MAN:	How much will you give me if I find your brother?

LUKE: All our money.

NARRATOR 1:   They eagerly opened their purses.

MAN: Well then . . .

NARRATOR 2:   He took the money and found a big stick.

MAN: Stand here in a line.

NARRATOR 1:   The brothers did so, and the gentleman bashed them all over the head.

MAN: ONE, TWO, THREE FOUR! You silly brothers, you forgot to count yourselves.

NARRATOR 2:   So, laughing and counting his newfound wealth, the gentleman rode off. The brothers were very happy to find that they were not lost after all. They waved their thanks to the gentleman, and set off for home, holding their heads and counting their bumps.

ALL: **ONE, TWO, THREE, FOUR.**

(All exit Left.)

(Musical interlude)

"The Four Silly Brothers."

The Clever Judge

NARRATOR 1:   This story is an old Russian folk tale. It shows that people who lie are very often caught by their own admissions. It is called "The Clever Judge."

NARRATOR 2:	There lived a man in the Russian steppes who was famous for his justice and wisdom. At that time, if a man was known for his fairness, people came to him from far and wide to ask him to settle their disputes. And so it was that one day two villagers appeared before this wise man and asked him to settle their quarrel.
JUDGE:	Tell me your story.
PLAINTIFF:	I had to leave my village for I had business elsewhere. All my wealth was one hundred gold coins. I did not come by them easily. I had to work hard for them, and I did not want them to be stolen while I was away. Nor did I care to carry so much money with me on my journey. So I entrusted these gold coins for safekeeping to this man here. When I got back from my journey, he denied that he had ever received the money from me.
JUDGE:	And who saw you give him these gold coins?
PLAINTIFF:	No one saw it. We went together to the heart of the forest, and there I handed him the coins.
JUDGE:	*(Turning to the Defendant.)* What have you to say to this?
DEFENDANT:	*(Shrugging his shoulders.)* I don't know what he is talking about. I never went to the forest with him. I never saw his gold coins.
JUDGE:	Do you remember the place where you handed over the money?
PLAINTIFF:	Of course I do. It was under a tall oak tree. I remember it very well. I can point it out with no trouble at all.
JUDGE:	So you do have a witness after all. Here, take my signet ring, go to the tall tree under which you stood when you handed over the money, set the seal of my signet ring against the trunk, and bid the tree appear before me to bear out the truth of your story.
NARRATOR 1:	The Plaintiff took the signet ring and went off to carry out the demands of the Judge. The Defendant remained behind and waited for his return. After some time had passed, the Judge again turned to the Defendant.
JUDGE:	Do you think he has reached the oak by this time?
DEFENDANT:	No, not yet.
NARRATOR 2:	After further time had passed, the Judge again turned to the Defendant.
JUDGE:	Do you think he has reached the tree by this time?
DEFENDANT:	Yes, by now he must have reached it.
NARRATOR 1:	Not long after, the Plaintiff returned.
JUDGE:	Well?

PLAINTIFF:　I did just as you said. I walked as far as the forest, and then I went on until I came to the tall oak under which we stood when I handed over my gold coins. I set the seal of your signet ring against the trunk of the tree and I bade it appear before you as a witness. But the tree refused to budge.

JUDGE:　Never mind. The oak tree has appeared before me and it has borne witness in your favor.

DEFENDANT:　How can you say such a thing! I have been here all this while, and no tree has stalked into the place.

JUDGE:　But you said that you had not been in the forest at all. And yet when I asked you whether the Plaintiff had reached the oak, first you answered that he could not have reached it, and the second time you said that he surely must have reached it. Therefore, you were in the forest and you remembered where the oak was under which you stood when the Plaintiff handed his gold coins to you for safekeeping. Now you must not only return him his hundred gold pieces, but you must also pay a fine for having tried to cheat him.

NARRATOR 2:　So the tree was a witness without budging, and justice was done.

(All exit Upstage.)

(Musical interlude)

"The Clever Judge."

The Little Girl and the Wolf

NARRATOR: James Thurber, an American writer, was so fond of Aesop's fables that he modernized them for our time. The one we will do is called "The Little Girl and the Wolf."

WOLF: One afternoon a big wolf waited in a dark forest for a little girl to come along carrying a basket of food to her grandmother.

GIRL: Finally a little girl did come along, and she was carrying a basket of food.

WOLF: "Are you carrying that basket to your grandmother?" asked the wolf.

GIRL: The little girl said yes, she was.

WOLF: So the wolf asked her where her grandmother lived, and the little girl told him, and he disappeared into the woods.

GIRL: When the little girl opened the door to her grandmother's house she saw that there was somebody in bed with a nightcap and nightgown on. She had approached no nearer than twenty-five feet from the bed when she saw that it was not her grandmother, but the wolf.

WOLF: For even in a nightcap a wolf does not look any more like your grandmother than the Metro-Goldwyn lion looks like Calvin Coolidge.

GIRL: So, the little girl took an automatic out of her basket and shot the wolf dead.

WOLF: Moral: IT'S NOT SO EASY TO FOOL LITTLE GIRLS NOWADAYS . . .

GIRL: AS IT USED TO BE.

(The entire cast enters and forms a line across the playing area.)

NARRATOR: Thank you for listening to our readers theatre. You were a good audience and we hope you enjoyed our folk tales. We would like to hear from you, be it fan mail or "pan" mail. Won't you please write to us and tell us what you thought of our presentation? The address is Room 209. Thank you.

(All bow and exit Right and Left.)

(Music up and out)

"The Little Girl and the Wolf."

Notes

1. Materials adapted from the following sources: "The Storyteller," in *The Fire on the Mountain and Other Ethiopian Stories*, ed. Harold Courlander and Wolf Leslau (New York: Henry Holt, 1950); "The Miller, His Son, and the Donkey" in *The Fables of Aesop,* ed. Joseph Jacobs (London: Macmillan, 1894); "The Stone-Cutter," in *The Crimson Fairy Book,* ed. Andrew Lang (London: Longman, Green, 1903); "Four Silly Brothers," in *The Wise Men of Gotham,* ed. Malcolm Carrick (New York: Viking, 1975); "The Clever Judge," in *Tales of Faraway Folk,* ed. Babette Deutsch and Avraham Yarmolinsky (New York: Harper, 1952); James Thurber, "The Little Girl and the Wolf," in *Fables for Our Time and Famous Poems* (New York: Harper & Bros., 1940).

Chapter 10

SAMPLE SCRIPT: REALLY FINE PEOPLE

Really Fine People[1]

Compiled and Adapted for Readers Theatre by Shirlee Sloyer

Cast of Characters

- **"You're a Good Man, Charlie Brown" by Clark Gesner**

    Patty, *a nice girl*
    Linus, *very smart*
    Schroeder, *helpful*
    Charlie Brown, *a good man*
    Lucy, *a very crabby person*
    Snoopy, *the all-American dog*

- **"How to Be a Hero" by Harvey Weiss**

    Voices 1, 2
    Hero, *very brave*
    Narrators 1, 2, *good storytellers*
    Moral, *always right*
    Another Moral, *also right*
    Gorilla, *mean and nasty*
    Aunt Beulah, *very loving*
    Questions 1, 2, 3, 4
    Answer

- **"The Three Wishes," an old Swedish folk tale**

    Fairy, *knows all*
    Martin, *a tired woodcutter*

Margaret, *his wife*

Sybil, *a friend*

• **"The Fisherman and His Wife" by Jacob Grimm and Wilhelm Grimm**

Narrator

Fisherman, *nice guy*

Wife, *greedy*

Flounder, *magical*

• **"Lovable Looey" by Shirlee Sloyer**

Narrators 1, 2

Sister

Brother

Flower

Father

Mother

Little Girl

Teacher

Production Notes

The following production can be played by an entire class divided into groups, or by as few as six readers, each student reading several parts. Characters from *"You're a Good Man, Charlie Brown"* provide transitional material for the various segments of the script and should be played by the same readers throughout.. The physical arrangement, headgear, props, and sound effects for each segment are included before each sequence.

Introduction: "You're a Good Man, Charlie Brown"

Physical Arrangement

Charlie Brown sits on tall stool, center. Snoopy sits on low stool to his left. Linus and Lucy stand to the right. Patty and Schroeder stand to the left. (See Figure 10.1.)

Lucy X Linus X	Charlie X Snoopy X	X Patty Shroeder X

Figure 10.1.

Headgear and Props

All wear baseball caps. Linus holds a blanket.

Sound Effects

A triangle "ping" signifies the beginning of the sequence.

PATTY: The only thing wrong with Charlie Brown is his lack of confidence; his inferiority and his lack of confidence; his clumsiness, his inferiority and his lack of confidence; his stupidity, his clumsiness, his inferiority, his foolishness . . . and

SCHROEDER: Did you know that Charlie Brown has never pitched a winning baseball game, never been able to keep a kite in the air, never won a game of checkers, and never successfully punted a football? Sometimes I marvel at his consistency.

LUCY: Now, Linus, I want you to take a good look at Charlie Brown's face. Would you please hold still a minute, Charlie Brown, I want Linus to study your face. Now this is what you call a Failure Face, Linus. Notice how it has failure written all over it. Study it carefully, Linus, you rarely get to see such a good example. Notice the deep lines, the dull vacant look in the eyes. Yes, I would say this is one of the finest examples of a Failure Face that you're liable to see for a long while.

LINUS: I'm sorry to have to say it right to your face, Lucy, but it's true. You're a very crabby person. I know your crabbiness has probably become so natural to you now that you're not even aware when you're being crabby, but it's true just the same. You're a very crabby person and you're crabby to just about everyone you meet. Now I hope you don't mind my saying this, Lucy, and I hope you'll take it in the spirit that it's meant. I think we should all be open to any opportunity to learn more about ourselves. I think Socrates was very right when he said that one of the first rules for anyone in life is "Know thyself."

LUCY: Well, what's Socrates got to do with it anyway, huh? Who was *he* anyway? Did he ever get to be king, huh? Answer me that, did he ever get to be king? Who was Socrates anyway? Know thyself, hmph!

CHARLIE BROWN: Say Snoopy, do you really think I'm a failure? Look at my face. Is this a failure face?

SNOOPY: My teeth are tingling again. I feel like I've just got to bite somebody before sundown or I shall go stark raving mad. And yet I know that society frowns on such an action. So what happens? I'm stuck with tingly teeth.

CHARLIE BROWN: Good grief!

SNOOPY: And you know what else? I hate cats. To me, cats are the crabgrass on the lawn of life. I am a cat-hater, a cat-despiser, and a cat-loather. I'm also scared to death of them.

PATTY: Lucy, why does your little baby brother, Linus, carry around that silly little blanket?

LINUS: *(Swings his blanket around like a cape.)* I am Count Dracula from Transylvania.

(Two Narrators enter to center stage. Other characters freeze in position until they react.)

NARRATOR 1: It appears Charlie Brown and his friends have many problems.

NARRATOR 2: Yes, they are complex.

NARRATOR 1: What's complex? Can you get a vaccination against it?

NARRATOR 2: No, silly. Complex means they have many sides to their character.

NARRATOR 1: I know. They're good sometimes.

ALL: *(React to good.)*

NARRATOR 2: And they're bad sometimes.

ALL: *(React to bad.)*

NARRATOR 1: They're heroic . . .

ALL: *(React to heroic.)*

NARRATOR 2: And they're scared . . .

ALL: *(React to scared.)*

NARRATOR 1: But the important thing is, they're really fine people. Right?

ALL: **Of course right!**

(Exit Left.)

Rehearsing "You're a Good Man, Charlie Brown."

How to Be a Hero

In this segment students may read more than one part. One reader may be assigned Voice 1, Question 1, and Answer, while another may read Voice 2, Question 2, Moral, and so on.

Physical Arrangement

Narrators 1 and 2 move DR standing close together. Hero sits on tall stool, DL (low stool is placed DR). All other readers stand in semicircle. (See Figure 10.2.)

	Other Readers X X	

Short Stool   X
      X
◯
	X
	     X
		Tall Stool
		◯

X X Narrators		X Hero

Figure 10.2.

Headgear and Props

Since one reader may read several characters, no hats or props are necessary.

Sound Effects

A triangle "ping" signifies the end of the sequence.

NARRATOR 1: There are many different kinds of heroes. There is the hero who jumps into the water to rescue a drowning puppy. There is the hero who flies solo across the Atlantic Ocean for the very first time.

NARRATOR 2: Charles Lindbergh did *that* in 1927.

NARRATOR 1: We all know about this kind of hero. But there are *many* other kinds of heroes, and many ways to be heroic. Let us look at some of the things that could happen to you in everyday life.

NARRATOR 2: Then we'll ask some questions which you should try to answer. The answer to these questions will be discussed and you will be able to decide for yourself whether you are a hero-type person.

NARRATOR 1: Let's take a situation you might find yourself in some day and see how you would act. Suppose you are flying across the South Pole in a dirigible carrying a cargo of seventy-four gorillas to a zoo in Budapest.

NARRATOR 2: Budapest is the capital of Hungary, which is a country in Europe.

NARRATOR 1: Then suddenly, one of the gorillas, the biggest and the meanest, breaks out of his cage and unlocks all the other cages. Then all the gorillas march into the pilot's compartment, here you are steering the dirigible through a terrible hurricane.

GORILLA: Take us back home or we'll set fire to the dirigible, says the meanest gorilla.

NARRATOR 2: Now, what would YOU do in a case like this? How you answer will show whether you are the stuff heroes are made of.

QUESTION 1: Question one. Do you say, "OK, you win. I'll take you back?"

QUESTION 2: Question two. Or would you pull out your automatic revolver and shoot all the gorillas?

QUESTION 3: Question three. Would you smile and talk to the gorilla in a peaceful way, explaining that the zoo in Budapest is a very cozy place and that gorillas are very well treated there and fed vanilla ice cream, cookies, and strawberries, not to mention *all* the bananas they can eat?

QUESTION 4:   Question four. Would you put on your parachute and quickly jump out the window?

ANSWER: If YOU are the hero-type person you wouldn't do any of these things. A *real* hero would refuse to get into the dirigible in the first place. A *real* hero doesn't take foolish chances. He would say:

HERO: I refuse to take up an overcrowded dirigible. I won't take more than fifty gorillas at one time!

MORAL: It takes courage to refuse to do foolish things.

ANOTHER MORAL: Don't *ever* take any gorillas anywhere! There will always turn out to be one or two in the group that are mean and nasty.

(To indicate a scene change, Narrator 1 crosses stage and sits on tall stool, DL. Hero crosses and sits on short stool, DR. Narrator 2 joins the other readers as they all walk once around in a circle ending up in the semicircle again. See Figure 10.3.)

	Other Readers X X X Narrator 2	
X X Short Stool		X X
Ⓧ Hero	Tall Stool Ⓧ Narrator 1	

Figure 10.3.

NARRATOR 1:   It's not difficult to be a hero when you are in a very dangerous or exciting situation. But it's *not* so easy in the normal, humdrum sort of life that most of us lead. For example, how can you be heroic on some dreary August afternoon when you are along on a visit to your Aunt Beulah's? And your Aunt Beulah talks about nothing but her collection of old silver teaspoons. What would you do?

QUESTION 1:   Question one. Would you simply sit there on the sofa and scratch and squirm and pretend you care about old silver teaspoons?

QUESTION 2:   Question two. Would you slowly slump down in your seat, then slide off onto the floor, then quietly roll over behind the sofa, then weedle out under the piano, crawl silently out the door, slither through the hallway, and sit on the front stoop cooling yourself in the breeze?

QUESTION 3:　Question three. Would you suddenly jump to your feet, waving your hands about wildly, and scream:

HERO:　*(Jumps up.)* I smell it. I smell it.

EVERYONE:　Smell what?

NARRATOR 1:　Everyone asks, much alarmed.

HERO:　Odorless hyena gas! It puts you to sleep. It can be fatal.

EVERYONE:　Where? Where? I don't smell it.

NARRATOR 2:　Everyone yells.

HERO:　Of course you can't smell it. It's odorless. Quick! Open the windows! Follow me.

(All walk around in a circle following hero. End in same place. Hero remains standing.)

NARRATOR 1:　Then you climb out of the window, leading everybody to safety.

HERO:　It does go away in three hours. Nobody can go into the house until then.

BEULAH:　My Hero! *(Kisses hero.)*

NARRATOR 2:　. . . your Aunt Beulah cries, hugging you. Then she takes you all out to a fancy restaurant for lobster tails and French fried potatoes, and then to a very good movie.

ANSWER:　Number one, sit there and pretend you care about old silver teaspoons, is the correct answer. Number two is not a very heroic way to act. No hero has ever been known to crawl, slither, weedle, or ooze. And number three is *much* too complicated. Your mother would probably say:

MOTHER:　Oh shut up and be still!

MORAL:　Even if you really think odorless hyena gas is escaping from somewhere, don't make a fuss about it. Nobody will believe you or do anything about it. Just sit still and try not to squirm too much. The *most* heroic acts are often performed during *very* unexciting times such as long dull visits to relatives.

Sound Effects: *(Triangle.)*

(All exit Right taking stools with them.)

Interlude 1: Charlie Brown Characters Followed by the Narrator

Physical Arrangement

The conversation begins as the characters enter, L. When they reach C, they pause long enough to complete their lines then exit, R. The effect should be casual. Two friends talking as they walk across the stage. The Narrator enters L quickly after Linus and Schroeder exit.

Headgear and Props

The Charlie Brown characters wear baseball caps. Linus holds a blanket.

Sound Effects

A triangle "ping" signifies the beginning of the sequence.

SCHROEDER: Linus, do you think I have a heroic character?

LINUS: Well not exactly, Schroeder. But I really don't think you have anything to worry about. After all, science has shown that a person's character isn't really established until he's at least five years old.

SCHROEDER: But I *am* five. I'm more than five.

LINUS: Oh well, that's the way it goes I guess.

(Exit Right.)

NARRATOR: Yes, Schroeder is right, a person's character takes time to develop. But I know a couple of characters who were very foolish. Listen to this fairy tale called "The Three Wishes."

(Exit Right.)

The Three Wishes

Physical Arrangement

Margaret, Sybil, and Fairy enter L, and take positions U, facing rear. Martin enters L, speaking as he walks. He stops C, faces front. Each of the four characters utilizes his vertical space, walking U, facing the rear when not in the scene, returning D, facing front when needed. (See Figure 10.4.)

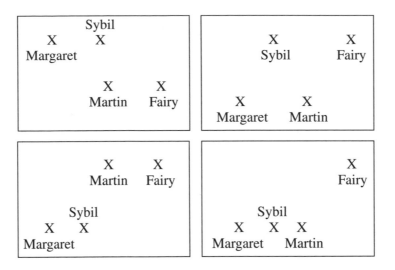

Figure 10.4.

Headgear and Props

Fairy wears headband with star and veiling. Martin wears a lumberjack hat. Margaret and Sybil wear mobcaps.

Sound Effects

Knocks on hollow block to represent chopping tree. Cymbal clash each time a wish is made. Triangle "ping" closes the segment.

MARTIN:	Martin, a tired woodcutter, has walked through the forest and sits down on a tree stump to rest.
FAIRY:	Martin! Martin!
MARTIN:	Hey there! Who's calling?
FAIRY:	I'm in the tree!
MARTIN:	Where? I don't see you.
FAIRY:	Listen Martin, I am an unfortunate fairy stuck in this tree. Cut a hole in the bark and let me out. But not too deep, you might hurt me.

Sound Effects: *(Three knocks on hollow block.)*

MARTIN:	Oh my goodness! A lady. Oh lady, please don't harm me!
FAIRY:	*Harm* you, I shall reward you with three wonderful wishes. Here is a ring. Whoever wears it may have three wishes come true, but only three, so be careful what you wish for. It's easy to waste wishes, but if you choose wisely, you're made for life. Choose wisely, Martin, *(Fading out.)*, wisely, wisely . . . *(Walks U, faces rear.)*
MARTIN:	Oh, thank you, thank you! *(Martin faces front, then R toward Margaret.)*

Hello there! Ha ha, corned beef and steak for me now, where's the butcher, call the butcher—ha!

(*Margaret turns, walks downstage.*)

MARGARET: What ails the man, home so early!

MARTIN: When luck comes into a house it tumbles in at the door and I've proved it. Margaret, I'm as grand a man as the Duke, or I will be. We've done with poverty. We've done with potatoes. Throw them to the neighbors' pigs. I'm drunk with joy!

MARGARET: (*Sobbing.*) Drunk!

MARTIN: Look, a ring. A beautiful fairy gave it to me. Look again at it. It's an enchanted wishing ring.

MARGARET: I don't believe it. What lady would give you a ring? You look like the back end of an old goat!

MARTIN: Three wishes she says.

MARGARET: Do you believe it, Martin? Let's try it now, let's wish that . . .

MARTIN: Hush, woman! Don't pop a wish out like that. I'm going to the Duke to find what the three grandest things are that a man can set his heart on.

MARGARET: Wait, Martin, someone might steal the ring. Leave it here with me.

MARTIN: Oh, all right, but be careful, it's a sacred charge, Margaret.

(*Martin turns, walks upstage. Sybil, Margaret's friend turns, joins others.*)

SYBIL: Good morning, Mistress Margaret, and where is Martin off to so early in the day?

MARGARET: He's gone to consult the Duke about an important matter, Sybil, but it's no use, I won't tell you.

SYBIL: Please, Margaret, I won't tell a soul, I promise.

MARGARET: Well, it's such good news I can't keep it. Look at this ring. It's a fairy gift. *Three* wishes!

SYBIL: Oh, what fine luck! Rare luck to drink to! I'm your friend, Margaret, drink to your luck any day. Don't forget that. Your old friend Sybil!

MARGARET: I'll be the finest lady in the village.

SYBIL: And me her best friend!

MARGARET: I'll have a carriage.

SYBIL: And me riding in it.

MARGARET: And horses . . .

SYBIL: And me behind them.

MARGARET: I'll have grand dinners.

SYBIL: I'll come to them. I will at that. Well, here's to good luck and long live the fairy! Say, Margaret, do you know what I feel like now? Let's have some sausages.

MARGARET: It's so long since I tasted sausages, I wouldn't know one if it looked me right in the face.

SYBIL: Yes, sausages!—nice, crisp, crackling, brown sausages.

MARGARET: Oh, I wish we had some sausages NOW!

Sound Effects: *(Cymbals.)*

SYBIL: What happened? It was like a flash of lightning! It left a pleasing smell, though. Sniff now. *(Both sniff.)* If I told you what my nose says, you'd laugh. *(She sniffs.)* It says sausages!

MARGARET: It does smell like sausages, just fried! Oh, oh, sausages *(crying.)* . . . it's a wish come true. Martin will have a fit. One wish is gone out of the ring—oh, oh.

SYBIL: Nothing is wrong with these sausages. They're good to eat!

MARGARET: *(Sobs.)* Oh dear! Oh dear!

SYBIL: It's true—you might have wished for a cartload. Martin couldn't have got mad at that! Let's sit down and eat the dish clean and not tell him a word about it. He'll think the fairy cheated him. You can't trust fairies these days.

MARGARET: Right! Hurry, sit down, eat quick and . . . oh . . . it's Martin . . .

(Martin turns, joins others.)

SYBIL: Oh, I just re-membered, I have a dentist appointment.

(Sybil turns, walks upstage.)

MARGARET: Come back, you coward, I won't take all the blame alone!

MARTIN: It's all settled in the wisest way. We're to have—What's that smell? Sausages! Where did they come from?

MARGARET: It was all Sybil's fault! Her mouth watered for sausages and before I knew it I was wishing for them!

MARTIN: You wished for sausages and you had the ring? *(He grabs it.)*

MARGARET: *(Sobbing.)* I forgot all about the ring.

MARTIN: So you've wasted a fairy wish—you doofus.

MARGARET: Oh Martin, two wishes are enough for a simple man like you. Be sensible. Sit down and eat the sausages.

MARTIN: What! Eat those sausages! I wish they were growing at the end of your nose!!

Sound Effects: *(Cymbals.)*

MARTIN: What was that?

MARGARET: Another wish come true!

MARTIN: Another wish, what wish?

MARGARET: That the sausages would grow on my nose. Oh-h-h . . . I'm a ruined woman. Look!!

MARTIN: They can't be growing on your nose. Pull them off.

MARGARET: Aw! They're hot! They burn me! *(sobbing)* Ohhh . . . I'm a ruined woman.

MARTIN: Stop that crying. Two wishes gone! Two—oh, what good's the third. What good to be rich like the Duke with that as a wife beside me. Look at her—look. An elephant with his nose in rollers. Stop swinging them, I say! I can't bear it! This ring has brought me nothing but torment. By magic they came and by magic they must go. I wish the sausages were off Margaret's nose!

Sound Effects: *(Cymbals.)*
(All face audience and freeze in position.)

FAIRY: *(Turns; walks D.)* So all three wishes got you nothing. I didn't think they would—for if you only *wish* for things, it will never do you good.

Sound Effects: *(Triangle.)*

(All exit Left.)

Interlude 2: "You're a Good Man, Charlie Brown"

Physical Arrangement

Linus enters first, R, takes his position as if watching television. Lucy enters L, talking as she does. (See Figure 10.5.)

	Linus Lucy X X	

Figure 10.5.

Headgear and Props

Baseball caps for both characters; a blanket for Linus.

Sound Effects

A triangle "ping" signifies the beginning of the sequence.

> LUCY: Linus, do you know what I intend? I intend to be a queen. When I grow up I'm going to be the biggest queen there ever was, and I'll live in this big palace with a big front lawn, and have lots of beautiful dresses to wear. And when I go out in my coach, all the people . . .

> LINUS: Lucy.

> LUCY: . . . all the people will wave and I will shout at them, and . . .

> LINUS: Lucy, I believe "queen" is an inherited title. *(Pause.)* Yes, I'm quite sure. A person can only become a queen by being born into a royal family of the correct lineage so that she can assume the throne after the death of the reigning monarch. I can't think of any possible way that you could ever become a queen. *(Pause.)* I'm sorry, Lucy, but it's true.

> LUCY: *(Silence, and then . . .)* And in the summertime I will go to my palace and I'll wear my crown in swimming and everything, and all the people will cheer and I will shout at them. . . . *(Pause.)* What do you mean, I can't be a queen?

> LINUS: It's true.

> LUCY: There must be a loophole. Nobody should be kept from being a queen if she wants to be one. IT'S UNDEMOCRATIC!

> LINUS: Good Grief.

> LUCY: It's usually just a matter of knowing the right people. I'll bet a few pieces of well-placed correspondence and I get to be a queen in no time.

> LINUS: I think I'll watch television. *(He returns to the set.)*

LUCY: I know what I'll do. If I can't be a queen, then I'll be very rich. I'll work and work until I'm very very rich, and then, I will buy myself a queendom.

LINUS: Good grief.

LUCY: Yes, I will buy myself a queendom and then I'll kick out the old queen and take over the whole operation myself. I will be head queen. And when I go out in my coach, all the people will wave, and I will . . . I will . . . *(She has glanced at the TV set and becomes engrossed. Pretty soon Linus turns and looks at her.)*

LINUS: What happened to your queendom?

LUCY: Huh?

LINUS: What happened to your queendom?

LUCY: Oh, that. I've given it up. I've decided to devote my life to cultivating my natural beauty.

(Lucy and Linus exit Right. Narrators 1 and 2 enter Left.)

NARRATOR 1: The trouble with Lucy, is she has a greedy side to her character.

NARRATOR 2: So what! It's better to be a greedy girl than a little dumb kid with a security blanket.

NARRATOR 1: Did you ever hear the story of the "Fisherman and His Wife?"

NARRATOR 2: What's it about?

NARRATOR 1: Being greedy.

(They exit Left.)

The Fisherman and His Wife

Physical Arrangement

All characters enter together, R, led by the narrator, who takes his position, DL. The three other characters stand in a row, C, Isabel and the Flounder alternate facing to the rear when they are out of the scene and to the Fisherman when in the scene. The Fisherman turns to each as he is required to speak to them.. When the Narrator speaks the line ending with ". . . they went to bed," both the Fisherman and his Wife let their heads fall on their chests in an exaggerated fashion. (See Figure 10.6.)

Isabel	Fisherman	Flounder	Narrator
X	X	X	X

Figure 10.6.

Headgear and Props

The Fisherman wears a rubber rain hat with a wide brim at back. The Flounder has a large scarf or string of scarves tied about his forehead. (For fun, the fish can wear a pair of snorkel goggles with a snorkel stuck in at the side.) The Wife should change her hats with the granting of each wish. First she wears an old scarf tied under her chin, then a garden hat, a riding helmet, a crown, and finally, a red velvet skull cap trimmed with sequins.

Sound Effects

A triangle "ping" ends the sequence.

NARRATOR. There once was a fisherman who lived with his wife in a miserable hovel by the sea and every day he went out fishing. Once, as he was sitting with his rod, looking at the clear water, his line suddenly went down far below, and when he drew it up again, he brought out a large flounder.

FLOUNDER: Hark, listen, fisherman, I am no common flounder. I am an enchanted prince. Please throw me back into the sea.

MAN: That's all right, I throw back all fish that can talk.

FLOUNDER: Thank you, thank you.

WIFE: Husband, did you catch anything today?

MAN: No. Well I did catch a flounder who said he was an enchanted prince so I threw him back into the water.

WIFE: Did you not wish for anything first?

MAN: What should I wish for?

WIFE: Isn't it bad enough we have to live in this miserable hovel? You might have wished for a nice clean cottage. He will certainly give us that. Go back and call him. You did catch him and let him go again, he is sure to do it. Now, be off.

MAN: I'm off.

Flounder, flounder in the sea,

	Come I pray thee here to me;
	Isabel my willful wife
	Does not like my way of life.
FLOUNDER:	Hello, fisherman.
MAN:	Hello, flounder. I had to call you back, my wife said I caught you and I should have wished for something.
FLOUNDER:	What would you have?
MAN:	She would like to live in a nice, clean cottage.
FLOUNDER:	Certainly. Return to your wife, she has her wish fully.
WIFE:	Husband, come inside.
NARRATOR:	There was a pretty sitting room and a bedroom . . .
MAN:	With a brass bed.
NARRATOR:	And a kitchen and outside there were chicks and hens and a great big fat rabbit . . .
MAN:	And a vegetable garden and a fruit tree.
WIFE:	Isn't this nice?
MAN:	This is nice. You and I will live in this cottage very happily.
WIFE:	We will think about that.
NARRATOR:	And with that they ate something and went to bed.
WIFE:	Husband.
MAN:	Yes.
WIFE:	This house is too cramped. Go to the flounder and tell him that I would like to live in a big stone castle.
MAN:	Oh, wife, this cottage is just right for us.
WIFE:	No, it's too cramped and I've changed my mind and the garden is too small. Now, get going!
MAN:	I don't want to go back to the flounder. *(Reluctantly.)*
	Flounder, flounder in the sea,
	Come I pray thee here to me;
	Isabel my willful wife
	Does not want my way of life.
FLOUNDER:	Fisherman, so we meet again.
MAN:	Hello.
FLOUNDER:	Give me some fin! *(They slap the palms of their hands together.)*
MAN:	The cottage was just right.
FLOUNDER:	You're welcome.
MAN:	But my wife changed her mind. She would like to live in a big stone castle.

FLOUNDER: So be it. Return to your wife. She awaits you at the gates of it.

WIFE: Husband.

MAN: Wife.

WIFE: Come inside with me.

NARRATOR: The walls were hung with beautiful tapestry.

WIFE: The floors were covered with rich, thick carpet.

NARRATOR: The rooms were furnished with golden chairs and golden tables.

WIFE: Crystal chandeliers hung from the ceiling.

NARRATOR: The tables were loaded with every kind of delicate food and the most costly wine.

WIFE: Outside there was a courtyard and beyond that forests and beyond that a park half a mile long.

NARRATOR: All kinds of animals roamed the grounds.

WIFE: And everything one could wish for. Now, is this not worth having?

MAN: Yes, this is worth having. You and I will live in this castle and be content.

WIFE: We will think about that.

NARRATOR: And with that they went to bed.

WIFE: Husband, peep out of that window, there, now wouldn't you like to be king over all this land. Go to the flounder and tell him that you consent to be king.

MAN: No, no wait, I don't want to be the king.

WIFE: You don't want to be the king?

MAN: No, no.

WIFE: That's all right, *I'll* be the king. GO!

MAN: Flounder, flounder in the sea,

Come I pray thee here to me;

Isabel my willful wife

Does not want my way of life.

FLOUNDER: What is it this time, fisherman?

MAN: My wife would be the king.

FLOUNDER: Return to your wife, she is the king.

MAN: Wife, are you now the king?

WIFE: Yes, I'm the king.

MAN: Wife, it is a fine thing for you to be the king.

WIFE: No, no husband. I find that time weighs heavy on my hands and I can't bear it any longer. I'm the king but it's not enough, I must be the Pope.

MAN: The Pope?

WIFE: The Pope.

MAN: Wife, this is something that is beyond the flounder.

WIFE: Nonsense, if he can make a king, he can make a Pope.

MAN: But it's not the same thing; there is only one Pope in the whole land.

WIFE: Are you forgetting who you are speaking to? I am the king and you are just my husband. You must obey. Beat it!

MAN: Flounder, flounder in the sea,

Come I pray thee here to me;

Isabel my willful wife

Does not want my way of life.

FLOUNDER: Now what does she want?

MAN: She would be the Pope.

FLOUNDER: Say that again.

MAN: My wife would be the Pope.

FLOUNDER: Go back to your wife, she is the Pope.

MAN: Wife, are you now the Pope?

WIFE: Yes, now we are the Pope.

MAN: Wife, I pray you now, content yourself to remain the Pope, higher you cannot go.

WIFE: We shall think about that.

NARRATOR: And with that they went to bed.

WIFE: Why can I not cause the sun and the moon to rise and set? Why? Husband, wake up. Go to the flounder. I will be the Lord of the Universe.

MAN: What are you saying?

WIFE: If I cannot cause the sun and the moon to rise and set, I shall not be able to bear it.

MAN: No, no, stay the Pope, you make a good Pope. Do not ask me to go to the flounder.

WIFE: Monous tumus scramus! Get out of here!

MAN: Flounder, flounder in the sea,

Come I pray thee here to me;

Isabel my willful wife,

Does not want my way of life.

FLOUNDER: Fisherman.

MAN: Flounder, she would be Lord of the Universe.

FLOUNDER: No, fisherman, this time it cannot be. Now you must return to your hovel by the sea.

NARRATOR: And there they are staying 'til this very day.

Sound Effects: *(Triangle.)*

(All exit Right.)

Interlude 3: "You're a Good Man, Charlie Brown"

Physical Arrangement

Lucy and Linus enter L immediately following the previous segment. They read their lines as they walk. Charlie Brown and the others enter L and form a huddle around Charlie. (See Figure 10.7.)

	Patty X	
Lucy X Linus X		Snoopy X Schroeder X
	Charlie X	

Figure 10.7.

Headgear and Props

Baseball caps for all.

Sound Effects

A triangle "ping" ends the sequence.

CHARLIE BROWN: All right, gang, I want this game to be our biggest and best game of the season, and I want everyone out there playing with everything he's got.

LUCY: Charlie Brown, I thought up some new strategy for you. Why don't you tell the other team that we're going to meet them at a certain place, only it isn't the real place, and then when they don't show up, we'll win by forfeit. Isn't that good strategy? Good Grief, I don't understand these managers who don't want to use good strategy.

SCHROEDER: Charlie Brown, is Lucy going to pitch again? Because if she does, I quit. Do you know what she does? She's always calling me out for a conference on the mound. I go out there, see? I go out there for a secret conference on the mound and do you know what she does? She kisses me on the nose.

ALL: **Ugh!**

CHARLIE BROWN: If we grit our teeth and bear down I'm sure we could finish this season.

LINUS: Perhaps you shouldn't be a playing manager, Charlie Brown. Perhaps you should be a bench manager.

PATTY. That's a good idea. You'd be a great bench manager, Charlie Brown. You could even be in charge of where we put the bench. When we get to the playing field, you could say, "Let's put the bench here," or "Let's put the bench there."

CHARLIE BROWN: I can't stand it.

LUCY: What's the sense of our playing when we know we're going to lose? If there was even a million to one chance we might win, it would make some sense.

CHARLIE BROWN: Well, there may not be a million to one chance, but I'm sure there is at least a billion to one chance. Now come on, Gimme a "T."

ALL: "T."

CHARLIE BROWN: Gimme an "E."

ALL: **"E."**

CHARLIE BROWN: Gimme an "A."

ALL: **"A."**

CHARLIE BROWN: Gimme an "M."

ALL: **"M."**

CHARLIE BROWN: What d'ya got?

ALL: **TEAM!!**

ALL: **There is no team like the best team, which is our team right here.**

LUCY: We will show you we're the best team in the very Little League this year.

ALL: **And in no time we'll be big time. With the big league baseball stars.**

LINUS: For all we have to do . . .

PATTY. Is win just one more game.

ALL: **And the championship is ours.**

CHARLIE BROWN: Three balls, two strikes, the bases were loaded with two men out. I pitched my curve, but somehow he hit it a good strong clout. "Lucy," I hollered, "It's coming right to you." She caught it as easy as pie—then dropped it.

ALL: **Ohhh!**

CHARLIE BROWN: I don't think it's good for a team's morale to see their manager cry.

SNOOPY:. Snoopy helped out by biting a runner and catching the ball in his teeth.

LINUS: Linus caught flies from a third-story window by holding his blanket beneath.

CHARLIE BROWN: Yes, we had fortitude. No one could argue with that. And one run would win us the game as I came up to bat.

LUCY: All right, Charlie Brown, we're all behind you—sort of. Now get a hit, Charlie Brown. This guy can't pitch. He pitches like my grandmother. We know you can do it if you just grit your teeth and bear down. Please, Charlie Brown, please . . .

LINUS: For all we have to do . . .

PATTY. Is win just one more game.

ALL: **And the championship is ours!**

(All freeze in position for a moment or two. Then a shift in position to show a slight passage of time.)

PATTY: Don't worry Charlie Brown. Heroes don't win all the time, sometimes they lose.

CHARLIE BROWN: All the time?

PATTY: Maybe.

CHARLIE BROWN: Oh, how could there possibly be one small person as thoroughly, totally, utterly BLAH as me.

(Charlie Brown and friends exit Right and Left. Narrators 1 and 2 enter and speak when they reach Center.)

NARRATOR 1: I guess it's possible for someone to be as totally blah as Charlie Brown but we all love him and that's what counts. Right?

NARRATOR 2: Of course right! He's lovable.

NARRATOR 1: Yeah! Just like lovable Looey. Listen.

(They exit Right.)

Lovable Looey

Physical Arrangement

All characters enter L and move to their positions, DR and DL. Father, Mother, Sister, and Brothers, in a group, RC. Flower, Teacher, Little Girl, in a line, LC. (See Figure 10.8.)

Headgear and Props

Father wears a man's felt hat. A large feathered hat is suitable for Mother. Sister wears a kerchief and Brother a baseball cap. The Flower can sport some petals around her face. The Teacher can wear a beanie or a mortarboard and the Little Girl, a big pink bow.

Father X Mother X	Sister X Brother X		Flower X	Teacher X	Little Girl X
Narrator 2 X					Narrator 1 X

Figure 10.8.

Sound Effects

A triangle "ping" ends the poem.

NARRATOR 1: Once there was a boy named Lovable Looey.

NARRATOR 2: He hated everyone!

FATHER: He didn't like his father.

MOTHER: He cared even less for his mother.

SISTER: He positively couldn't stand his sister.

EVERYONE: **Ugh!**

BROTHER:	And he never did dig his brother.
NARRATOR 1:	Lovable Looey despised dogs.
NARRATOR 2:	He detested cats.
FLOWER:	He would never smell a flower or stop along the way for friendly chats . . .
EVERYONE:	**With friends.**
TEACHER:	Lovable Looey thought his teacher was dreadful.
LITTLE GIRL:	And the little girl in his class with the big pink bow and the adorable dimple in her chin . . .
NARRATOR 1:	Was definitely not his type.
NARRATOR 2:	But the funny thing is, everyone . . .
EVERYONE:	**Simply everyone!**
NARRATOR 1:	Loved Looey.
NARRATOR 2:	Because he had freckles and even with this Women's Liberation thing . . .
NARRATOR 1:	He always opened doors for all the ladies!!

Sound Effect: *(Triangle.)*

(All exit Left.)

Conclusion: Charlie Brown Characters and Narrators

Physical Arrangement

The characters enter R and move into a huddle position around Schroeder and Snoopy. (See Figure 10.9.)

Patty X	Linus X Lucy X	Charlie X
	Scroeder X Snoopy X	

Figure 10.9.

Headgear and Props

Baseball caps for ALL: A blanket for Linus.

Sound Effects

Triangle "ping" ends the production.

NARRATOR 1:	So you see gang. People are complex—we're complicated with lots of sides to our character.
NARRATOR 2:	We're good.
ALL:	***(React to good.)***
NARRATOR 1:	And we're bad.
ALL:	***(React to bad.)***
NARRATOR 2:	But the main thing is we're all really very fine people. Right, Snoopy?
SNOOPY:	I don't know. Yesterday I was a dog. Today I am a dog. Tomorrow I'll probably still be a dog. There's just so little hope of advancement.
ALL:	**Good Grief!**

(The entire company enters Right and Left.)

Physical Arrangement

"Charlie Brown" characters remain DC, "Three Wishes" in a line, DR, "Fisherman and His Wife," DL, "Lovable Looey" and "How to Be a Hero" in a double line across the upper stage. (See Figure 10.10.)

	"How to Be a Hero" X X X X X X X X X X X X X X	
	"Lovable Looey"	
	X X X X X X X X X X X X X	
"Three Wishes"	"Charlie Brown" X X	"Fisherman"
X X X X	X X X X X	X X X X

Figure 10.10.

NARRATORS 1 and 2:	The thing is . . .
ALL:	*(Shout.)* **We're really fine people!**

Sound Effects: (Triangle.)

(All bow then exit Right and Left.)

Notes

1. Includes excerpts from Clark Gesner's "*You're a Good Man, Charley Brown*" (New York: Random House, 1967); Harvey Weiss's *How to Be a Hero* (New York: Parents' Magazine Press, 1968); "The Three Wishes," in *Favorite Stories Old and New,* comp. Sidonie Matsner Gruenberg (Garden City, NY: Doubleday, 1955), 344–346; "The Fisherman and His Wife," in *Grimm's Household Tales* (London: George Bell, 1884); unpublished poem, "Lovable Looey," by Shirlee Sloyer.

Chapter 11

SAMPLE SCRIPT: THE BRIDGE

The Bridge

Written for Readers Theatre by Shirlee Sloyer

Cast of Characters

Newspaper Reporter
Hairdresser
Panhandler
Roto Rooter Man
Prizefighter
School Teacher
Private Eye
Little Girl

Production Notes

Eight small, low library chairs are set up in a line. The Newspaper Reporter stands on the first chair in the row. Each character enters in turn. As a character is invited to join the others, he or she stands on a chair until all the characters are on the chairs. The characters wear hats that represent their jobs. For example, the Newspaper Reporter wears a man's hat with a sign "Press" placed in the band of the hat. He or she carries a notepad and pencil. (The jobs can be changed and/or added or subtracted.)

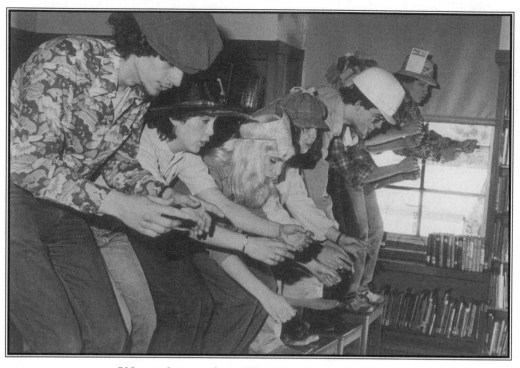

Older students perform "The Bridge" for lower grades.

NEWSPAPER REPORTER:	I'm a newspaper reporter and I can't find any stories to report, so I'm going to jump off this bridge and end it. One, two, . . .
PANHANDLER:	Hey, what are you doing?
REPORTER:	I'm a newspaper reporter and I can't find any stories to report, so I'm going to jump off this bridge and end it.
PANHANDLER:	Well, I'm a panhandler and I can't find any pans to handle. May I join you?
REPORTER:	Why certainly!
BOTH:	**One, two, . . .**
PRIZEFIGHTER:	Hey, what are you doing?
REPORTER:	I'm a newspaper reporter and I can't find any stories to report.
PANHANDLER:	And I'm a panhandler and I can't find any pans to handle, so we are going to jump off this bridge and end it.
PRIZEFIGHTER:	Well, I'm a prizefighter and I can't find any prizes to fight. May I join you?
REPORTER and PANHANDLER:	**Why certainly!**
ALL:	**One, two, . . .**
PRIVATE EYE:	Hey, what are you doing?

REPORTER:	I'm a newspaper reporter and I can't find any stories to report.
PANHANDLER:	And I'm a panhandler and I can't find any pans to handle.
PRIZEFIGHTER:	And I'm a prizefighter and I can't find any prizes to fight, so we're going to jump off this bridge and end it.
PRIVATE EYE:	Well, I'm a private eye and I can't find any privates to eye. May I join you?
OTHERS:	**Why certainly!**
ALL:	**One, two, . . .**
HAIRDRESSER:	Hey, what are you doing?
REPORTER:	I'm a newspaper reporter and I can't find any stories to report.
PANHANDLER:	And I'm a panhandler and I can't find any pans to handle.
PRIZEFIGHTER:	And I'm a prizefighter and I can't find any prizes to fight.
PRIVATE EYE:	And I'm a private eye and I can't find any privates to eye, so we're going to jump off this bridge and end it.
HAIRDRESSER:	Well, I'm a hairdresser and I can't find any hairs to dress. May I join you?
OTHERS:	**Why, certainly.**
ALL:	**One, two, . . .**
ROTO ROOTER MAN:	Hey, what are you doing?
REPORTER:	I'm a newspaper reporter and I can't find any stories to report.
PANHANDLER:	And I'm a panhandler and I can't find any pans to handle.
PRIZEFIGHTER:	And I'm a prizefighter and I can't find any prizes to fight.
PRIVATE EYE:	And I'm a private eye and I can't find any privates to eye.
HAIRDRESSER:	And I'm a hairdresser and I can't find any hairs to dress, so we're going to jump off this bridge and end it.
ROTO ROOTER MAN:	Well, I'm a roto rooter man and I can't find any rotos to root. May I join you?
OTHERS:	**Why certainly!**
ALL:	**One, two, . . .**

SCHOOL TEACHER:	Hey, what are you doing?
REPORTER:	I'm a newspaper reporter and I can't find any stories to report.
PANHANDLER:	And I'm a panhandler and I can't find any pans to handle.
PRIZEFIGHTER:	And I'm a prizefighter and I can't find any prizes to fight.
PRIVATE EYE:	And I'm a private eye and I can't find any privates to eye.
HAIRDRESSER:	And I'm a hairdresser and I can't find any hairs to dress.
ROTO ROOTER MAN:	And I'm a roto rooter man and I can't find any rotos to root, so we're going to jump off this bridge and end it.
SCHOOL TEACHER:	Well, I'm a school teacher and I can't find any schools to teach. May I join you?
OTHERS:	**Why certainly!**
ALL:	**One, two, . . .**
LITTLE GIRL:	Hey, what are you doing?
REPORTER:	I'm a newspaper reporter and I can't find any stories to report.
PANHANDLER:	And I'm a panhandler and I can't find any pans to handle.
PRIZEFIGHTER:	And I'm a prizefighter and I can't find any prizes to fight.
PRIVATE EYE:	And I'm a private eye and I can't find any privates to eye.
HAIRDRESSER:	And I'm a hairdresser and I can't find any hairs to dress.
ROTO ROOTER MAN:	And I'm a roto rooter man and I can't find any rotos to root.
SCHOOL TEACHER:	And I'm a school teacher and I can't find any schools to teach, so we're going to jump off this bridge and end it.
LITTLE GIRL:	Well, I'm just a little girl and I have nothing to do. May I join you anyway?
OTHERS:	**Why certainly!**
ALL:	**One, two, . . . THREE!**

(All jump off chairs except the reporter. All crouch down and stay.)

REPORTER: WOW! *(Writes on pad)* WHAT A STORY!

(All, in a line, bow and exit Right and Left.)

Audience members enact "The Bridge."

Chapter 12

SAMPLE SCRIPT: THE LEGEND OF LIGHTNING LARRY

The Legend of Lightning Larry*

By Aaron Shepard

Cast of Characters

Citizen 1, 2, 3, 4, 5, 6, 7, 8
Raunchy Ralph
Lightning Larry
Grimy Greg
Crooked Curt
Creepy Cal
Evil-Eye McNeevil
Moldy Mike
Dismal Dan
Lousy Luke
Devilish Dick
Gruesome Gus
Dreadful Dave
Stinky Steve
Sickening Sid
Other Citizens

> (Musicians)
>
> (Bartender)
>
> (Bank Teller)

Production Notes

Citizens serve as narrators. Citizens 1 through 4 are at Stage Right, Citizens 5 through 8 at Stage Left. They can be standing on risers at various levels. Male Citizens wear three-cornered hats or other period headgear. Females wear bonnets or head scarves. Other characters wear cowboy hats or old felt country hats and red or blue bandannas. Musicians, Bartender, and Bank Teller may be added where appropriate.

CITIZEN 1: Well, you've heard about gunfighting good guys like Wild Bill Hickock and Wyatt Earp.

CITIZEN 8: But we'll tell you a name that strikes even greater fear into the hearts of bad men everywhere.

ALL (except LARRY): Lightning Larry!

CITIZEN 2: We'll never forget the day Larry rode into our little town of Brimstone and walked into the Cottonmouth Saloon. He strode up to the bar, smiled straight at the bartender, and said,

LIGHTNING LARRY: Lemonade, please!

CITIZEN 7: Every head in the place turned to look.

CITIZEN 3: Now, standing next to Larry at the bar was Crooked Curt.

CITIZEN 6: Curt was one of a band of rustlers and thieves that had been terrorizing our town, led by a ferocious outlaw named Evil-Eye McNeevil.

CITIZEN 4: Curt was wearing the usual outlaw scowl.

CITIZEN 5: Larry turned to him and smiled.

LIGHTNING LARRY: Mighty big frown you got there, mister!

CROOKED CURT: What's it to *you*?

LIGHTNING LARRY: Well, maybe I could help remove it!

CROOKED CURT: I'd like to see you try!

CITIZEN 1: The rest of us got out of the way, real fast.

CITIZEN 8: The bartender ducked behind the bar.

CITIZEN 2: Larry and Curt moved about ten paces from each other, hands at the ready.

CITIZEN 7: Larry was still smiling.

CITIZEN 3: Curt moved first. But he only just cleared his gun from its holster before Larry aimed and fired.

LIGHTNING LARRY: *Zing!*

CITIZEN 6: There was no bang and no bullet. Just a little bolt of light that hit Curt right in the heart.

CITIZEN 4: Curt just stood there, his eyes wide with surprise. Then he dropped his gun, and a huge grin spread over his face.

CITIZEN 5:	He rushed up to Larry and pumped his hand.
CROOKED CURT:	I'm mighty glad to know you, stranger! The drinks are on me! Lemonade for everyone!
CITIZEN 1:	When Evil-Eye McNeevil and his outlaw gang heard that Crooked Curt had gone straight, they shuddered right down to their boots.
CITIZEN 8:	Most any outlaw would rather die than smile!
CITIZEN 2:	Evil-Eye's men were shook up, but they weren't about to let on.
CITIZEN 7:	The very next day,
DISMAL DAN:	Dismal Dan!
DEVILISH DICK:	Devilish Dick!
DREADFUL DAVE:	And Dreadful Dave!
CITIZEN 7:	Rode into Brimstone, yelling like crazy men and shooting wild.
DAN, DICK, AND DAVE:	(*Hoot and holler, prance, wave guns and shoot.*)
CITIZEN 3:	Windows shattered,
CITIZEN 6:	and citizens scattered.
CITIZEN 4:	Then Lightning Larry showed up. He never warned them.
CITIZEN 5:	Never even stopped smiling.
CITIZEN 1:	Just shot three little bolts of light.
LIGHTNING LARRY:	*Zing! Zing! Zing!*
DAN, DICK, AND DAVE:	(*Stop and fall when hit.*)
CITIZEN 8:	Hit those outlaws right in the heart.
CITIZEN 2:	Larry's shots knocked the outlaws to the ground. They lay there trying to figure out what had hit them. Then they got up and looked around.
DISMAL DAN:	Looks like we did some damage, boys.
CITIZEN 7:	. . . said Dismal Dan.
DEVILISH DICK:	Hope nobody got hurt!
CITIZEN 3:	. . . said Devilish Dick
DREADFUL DAVE:	We'd better get to work and fix this place up.
CITIZEN 6:	. . . said Dreadful Dave.
CITIZEN 4:	They spent the rest of the day replacing windows and apologizing to everyone who'd listen.
CITIZEN 5:	Then for good measure, they picked up all the trash in the street.
CITIZEN 1:	Evil-Eye McNeevil had lost three more of his meanest men,
CITIZEN 8:	and he was furious!
CITIZEN 2:	He decided to do something *really* nasty.
CITIZEN 7:	The next day,

STINKY STEVE:	Stinky Steve!
SICKENING SID:	And Sickening Sid!
CITIZEN 7:	Walked into the 79th National Savings and Loan, with guns in hand.
CITIZEN 3:	They wore masks,
CITIZEN 6:	but everyone knew who they were – from the smell.
STINKY STEVE:	Stick up your hands.
CITIZEN 4:	. . . said Stinky Steve.
SICKENING SID:	Give us all the money in your vault.
CITIZEN 5:	. . . ordered Sickening Sid.
CITIZEN 1:	They were just backing out the door with the money bags, when Lightning Larry strolled by.
CITIZEN 8:	Didn't even slow his step.
CITIZEN 2:	Just shot those bandits in the back.
LIGHTNING LARRY:	*Zing! Zing!*
CITIZEN 7:	Went right through to the heart.
CITIZEN 3:	The puzzled outlaws stopped and looked at each other.
STINKY STEVE:	Seems a shame to steal the money of hardworking cowboys.
SICKENING SID:	Wouldn't want to make their lives any harder.
CITIZEN 6:	They holstered their guns and walked back to the teller.
CITIZEN 4:	They plunked the money bags down on the counter.
SICKENING SID:	Now, you keep that money safe.
CITIZEN 5:	Then they pulled out their wallets and opened up accounts.
CITIZEN 1:	That was the last straw for Evil-Eye McNeevil. It was time for a showdown!
CITIZEN 8:	The next day, at high noon, Larry was sipping lemonade at the Cottonmouth Saloon. Evil-Eye burst through the doors and stamped up to him.
EVIL-EYE McNEEVIL:	I'm Evil-Eye McNeevil!
LIGHTNING LARRY:	(*with a huge smile*) Hello, Evil-Eye! Can I buy you a lemonade?
EVIL-EYE McNEEVIL:	This town ain't big enough for the both of us.
LIGHTNING LARRY:	Seems pretty spacious to me!
EVIL-EYE McNEEVIL:	I'll be waiting for you, down by the Okey-Dokey Corral.
CITIZEN 8:	And Evil-Eye stamped out.
CITIZEN 2:	Larry finished his lemonade and walked out onto Main Street.
CITIZEN 7:	Evil-Eye was waiting for him. But Evil-Eye wasn't alone.
CITIZEN 3:	There on either side of him were
RAUNCHY RALPH:	Raunchy Ralph!

GRIMY GREG:	Grimy Greg!
CREEPY CAL:	Creepy Cal!
MOLDY MIKE:	Moldy Mike!
LOUSY LUKE:	Lousy Luke!
GRUESOME GUS:	And Gruesome Gus!
CITIZEN 6:	And not a one of them looked friendly.
LIGHTNING LARRY:	Nice day for a stroll!
CITIZEN 4:	. . . called Larry.
EVIL-EYE McNEEVIL:	Draw!
CITIZEN 5:	. . . said Evil-Eye.
CITIZEN 1:	All of us citizens of Brimstone were lining Main Street to see what would happen.
CITIZEN 8:	Larry was still smiling, but we knew even Larry couldn't outshoot all those outlaws together.
CITIZEN 2:	Just then, a voice came from the Cottonmouth Saloon.
CROOKED CURT:	Like some help, Larry?
LIGHTNING LARRY:	Wouldn't mind it!
CITIZEN 7:	Out stepped . . . Crooked Curt! And right behind him were Dismal Dan, Devilish Dick, Dreadful Dave, Stinky Steve, and Sickening Sid.
CITIZEN 3:	They all took places beside Larry.
CROOKED CURT:	Hello, Evil-Eye!
CITIZEN 6:	. . . called Curt.
EVIL-EYE McNEEVIL:	Traitors!
CITIZEN 4:	. . . yelled Evil-Eye.
LIGHTNING LARRY:	Draw!
CITIZEN 5:	. . . said Larry, with a smile.
CITIZEN 1:	Evil-Eye and his men drew their guns,
CITIZEN 8:	but Larry and his friends were an eye-blink quicker.
CITIZEN 2:	Their guns fired seven little bolts of light.
LARRY AND FRIENDS:	*Zing!*
CITIZEN 7:	Hit those outlaws right in the you-know-what.
EVIL-EYE McNEEVIL:	YIPPEE!
CITIZEN 3:	. . . yelled Evil-Eye.
CITIZEN 6:	He shot in the air.
EVIL-EYE McNEEVIL:	*Zing!*
CITIZEN 4:	There was no bang and no bullet.
CITIZEN 5:	Just a little bolt of light.

LIGHTNING LARRY: All right, men! Let's clean up this town, once and for all!

LARRY AND ALL OUTLAWS: *(Shoot at all others) Zing! Zing! Zing! . . .*

CITIZEN 1: And before we could duck for cover,

CITIZEN 8: Larry and Evil-Eye and the others

CITIZEN 2: turned their guns on the *rest* of us.

CITIZEN 7: Bolts of light flew everywhere.

CITIZEN 3: *No* one was spared—

CITIZEN 6: not a man,

CITIZEN 4: woman,

CITIZEN 5: or child!

ALL: (except LARRY). YIPPEE!

CITIZEN 1: You never saw such a happy crowd!

CITIZEN 8: We all rushed around

CITIZEN 2: and pumped each other's hands

CITIZEN 7: and hugged each other.

CITIZEN 3: Then the musicians got out instruments, and we had dancing, too. Main Street was one huge party,

CITIZEN 6: all the rest of that day,

CITIZEN 4: and on through the night.

CITIZEN 5: We never drank so much lemonade in all our days!

CITIZEN 1: With all the commotion, only a few of us saw Larry ride into the sunset.

CITIZEN 8: Can't say where he went.

CITIZEN 2: Can't say what he's doing now.

CITIZEN 7: But we bet he still aims for the heart.

ALL: *(Shooting at audience.) Zing!*

(All bow and exit Right and Left.)

Chapter 13

SAMPLE SCRIPT: THE BULLY

The Bully

Written for Readers Theatre by Shirlee Sloyer

After its enactment, this script should spark a discussion with cast and audience about bullies and bullying.

Cast of Characters

Narrators 1, 2, 3, 4
Jake, *the bully*
Jane, *a classmate*
Marge, *a classmate*
Jamal, *a classmate*
Dan, *a classmate*
Mike, *a classmate*
Ari, *a classmate*

Production Notes

The Narrators are the storytellers. They talk to the audience as does Jake, the bully, in the first scene. In Scenes 2, 3, and 4, Jake interacts with his classmates. In Scene 6, as in Scene 1, Narrators and Jake talk to the audience. The various locales change. The Narrators set each scene.

Scene from "The Bully."

Scene 1

*(Four narrators stand in a line across the playing area. Jake, Downstage Right. Three chairs are arranged behind the speakers to suggest seats on a bus.***)**

NARRATOR 1:	This is the story of a boy named Jake.
JAKE:	That's me.
NARRATOR 2:	He's big.
JAKE:	Yeah. (*Stands on his toes.*)
NARRATOR 3:	He's strong.
JAKE:	You're talkin' muscles man! (*Flexes his muscles.*)
NARRATOR 4:	He's smart.
JAKE:	Check out the I Q. I'm the genius meister. (*Thumbs lift lapels.*)
NARRATOR 1:	And . . .
ALL NARRATORS:	**HE'S A BULLY!**
JAKE:	Say what?
NARRATOR 1:	Here is what happens on the bus almost any day.

(Narrators turn, move upstage. Stay with backs to audience.)

The bully shows his muscle.

Scene 2

(Jamal and Mike enter, take seats on bus. Jake sits in the seat behind them.)

JAKE: *Hey Jamal, whaddya' got in that bag?*

JAMAL: It's my collection of old toys.

JAKE: Ha! Mama's baby needs to take his toys to school.

JAMAL: They're antiques. Very old. I'm going to talk about them in class.

JAKE: No one wants to hear about your silly junk, stupid.

MIKE: Come on Jake, leave him alone.

JAKE: Mind your own business, fatty.

MIKE: Hey, who ya callin' fatty?

JAKE: I dunno. What's your name? *(Has a fit of laughter.)*

(Jamal and Mike turn chairs to the rear and exit right. Jake turns his back to audience, stays. Narrator 1 turns, walks downstage.)

NARRATOR 1: Well, that's how it is on the bus. Now lets us look in on Jake as he walks into school.

(Narrator 1 turns, walks upstage.)

Scene 3

(Marge and Jane, carrying lunch bags, enter left talking to each other. Jake turns and follows them mockingly.)

MARGE: I'm glad we didn't have any homework last night. I got to watch TV.

JANE: Yeah. Me too.

JAKE: Watchya' got for lunch Ma-a-a-r-ger-r-i-e-e-e.

MARGE: None of your business.

JAKE: Oh yeah, well I like Twinkies and you always get Twinkies.

JANE: Leave us alone, Jake.

JAKE: No one asked you, Jane. Now give over the Twinkies, Ma-a-a-r-ger-ri-e-e-e.

MARGE: No way.

JAKE: You're forcing me to get them for myself. Right Jane?

JANE: Not right Jake.

JAKE: Okay. You asked for it.

(Jake pulls bag from Marge, laughs, and runs out left. Marge and Jane, disturbed, exit right. Narrator 2 turns, comes downstage.)

NARRATOR 2: It seems there's no stopping Jake. Let's check him out during recess in the school yard.

(Narrator 2 turns, walks upstage.)

Scene 4

(Dan and Ari, holding soccer ball, enter right. Jake enters left.)

JAKE: You wimps gonna choose me for the game.

DAN: Maybe.

JAKE: Whaddya' mean, *maybe*?

ARI: You made us lose the last time trying to be funny.

JAKE: I wasn't trying. I *was* funny. Everyone laughed.

DAN: Yeah and while you were joking, the other team scored.

JAKE: You guys are too skinny and weak to play soccer. Give it up.

ANDY: Cool it Jake.

JAKE: No one tells Jake to cool it. I can beat you both up with one hand tied behind my back.

DAN: Let's go, Ari.

JAKE: Sure, scaredy cats. Run away. Here take this with you.

(Jake punches each one on the arm and exits right, laughing. Dan and Ari remain.)

Scene 5

(Jamal, Mike, Marge, and Jane join Dan and Ari.)

JAMAL:	What can we do to stop getting bullied?
MIKE:	We tell on the bully.
MARGE:	I'm scared to tell.
JANE:	Yeah, if we tell we'll really have trouble with the bully.
ARI:	Anyway they'll say it's *our* fault, not his.
DAN:	No! Bullying gets worse when bullies get away with it.
JANE:	But we can't fight back.
JAMAL:	No, but we can stick together. Never let him get us alone.
MARGE:	You're right. And if the bully hits you, get away from him.
DAN:	And get help.
MIKE:	Yes, get help. Telling on a bully isn't snitching.
ARI:	That's right. The bullies need help too.
JANE:	So we tell someone?
ALL:	**Right!!**

(All exit.)

Scene 6

(All Narrators return downstage. Stand in line.)

NARRATOR 1:	What is a bully?
NARRATOR 2:	Anyone who tries to hurt you.
NARRATOR 3:	Or makes you feel bad.
NARRATOR 4:	Or unhappy.
NARRATOR 1:	Why do kids become bullies?
NARRATOR 2:	Let's ask Jake. *(Calls.)* Hey Jake!

(Jake enters right.)

NARRATOR 3:	Why are you a bully?
JAKE:	I get to feel important. When *you* feel small, *I* feel big.
NARRATOR 4:	Is that what you want?
JAKE:	Sure, I like feeling more important than other people.
NARRATOR 1:	Why?

JAKE: Well, sometimes I feel unhappy inside. And sometimes I feel jealous of kids. So if I spoil their fun or get them mad, I feel better.

NARRATOR 1: Were you ever bullied?

JAKE: Sure, my big brother bullies me at home all the time.

NARRATOR 2: How do you feel then?

JAKE: How do you think I feel? I hate it.

(Jake exits Left.)

ALL: Imagine that!

NARRATOR 3: Maybe kids bully other kids because *they* themselves were bullied.

ALL: **Could be.**

NARRATOR 4: Maybe bullies pick on other kids 'cause those kids are different

ALL: **But we're *all* different!**

NARRATOR 1: Right. So, if you are ever bullied . . .

ALL: **DON'T FIGHT BACK!**

NARRATOR 2: Ignore the bully. Then tell someone who can help.

ALL: **Like your teacher.**

NARRATOR 3: Or your mother or father.

ALL: **DON'T BE AFRAID!**

NARRATOR 4: Remember, it's never *your* fault if you get bullied.

NARRATOR 1: So let's work together.

(All the characters enter. Join narrators in line.)

EVERYONE: **PUT A STOP TO BULLYING!!**

(All bow and exit Right and Left.)

Chapter 14

SAMPLE SCRIPT: HOUSEWORK

Housework*

By Sheldon Harnick

Adapted for Readers Theatre by Shirlee Sloyer

This script can be included in a readers theatre presentation of poetry or used as a stimulus for a discussion about gender.

Cast of Characters

Narrators 1, 2, 3, 4
Male Voice 1, 2, 3, 4, 5, 6, 7
Lady 1, 2, 3, 4
Female Voice 1, 2, 3, 4, 5, 6, 7

Production Notes

The four Narrators and the four Ladies sit on high stools, two on each side of the playing area. Those playing male voices are posing, statue-still, in a line across the stage, displaying the items mentioned in the script. They become animated when they speak, holding up their products even more prominently, and return to their poses quickly thereafter. The female voices, wearing head scarves, are on their knees in front of the males. They hold dust cloths, etc. and are also motionless until they speak, at which time they enact the job they represent, such as dusting an imaginary wall or scrubbing the floor. It is best if both the male and female voices have their parts memorized to allow them to have their hands free. All stand for the last line of the poem.

NARRATOR 1: You know, there are times when we happen to be just sitting there quietly watching TV,

NARRATOR 2: when the program we're watching will stop for awhile and suddenly someone appears with a smile,

NARRATOR 3:	and starts to show us how terribly urgent it is to buy some brand of detergent,
MALE VOICE 1:	or soap,
MALE VOICE 2:	or cleanser,
MALE VOICE 3:	or cleaner,
MALE VOICE 4:	or powder,
MALE VOICE 5:	or paste,
MALE VOICE 6:	or wax,
MALE VOICE 7:	or bleach,
ALL MALE VOICES:	**to help with the housework.**
NARRATOR 4:	Now, most of the time it's a lady we see who's doing the housework on TV.
LADY 1:	She's cheerfully scouring a skillet or two, or she's polishing pots 'til they gleam like new,
LADY 2:	or she's scrubbing the tub, or she's mopping the floors, or she's wiping the stains from the walls or the doors,
LADY 3:	or she's washing the windows, the dishes, the clothes, or waxing the furniture 'til it just glows,
LADY 4:	or she's cleaning the "fridge," or the stove or the sink with a lighthearted smile and a friendly wink and she's doing her best to make us think that *her* detergent,
MALE VOICE 1:	or soap,
MALE VOICE 2:	or cleanser,
MALE VOICE 3:	or cleaner,
MALE VOICE 4:	or powder,
MALE VOICE 5:	or paste,
MALE VOICE 6:	or wax,
MALE VOICE 7:	or bleach,
ALL MALE VOICES:	**is the best kind of detergent,**
MALE VOICE 1:	or soap,
MALE VOICE 2:	or cleanser,
MALE VOICE 3:	or cleaner,
MALE VOICE 4:	or powder,
MALE VOICE 5:	or paste,
MALE VOICE 6:	or wax,
MALE VOICE 7:	or bleach,
ALL MALE VOICES:	**that there is in the whole world!!**
NARRATOR 1:	And maybe it is . . .
NARRATOR 2:	and maybe it isn't . . .

NARRATOR 3: and maybe it does what they say it will do . . .

NARRATOR 4: but I'll tell you one thing I *know* is true:

LADY 1: The lady we see when we're watching TV—The lady who smiles as she scours,

FEMALE VOICE 1: or scrubs,

FEMALE VOICE 2: or rubs,

FEMALE VOICE 3: or washes,

FEMALE VOICE 4: or wipes,

FEMALE VOICE 5: or mops,

FEMALE VOICE 6: or dusts,

FEMALE VOICE 7: or cleans—

LADY 2: or whatever she does on our TV screens—that lady is smiling because she's an actress.

LADY 3: And she's earning money for learning those speeches that mention those wonderful detergents,

MALE VOICE 1: and soaps,

MALE VOICE 2: and cleansers,

MALE VOICE 3: and cleaners,

MALE VOICE 4: and powders,

MALE VOICE 5: and pastes,

MALE VOICE 6: and waxes,

MALE VOICE 7: and bleaches.

LADY 4: So the very next time you happen to be just sitting there quietly watching TV,

LADY 1: and you see some nice lady who smiles as she scours,

FEMALE VOICE 1: or scrubs,

FEMALE VOICE 2: or rubs,

FEMALE VOICE 3: or washes,

FEMALE VOICE 4: or wipes,

FEMALE VOICE 5: or mops,

FEMALE VOICE 6: or dusts,

FEMALE VOICE 7: or cleans,

ALL FEMALE VOICES: **remember:**

LADY 1: Nobody smiles doing housework but those ladies you see on TV.

LADY 2: Because even if the detergent,

MALE VOICE 1: or soap,

MALE VOICE 2: or cleanser,

MALE VOICE 3:	or cleaner,
MALE VOICE 4:	or powder,
MALE VOICE 5:	or paste,
MALE VOICE 6:	or wax,
MALE VOICE 7:	or bleach,
LADY 3:	that you use is the very best one—
LADY 4:	housework
ALL LADIES AND FEMALE VOICES:	(*shouting*) **is just not fun!!!**
NARRATOR 1:	Children, when you have a house of your own,
NARRATOR 2:	make sure, when there's housework to do, that you don't have to do it alone.
NARRATOR 3:	Little boys, little girls, when you're big husbands and wives,
NARRATOR 4:	if you want all the days of your lives to seem sunny as summer weather,
LADY 1:	make sure, when there's housework to do,
ENTIRE CAST.	(*All stand.*) **THAT YOU DO IT TOGETHER!!!**

(Entire cast bows and exits Right and Left.)

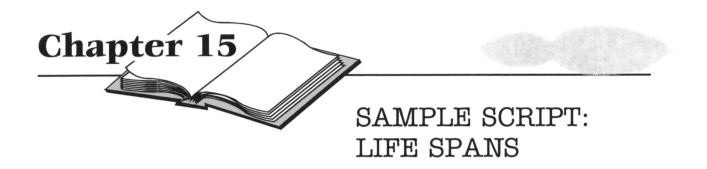

Chapter 15

SAMPLE SCRIPT: LIFE SPANS

Life Spans

Adapted from an Old Folk Tale for Readers Theatre by Shirlee Sloyer

Cast of Characters

Prologue
The Lord
Donkey
Dog
Monkey
Man
Epilogue

Production Notes

The Prologue and the Epilogue can be played by the same person. He or she is at a lectern, stage left. The Lord is seated on a high stool or chair, throne-like. He wears a crown. The Donkey, Dog, and Monkey wear appropriate headpieces. They enter one after the other from stage right and exit stage left. As each enters he oe she makes the sound specific to his or her breed animal: the Donkey brays, the Dog barks, the Monkey chatters. Man wears a baseball cap and enters whistling or humming.

PROLOGUE: It is almost the end of the sixth day of the first week of the world and The Lord is seated on his throne thinking about what he will do next.

THE LORD: Now that I have created the heaven and the earth I have but one more task. I must assign a life span for each of my creatures. Ah, here comes the Donkey.

(Donkey enters stage right.)

DONKEY: *(brays)* Hi Lord, how goes it?

THE LORD: I've had a busy week. But I will get a much-needed rest tomorrow. What's up, Donkey?

DONKEY: Well I was wondering if you were assigning life spans.

THE LORD: Of course, my friend. I was just contemplating that very thing.

DONKEY: Have you figured out how long I will live?

THE LORD: How does thirty years sound to you?

DONKEY: Thirty years!!! That's a lot of living. Just think of my life style and how much I have to put up with. Morning to night. Night to morning. Trudging! Shlepping! Carrying bags of grain to the mill!

THE LORD: My, my!

DONKEY: And that's not all. In the morning they wake me with a kick. If I'm tired they provide energy with a whip. Give me a break Lord, thirty years is too long to put up with that kind of strain.

THE LORD: Poor Donkey. I understand. How about eighteen years?

DONKEY: Cool! Thanks Lord, you're a good man. Er . . . I mean you're a good Lord. *(Brays and exits stage left.)*

THE LORD: Do I hear barking?

(Dog enters stage right.)

DOG: *(Barks)* That you do. It's me, the Dog.

THE LORD: How are you, Doggie?

DOG: Fine, Lord, but I want to ask about my life span. How long shall I live?

THE LORD: I was thinking of giving you thirty years.

DOG: *(Howls.)* Thirty years? Thirty years?

THE LORD: That's what I said. Thirty years. I guess your ears must lap?

DOG: Do you realize how many sticks I would have to fetch in thirty years? How many frisbees I'd have to catch?

THE LORD: So what's so bad about that?

DOG: And when I lose my bark and my bite, I'll have to go around snarling and snapping at everything. That's a dog's life!

THE LORD: Well then, what would you have me do?

DOG: Make it less, Lord, less than thirty years. I'll be your best friend. *(Panting, he nuzzles The Lord.)*

THE LORD: No problem. I'll give you twelve years instead.

DOG: You're a pal, Lord. I won't forget this. *(Exits, skipping, stage left.)*

THE LORD: Now who's coming?

(*Monkey enters stage right.*)

MONKEY: (*Chatters*) It's me, Monkey.

THE LORD: Ah, my good buddy. How's the monkey business?

MONKEY: Pretty tricky. But I'm holding on.

THE LORD: Good. What can I do for you?

MONKEY: Have you figured out how many years I will live?

THE LORD: Well, everyone else thought thirty years was too long, but you have lots of fun, you shouldn't mind.

MONKEY: (*Chattering.*) Mind! Do you know what it's like to hang around on your tail for thirty years? And besides to see no evil, speak no evil, and hear no evil? That's sheer torture!

THE LORD: Mercy! That does seem to be a bad scene. Okay. How about twenty years?

MONKEY: Thanks, Lord. I knew we would get along. (*Exits stage left, chattering as he goes.*)

(*Man enters stage right, whistling or humming.*)

THE LORD: Hey Man, give me some skin! (*They slap each other's hand.*) How have you been?

MAN: Fine, Lord. Eden was a fabulous place. But you should see *my* garden. I've planted all kinds of stuff. And my house is coming along too. I'm working on putting in a fireplace.

THE LORD: Sounds like all is well outside of paradise.

MAN: Right on! But what can I look forward to?

THE LORD: I've decided that man shall live for thirty years.

MAN: Mmmm. Well . . . er . . . er . . .

THE LORD: You look pale. What's wrong?

MAN: Thirty years is not very much. I'm just getting started.

THE LORD: Well, I could give you the eighteen years that the Donkey didn't want.

MAN: That's super Lord, but that makes only forty-eight and I still have more to accomplish.

THE LORD: Okay. Then I can give you the twelve years the Dog didn't take.

MAN: Fantastic! That makes sixty. But a big shot like you surely could do better.

THE LORD: Well . . . I don't know . . .

MAN: Make it longer and I'll give you one day out of every week. Whaddya say?

THE LORD: Fine. I will give you the ten years that the Monkey couldn't use. But that's my final answer.

MAN: Thanks dear Lord. I'll remember you in my prayers.

(Man exits happily, whistling or humming as he goes.)

EPILOGUE: So man lives about seventy years. The first thirty he is strong and happy. The next eighteen are those of a donkey, when load after load is placed on his back. Then he lives twelve years like a dog. He snaps and snarls at everything, but has no teeth to bite with. And, finally, the ten years of the monkey, when he becomes feeble-minded and foolish and does silly things, and children laugh at him.

(The Lord and the Prologue exit together, laughing.)

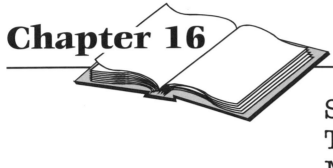

Chapter 16

SAMPLE SCRIPT: THE EMPEROR'S NEW CLOTHES

The Emperor's New Clothes

By Hans Christian Andersen

Adapted for Readers Theatre by Shirlee Sloyer

Cast of Characters

Storyteller 1 and 2
Officer
Minister
Man
Emperor
Woman
Rogue 1 and 2
Child

Production Notes

Storytellers 1 and 2 are positioned throughout the script in front of music stands on either side of the stage. They wear velvet tams to suggest Pages to the Emperor. The Emperor, wearing an elaborate crown and possibly a fur piece around his neck, sits on a high stool, left stage, while the two Rogues occupy right stage. The Rogues wear old felt hats pulled down on their foreheads. The Minister, wearing a skull cap with a large, flashy pin affixed, and the Officer, wearing a helmet, flank the Emperor. When they are called on to visit the Rogues, they walk to right stage. All the characters are on stage for the procession. The Emperor stands center stage, flanked by the Minister and the Officer. The Man (straw hat), Woman (head scarf), and Child (bow or baseball cap, carrying a balloon), stand to the side. The Rogues exit, running across the length of the stage area before the procession segment begins.

STORYTELLER 1:	Many years ago there lived an Emperor, who was so extremely fond of grand new clothes that he spent all his money on them. He had a new costume for every hour of the day.
STORYTELLER 2:	One day, two clever rogues came to the kingdom. They pretended to be weavers and declared they could weave the finest stuff anyone could imagine.
MINISTER:	Your majesty, there are two weavers outside who claim they make a magic cloth. The cloth becomes invisible to anyone who is unfit for his job or is terribly stupid.
EMPEROR:	Do you mean to say that if you look at this cloth and do not see it, you are very stupid or unfit for your job?
MINISTER:	Yes, your Majesty.
EMPEROR:	Those would be extraordinary clothes. *(Aside.)* If I wore those clothes, I should be able to find out which men in my empire are not fit for the place they have. I could tell the clever from the dunces. *(To Minister.)* Yes, the stuff must be woven for me directly. Give these weavers all the gold they need, that they might begin their work at once.
ROGUE 1:	So the rogues put up two looms, and pretended to be working; but they had nothing at all upon their looms.
ROGUE 2:	They at once demanded the costliest silk and finest gold; these they put into their own pockets and worked at the empty looms until late into the night.
EMPEROR:	Then the emperor sent the minister to see how the weavers were getting on with the cloth.
MINISTER:	*(Aside.)* Mercy on us, thought the old Minister, and he opened his eyes wide. *(Aside.)* I cannot see anything at all.
ROGUE 1:	Be so good as to come nearer. Don't you approve of the colors? And look, what do you think of the pattern?
MINISTER:	Can I indeed be so stupid? I never thought that, and not a soul must know it. Am I not fit for my job? No, it will never do for me to tell that I could not see the stuff.
ROGUE 2:	Have you nothing to say?
MINISTER:	Oh, it is charming—quite enchanting. What a fine pattern. And what colors. Yes, I shall tell the emperor I am very much pleased.
ROGUE 1:	Well, we are glad of that. See the red, the gold, the blue, and the intricate pattern?
MINISTER:	Oh, yes, yes. I'll go tell the emperor.
EMPEROR:	Next the emperor sent his officer to see the weaving.

OFFICER:	The officer looked and looked, just like the minister, but as there was nothing there to see but empty looms, he could see nothing.
ROGUE 1:	Is that not a pretty piece of cloth?
OFFICER:	*(Aside.)* I am not stupid, thought the officer, but I can't see the stuff, so it must be the job for which I'm unfit. I must not let it be noticed. *(To the Rogue.)* Yes, I am very pleased by it. They are such beautiful clothes, and what a charming pattern. It is enchanting. A most pretty piece of stuff.
STORYTELLER 1:	The whole city was talking of the splendid cloth. They knew what strange power the stuff possessed, and all were anxious to see how bad or how stupid their neighbors were. And finally, the Emperor said . . .
EMPEROR:	I wish to see it myself, while it is still upon the loom. So he went to the weavers.
ROGUE 2:	Isn't the cloth splendid? Doesn't your Majesty like the pattern? And the colors? he said, pointing to the empty loom.
EMPEROR:	*(Aside.)* What's this? thought the Emperor. I can see nothing at all. That is terrible. Am I stupid? Am I not fit to be Emperor? That would be the most dreadful thing that could happen to me. *(To all.)* Oh, it is very pretty. That *is* pretty. It is splendid. Excellent.
ROGUE 1:	I hope you will wear the splendid new clothes for the first time at the great procession tomorrow.
EMPEROR:	Indeed, I will. And as a reward for such beautiful work I hereby bestow the title of Imperial Court Weavers upon you both.
ALL.	*(Cheer.)*
STORYTELLER 2:	The whole night before the morning of the procession the rogues were up, so the people would see that they were hard at work completing the Emperor's new clothes.
STORYTELLER 1:	They pretended to roll the cloth off the loom, they made great cuts in the air with great scissors, they sewed with needles without thread, and at last they said,
ROGUE 2:	The clothes are ready.
ROGUE 1:	See, here are the trousers! Here is the coat.
ROGUE 2:	Here is the cloak . . . it is light as a spider's web. One would think one had nothing on. But that is just the beauty of it.
ROGUE 1:	Will your Imperial Majesty be so kind as to take off your clothes? said the rogue.

ROGUE 2: Then we will put on the new clothes here in front of the great mirror.

STORYTELLER 2: The Emperor took off his clothes. The rogues pretended to put on him each new garment as it was ready; and the Emperor turned round and round before the mirror.

MINISTER: Oh, how well they look!

OFFICER: How wonderfully they fit!

MINISTER: What a pattern!

OFFICER: Splendid!

EMPEROR: Well, I am ready.

STORYTELLER 1: So the Emperor went in procession, and everyone in the streets said . . .

MAN: Oh, how beautiful are the Emperor's new clothes!

WOMAN: What a magnificent train to his cloak. How it fits him!

STORYTELLER 2: No one would let it be known that he could not see the clothes, for that would have shown he was not fit for his job or was very stupid. No clothes of the Emperor had ever had such a success as these new clothes.

ALL: *(Cheer.)*

STORYTELLER 1: Suddenly a little child cried out . . .

CHILD: But, he has nothing on.

ALL: What? What?

MAN: Just hear what the little child says!

WOMAN: Listen to the child.

CHILD: But he has nothing on!

STORYTELLER 2: It seemed to the Emperor that the child was right. He too, thought to himself, that he had nothing on.

EMPEROR: But I must go through with the procession.

STORYTELLER 1: And so he held himself a little higher, and the chamberlains held on tighter than ever, and carried the cloak that did not exist at all.

(The cast returns to center stage for a bow. Exit Right and Left.)

Chapter 17

SAMPLE SCRIPT: HE MAIL/SHE MAIL

He Mail/She Mail*

By Ted K. Hechtman

Cast of Characters

Susan (Squidget@aol.com), *a sixth-grade girl*
Max (Binkus@aol.com), *a sixth-grade boy*

Production Notes

The two students are writing to each other. They read out loud as they create the notes. Max is seated at a desktop computer on his desk. We can see Max's keyboard, but the monitor is just a square frame so that we can see his face. Susan is using a laptop computer that is sitting on the floor. She sits cross-legged in front of it. They are both facing the audience. Max is wearing a baseball cap, backwards.

SUSAN: Dear Binkus@aol.com, I can't believe it. I cannot for one moment believe it. I do not believe it. Who doesn't know that I know more about chemistry and biology than anyone else in the class. Who doesn't know that. I know who doesn't know that. *You* seem not to know it. My oldest friend. We have been friends for our whole lives and you choose two people to work on the project with and none of them are me? Ali Feuerstein . . . Ali Feuerstein and Mike Potters? Mike Potters has trouble figuring out how to use the water fountain in the hall. I hope all your fungi just . . . well . . . just wither and die! Squidget@aol.com.

* Used by permission of Ted K. Hechtman.

MAX: Dear Squidget@aol.com, *You* wanted to do the project about pond water and I do not want to work on that. Danny Smythe worked on that last year and it was BORING! I mean who wants to do a project that was done last year. Anyway, you're working with Jessica Harding and Irving Johnson. And Irving is a jock. He plays football! He wouldn't know a protozoa from a pro line backer! Go ahead and waste your time with cloudy water full of . . . full . . . well . . . full of whatever pond water is full of. Be careful nothing climbs out of the pond and absorbs you! Binkus etc.

SUSAN: Thought I would let you know that this weekend my dad is driving me and Jessica and Irving upstate to collect pond water. We're all going to stay at Jessica's parents place in the mountains. I just checked the weather and it's going to be a beautiful day. We are going to have a good time. Hope you and your fungi are doing well in some dark hole.

MAX: I just wanted to let you know that this Friday the Discovery Channel is going to have a show all about the ocean. My mom and dad invited Ali and Mike to come over and have dinner with us and then we could all watch the show together. My mom asked if you wanted to come over and see it with us, but I told her you had to go upstate and squish around in some swamp.

SUSAN: Hope you enjoyed just sitting around INSIDE while I was in the beautiful mountains this weekend. It didn't even matter that it rained. We went out anyway. We went to three different ponds. The rain didn't even matter. Our clothes dried on the way home . . . in the car. Dr. Sternberg says I can go back to school on Tuesday. Or maybe Wednesday when the fever goes down. Could you get my homework for me?

MAX: Sure I can get your homework for you, but wouldn't you rather ask your new best friends like Jessica or Irving to do it for you? Oh . . . I just remembered Jessica was out sick today also. So I'll give it to Irving and he can drop it off and catch whatever strange germs you got in the swamp. Do you have any *National Geographics* or *Scientific Americans* that have any articles about fungi, mushrooms? If you do, could you give them to Irving when he drops off your homework?

SUSAN: Binkus . . . I was nice enough to send over the magazines you wanted with my brother since Irving NEVER CAME with my homework. Couldn't you see your way clear to do one little favor for an ex-friend? I'm changing my screen name and my profile. You are blocked, blocked, blocked!!!

MAX: Irving wasn't in school today either and Mike is sick too. I couldn't give them your stupid homework. Even though we are not on the same project, I don't see why you have to be so—well mad. Anyway I hope your hard drive crashes. I would have dropped off your homework myself, but my mom says you must be infectious.

SUSAN (*sarcastic*): Thanks. I am sure that your good wishes are what gave my computer a virus. In fact, my hard drive *did* crash! And I'm not infectious!

MAX: Sorry about your hard drive. Do you need any help? I mean, if you needed any help I could . . . well . . . help.

SUSAN (*softening*): Thanks. Sorry for all the stuff about fungi. You really are fun guy. Hah! Hah! So . . . Mike's sick. Irving's sick. Ali's sick. What about our projects?

MAX: *We* could join up. How about FUNGI GROWTH IN A POND VICINITY?

SUSAN: No way! It's got to be THE EFFECT OF A POND ON NEARBY FUNGI GROWTH.

MAX: It's a deal! Library?

SUSAN: Tomorrow?

MAX: Okay. Friends?

SUSAN: Sure.

"Dear Binkus@aol.com . . ." from *He Mail/She Mail.*

Chapter 18

SAMPLE SCRIPT: EXCERPT FROM THE PRINCE AND THE PAUPER

Excerpt from *The Prince and the Pauper*[1]

by Mark Twain

Adapted for Readers Theatre by Shirlee Sloyer

Cast of Characters

Narrators 1 and 2, *the storytellers*
Soldier, *a palace guard*
Crowd, *the rabble of old London*
Prince, *the Prince of Wales*
Father, *Tom Canty's mean dad*
Lady Jane Grey, *lady at the court*
Tom Canty, *the beggar boy*

Production Notes

Narrators 1 and 2 stand on either side of the stage area in front of music stands throughout the performance. The Crowd (any number of students) may enter and leave as instructed in the script, or they can be seated on two benches, one on either side of the stage, much like a Greek chorus. They rise when they speak their lines and return to their seats when they are offstage. Father, Soldier, and Lady Jane Grey are seated on stools up stage with their backs to the audience until they speak. At that time they leave their stools and come downstage. Tom Canty and the Prince are seated on high stools center stage. These characters are also turned away from the audience until they speak. When they converse with each other they rise from the stools. Old hats for the boys and head scarves for the girls may be used by the Crowd. Father wears a scarf tied around his forehead. Tom wears a battered hat with a feather. The Prince sports a fancy crown while the Soldier wears a military hat. Lady Jane Grey wears a tiara.

NARRATOR 1: In the ancient city of London, on a certain autumn day in the second quarter of the sixteenth century, a boy by the name of Tom Canty was born to a poor family who did *not* want him.

NARRATOR 2: On the same day another English child was born to a *rich* family by the name of Tudor, who *did* want him.

NARRATOR 1: All England wanted him too, for he would be heir to the throne.

NARRATOR 2: England had so longed for him, and hoped for him, and prayed God for him, that, now that he was really come, the people went nearly mad for joy.

CROWD: (*Cheering.*) Hip hip hooray! Hip hip hooray! Hip hip hooray! Long live the little prince. God bless The Prince of Wales.

(*The crowd turns to face the rear.*)

NARRATOR 1: Let us now *skip* a number of years.

NARRATOR 2: Tom Canty lived with his family in a run-down section of London, called Offal Court, out of Pudding Lane. It was a small, decayed, and rickety place packed full of wretchedly poor families.

NARRATOR 1: His mother and his twin sisters were kindly toward him but his father and grandmother were cruel and mean.

NARRATOR 2: Tom's father was a thief, and although Tom was never taught to steal, his father forced him to beg and beat him often if he didn't obey.

FATHER: Tom Canty, I will give you a fair beating if you don't go out there and do the begging.

TOM: Father, please do not make me beg. I will work. I will earn my keep.

FATHER: Nonsense! Do as I say. Get to the streets!

NARRATOR 2: One January day, when Tom was begging, barefoot and cold, he found himself in the vicinity of the majestic palace, Westminister.

(*Soldier and Crowd turn to face audience.*)

NARRATOR 1: He hoped, beyond hope, to see the Prince passing by.

NARRATOR 2: And lo and behold on that cold January day the Prince appeared at the front gate.

(*Prince turns to audience.*)

CROWD: (*cheering*) Hail to the Prince. Hooray!!

NARRATOR 1: Tom's heart beat fast as he pressed his face against the gate bars to get a better look. But a soldier guarding the palace screamed at him.

SOLDIER:	Get away from the gate, you young beggar!
CROWD:	Yeah! Get away! You don't belong here! Beat it!
NARRATOR 2:	The crowd jeered and laughed, but the young Prince sprang to the gate. He was indignant as he cried out,
PRINCE:	How dare you treat a poor lad like that! He is the King's subject just like you. Open the gates and let him in!
CROWD:	(*Reacts.*) Oh, the Prince is so kind. He's allowing the beggar boy entry. Long live the Prince of Wales!
PRINCE:	(*To Tom.*) You look tired and hungry. You were not treated nicely out there. Come with me.

(*They stroll to another part of the stage. Crowd and Soldier exit.*)

PRINCE:	What is your name?
TOM:	Tom Canty, sire.
PRINCE:	And where do you live?
TOM:	Offal Court, sire. Out of Pudding Lane.
PRINCE:	Have you parents?
TOM:	Oh yes, sire. I have parents, a grandmother, and twin sisters.
PRINCE:	Are they good to you.
TOM:	Well, sire . . .
PRINCE:	Yes, I see. They are not kind to you.
TOM:	My mom and sisters are good people but . . .
PRINCE:	I take it your father is a brute. And your grandma?
TOM:	She's not so nice.
PRINCE:	A mean old lady?
TOM:	I'm afraid that's true, sire.
PRINCE:	But you are free to roam the city and see the puppet shows, and the monkeys at the zoo.
TOM:	Oh yes, sire. But I am hungry all the time.
PRINCE:	How I wish to be on my own, without my Chamberlains, to see the delights of the world.
TOM:	And how I wish I could be dressed like you, just once, in fine silks and satins, and *shoes.*
PRINCE:	Say no more! Let us switch our clothes.
TOM:	Oh, sir. You can't mean it.
PRINCE:	Yes I mean it! Let's do it. Let's switch.

(*Tom and the Prince exchange hats.*)

NARRATOR 1:   And so the Prince of Wales was dressed in Tom's shabby odds and ends.

NARRATOR 2:   While the little beggar, Tom, was decked out in the gaudy plumage of royalty.

NARRATOR 1:   They stood side by side and stared at each other in the mirror.

PRINCE: What do you make of it?

TOM: It is not for me to say, sire.

PRINCE: Then I shall say it. You look exactly like me. The same hair, the same eyes, the same voice and manner. Your face and mine are the same. If we walked naked down the hall no one could tell us apart.

TOM: It is hard to believe, sire, but it is true.

PRINCE: Is that a bruise I see on your arm?

TOM: Yes, it was the soldier who pulled me away from the gate, sire. But it's nothing.

PRINCE: Nothing? No, no. It is shameful that a man-at-arms in my father's kingdom should inflict such harm on a citizen. I shall go immediately and take care of him.

NARRATOR 1:   So the prince was out the door before Tom could object, dressed in Tom's dirty rags. With a hot face and glowing eyes he flew out of the palace.

NARRATOR 2:   As soon as he reached the gate, he seized the bars, and tried to shake them shouting:

(Soldier and Crowd return.)

PRINCE: Open! Unbar the gates!

NARRATOR 1:   The soldier who maltreated Tom obeyed. But as soon as the prince exited the grounds, the soldier boxed him on the ear and sent him whirling to the roadway.

SOLDIER: Take that, you beggar. You think because you got in to see his highness that you're special? Forget it.

CROWD: *(Roaring with laughter.)* Yeah! Yeah! You're just like everyone else, only worse. Beggar! Beggar boy!

PRINCE: I am the Prince of Wales. My person is sacred and you shall hang for laying your hands upon me!

SOLDIER: *(Mockingly.)* Sure, sure your royal highness. Now be off, you crazy rubbish!

CROWD: *(Jeering.)* Make way for his royal highness. Make way for the beggar Prince of Wales. Ha, ha, ha.

NARRATOR 1:   After hours of persecution by the rabble, the little Prince was at last left alone.

NARRATOR 2: He could not go back to the palace dressed in rags. No one believed he was the Prince.

PRINCE: What shall I do? Where shall I go? Offal Court. That is where Tom said he lived. If I can find it before my strength gives out I shall be saved. They will surely know that I am not one of theirs, but the true Prince.

(Prince freezes in position until spoken to by Father.)

NARRATOR 1: Now listeners, do you really think Tom's family will see this beggar in rags as a true Prince? You're right, they don't. After all, he is the spitting image of Tom Canty.

FATHER: Well, Tom Canty, you're back. Late. Very late. For that you'll be beaten and no supper.

NARRATOR 2: And so the Prince is taken to be Tom Canty, who lives in a hovel in Pudding Lane.

NARRATOR 1: He is treated cruelly by Tom's father, who beats him and sends him out to beg.

(Prince turns away from audience.)

NARRATOR 2: Meanwhile, back in the palace, everyone thinks Tom Canty is the Prince.

(Tom enters.)

TOM: It appears that all around me think I am the Prince. Surely they will see that I am just a beggar boy from the other side of London and they will punish me severely.

(Lady Jane Grey enters.)

LADY JANE GREY: Good day, my lord!

TOM: Please fair lady, I am no lord but only Tom Canty of Offal Court. Pray let me see the Prince and he will give me back my rags and let me go.

LADY JANE GREY: What's wrong, my lord? Are you ill?

TOM: You must believe me. I am not the Prince.

LADY JANE GREY: But of course you are. Why are you acting this way?

TOM: Oh, I am in deep trouble. Please, please find the Prince.

(Tom freezes in position.)

NARRATOR 1: So naturally the Lady Jane Grey thought to herself:

LADY JANE GREY: The Prince has gone mad. Oh dear, the Prince has gone mad.

NARRATOR 2: She tells the king, who insists it be kept a secret. He will help the Prince overcome his malady.

NARRATOR 1:   Well, listeners, here we have it. The Prince is now roaming the city in rags and Tom Canty, the beggar boy, is firmly established in the palace as the Prince. What a dilemma!

NARRATOR 2:   The story of what finally happens to these two hapless boys is definitely a fascinating one.

NARRATOR 1:   We are sure you will want to learn about the outcome. So, we invite you to read the classic story by Samuel L. Clemens. You know him better as Mark Twain. The book is called *The Prince and the Pauper.* You will find it on your library shelf.

NARRATOR 2:   Write to us and tell us what you think.

NARRATORS 1 and 2:   **Have fun reading!**

(The entire cast comes downstage for a bow.)

Notes

1. Mark Twain, *The Prince and the Pauper* (New York: Harper & Row, 1817), 1–34.

Chapter 19

SAMPLE SCRIPT: THE ASSIGNMENT

The Assignment

Written for Readers Theatre by Shirlee Sloyer

This script demonstrates how social studies may be integrated with the language arts program in a readers theatre presentation.

Cast of Characters

Adam, *an eighth-grade boy*
Harriet Tubman
Evelyn, *an eighth-grade girl*
Gotama, the Buddha
Abraham Lincoln
George Herman Ruth (Babe Ruth)
Winston Churchill
Harry S. Truman
Madame Curie
Lou Costello and Bud Abbott

Production Notes

Adam and Evelyn are on opposite sides of the performing area. Each is sitting on a high stool facing out, away from each other. They are talking on the telephone. The other characters enter as directed. They take their prescribed places, slightly upstage of Evelyn and Adam. Once each pair has spoken they turn their backs and walk upstage, one to the right, the other to the left. Their backs remain toward the audience until directed (see script directions). The historical characters may wear hats such as a stovepipe hat for Lincoln, baseball cap for Ruth, bowler hat for Churchill, and the like. A sign "Hello My Name Is . . . " will do nicely as well.

Scene 1

(Adam and Evelyn are on the telephone.)

ADAM:	Hi Evelyn, it's me, Adam.
EVELYN:	Hi Adam, what's up?
ADAM:	Did you get the assignment today?
EVELYN:	You were in school, didn't you get it?
ADAM:	I guess I lost it. Or maybe I was just bored and stopped listening.
EVELYN:	Well, it's a weird assignment. We have to say how we would make the world a better place.
ADAM:	Another dumb one. How are we supposed to know how to make the world a better place when all those guys in Washington don't know how to do it?
EVELYN:	Anyway, we have to think of something. It's due Monday. We only have the weekend to work on it.
ADAM:	Can we do it together?
EVELYN:	Mrs. Samuels said we could work with someone else in the class if we want to.
ADAM:	Cool. Can you think of anything we can do?
EVELYN:	No. I'm clueless. I'm really no great thinker.
ADAM:	That's it. You got it. That's a super idea!
EVELYN:	What? What idea? I didn't come up with anything.
ADAM:	Oh, but you did. Great thinker. You said you're not a great thinker.
EVELYN:	So? How is that an idea?
ADAM:	Don't you see? We should call on the great thinkers. They'll know how to make the world better.
EVELYN:	Yeah, right. Just call 'em up and tell them about our assignment. They'll just come over and help us.
ADAM:	Exactly. We get on the computer and collect a virtual group of great minds from the past and ask them what they would do today to make the world a better place.
EVELYN:	Awesome. Let's do it.

Scene 2

(Adam and Evelyn remain in place, in a freeze position, while the historical people say their lines. They become animated again when their conversation continues. Each of the famous characters enters at his or her turn to speak. When they finish they turn away from the audience.)

ABRAHAM LINCOLN: "A house divided cannot stand." I, Abraham Lincoln, said this in one of my debates with Stephen Arnold Douglas in 1858. I was referring to the fact that a nation cannot be united and strong when some states are for slavery and some against. And although slavery is long gone, if I were living today I would speak out against discrimination. Now, as then, our country cannot be powerful and influential when the people within the land are distant and hostile toward one another.

WINSTON CHURCHILL: You speak the truth, Mr. Lincoln. You do not know me because I was born ten years after you were assassinated. My name is Winston Churchill, and we have many things in common. I, too, was in politics. I was the prime minister of England when we were involved in World War II. And just like you, we fought for a democratic form of government. Hitler was an anti-Semitic tyrant who tried to conquer all of Europe. Human rights were threatened. And now, in the twenty-first century, some folks are still not free to speak out and live decent, peaceful lives. To make a better world, we must help people fight for their rights. Yes, even if it takes "blood, sweat and tears."

(*Lincoln and Churchill turn their backs to audience*)

ADAM: Evelyn, did you hear them? I called on Lincoln and Churchill.

EVELYN: Yeah, Adam, but they talk like all those other politicians—in generalities.

ADAM: Whatdya' mean?

EVELYN: Let's cure the world of hostility! Let's fight for our rights! The only right I can fight for is to get a seat on the bus. Those guys aren't talking about *our* world.

ADAM: Well, who would you choose?

EVELYN: Listen.

MADAME CURIE: My name is Marie Sklowdowska. But you know me by my married name, Madame Curie. I came from a poor Polish family. My father was a mathematics teacher who scraped together what little he had to give me an education. I went to the Sorbonne in Paris. I loved science. When I finally married Pierre, we labored for four years to prove the existence of polonium and radium. We worked in a miserable old shed, but those were the happiest years of my life. We were entirely dedicated to our work Then we had to make a choice: become the inventors of radium, patent the technique, and get rich or describe the results of our research to American engineers and get little monetary reward. We chose the latter because to do otherwise would be contrary to the scientific spirit. We made our contribution to the world, and now we would advise all scientists to help each other to find cures for the illnesses that plague your world: cancer and AIDS. There can be no nobler effort.

HARRIET TUBMAN: I am a black woman, Harriet Tubman. Many years ago, because my skin was not white, I could be bought and sold like a horse or a cow. I had no rights. I could not marry legally. My children did not belong to me but to the master, who could sell them for money when he wanted to. But I found a way to lead over 300 slaves up to freedom. Yes, I was a kind of spy and I helped nurse people to health. I overcame every obstacle because I had faith in God. For a better world, try having the courage to break out of the mold. There is a promised land out there. Go get it!

(Curie and Tubman turn their backs to the audience.)

EVELYN: Well, what do you think?

ADAM: I think they're great women who did a lot for the world but . . .

EVELYN: But what?

ADAM: They are telling us to combat disease, have courage, and go out into the promised land. Get real!

EVELYN: Okay, Mr. Smarty, you get to pick next. Who'll it be?

GOTAMA, THE BUDDHA: Thank you for calling on me, Gotama, the Buddha. I have over 400 million followers today, more than any other religion in history. And you ask how I would improve the world. Perhaps you seek nirvana, a sublime peace. This state can only be achieved by understanding what is important in life. We must abandon ignorant cravings. Craving to be rich, famous, better than our neighbors. We must learn to love one another, to interact with the world and be a humble part of it. In this lies peace and perfect happiness.

GEORGE HERMAN RUTH (BABE RUTH): Well, Buddha, have it your own way. But I, Babe Ruth, can't say that one shouldn't strive to be the best. The world would surely be a better place if people tried harder to succeed in what they do. Look at me. No, I'm not a Buddha, but I am a Sultan, The Sultan of Swat. Sure, I wanted money and fame, but I worked tirelessly to be the greatest hitter ever to hold a bat. And as a result I am recognized as the player who made baseball the American national sport. My history shows that people can rise above humble beginnings and make a difference

(Buddha and Ruth turn their backs to the audience.)

EVELYN: Yeah, well the Buddha left his family, and Babe Ruth had a drinking problem.

ADAM: So, none of us is perfect. We all have problems. That's part of being in the world.

EVELYN: Yes, I guess you're right. It's just that we have to recommend ways *we* can make the world a better place. I can see plenty of problems, but so far I can't see how they concern us.

HARRY S. TRUMAN: Hold on, kids. Perhaps you *should* be concerned. Look at me, Harry S. Truman. I really had to make some difficult decisions. Can you imagine waking up one day and finding out that you are the president of the United States? Well, when President Franklin D. Roosevelt died unexpectedly, that is what happened to me. Believe me, it wasn't easy to fill a great president's shoes. But someone had to do it, so it was me. I guided my country through some very difficult years. I made the heavy decision to use the atomic bomb against Japan to bring the war to a close. I never regretted it. As to my ideas about the world, I think you should try to make sense of what's going on around you. The more people who know and understand their government, the better government they will have. I have no sympathy with anyone who complains about what's done when he never takes any interest in it.

(*Truman turns his back to the audience.*)

EVELYN and ADAM: **Wow**!

ADAM: Truman is right. We have to take an interest in our government and our world.

EVELYN: Sure, like Mrs. Samuels said, we are the world's future.

ADAM: So what should we do about the assignment?

EVELYN: I'm still uncertain, but I'm beginning to get it.

ADAM: What are you thinking about? Who will we use to give us the answer?

EVELYN: Who?

LOU COSTELLO: Hey Abbott, who's on first?

BUD ABBOTT: Yes.

LOU COSTELLO: I mean the fellow's name on first base.

BUD ABBOT: "Who."

LOU COSTELLO: The fellow's name on first base for St. Louis.

BUD ABBOTT: "Who." And that's the way our famous baseball routine began. I tried to tell Lou Costello that the names of the players on the St. Louis team were peculiar. "Who's" on first, "What's" on second, and "I Don't Know's" on third.

This caused confusion and lots of laughter. It made us famous. It remains a classic to this day.

LOU COSTELLO: Bud Abbott could make the most outrageous statement seem sound and logical. He really made you believe that the first baseman's name was "Who."

BUD ABBOTT: And Lou's comic asset was his credibility as the gullible one.

LOU COSTELLO: So what we want to bring out here for a better world is two things. First of all, the world needs humor. Without some laughs the world would be a dull place. And second, each person needs someone to depend on. This was our formula for success as a comedy team.

(Abbott and Costello turn their backs to the audience.)

EVELYN: Exactly. John Donne said, "No man is an island." We need each other. We can't cure the world of all its problems but, together, we can begin to try and make it a better place.

(Abraham Lincoln turns to face audience.)

ADAM: Yeah. One step at a time. Little things like being careful about another guy's feelings.

(Winston Churchill turns to face audience.)

EVELYN: And giving up that seat on the bus to someone who needs it more.

(Madame Curie and Harriet Tubman turn to face audience.)

ADAM: And stop complaining about stuff and blaming others.

(Gotama, the Buddha turns to face audience.)

EVELYN: We need a positive attitude.

(Babe Ruth turns to face audience.)

ADAM: Yeah. Getting angry doesn't help anyone.

(Harry Truman turns to face audience.)

EVELYN: And don't forget (pause) . . . to laugh.

(Bud Abbott and Lou Costello turn to face audience.)

ADAM: Hey Evelyn, who's on first?

EVELYN and ADAM: *(Laugh)* **I think we did it!**

(All readers form a line across the playing area. They bow and exit Right and Left.)

Chapter 20

SAMPLE SCRIPT: MIDDLE SCHOOL MEMOIRS

Middle School Memoirs[1]

Compiled and Adapted by Shirlee Sloyer

Cast of Characters

- ***The D- Poems of Jeremy Bloom* by Gordon Korman and Bernice Korman**

    Narrator 1,2
    Jeremy Bloom, *student*
    Ms. Terranova, *teacher*

- ***Nothing But the Truth* by Avi**

    Miss Narwin, *teacher*
    Student 1 (Lisa)
    Student 2 (Gloria)
    Allison Doresett, *student*
    Student 3 (Joseph)
    Phillip Malloy, *student*

- ***Hey World, Here I Am* by Jean Little**

    Kate Bloomfield 1, 2, 3, *student*
    Mr. Entwhistle, *substitute teacher*

- ***How to Eat Like a Child* by Delia Ephron**

    Student 1, 2, 3, 4, 5, 6, 7, 8, 9, 10

- *Class Dismissed!* **by Mel Glenn**

  Eleanor Paine, *student*

  Lisa Goodman, *student*

  Ellen Winters**,** *student*

- *For Your Eyes Only* **by Joanne Rocklin**

  Lucy 1, 2, *student*

- *My Friend's Got This Problem, Mr. Candler*, **by Mel Glenn**

  Patrick DeShannon, *student*

  Melissa Cohen, *student*

- *Up the Down Staircase* **by Bel Kaufman**

  Student 1, 2, 3, 4, 5, 6, 7, 8, 9, 10

- *The Yearbook* **by Shirlee Sloyer**

  Editor

  Biggest Sycophant

  Best Athlete

  Most Likely to Succeed

  Biggest Ego

  Best Dressed

  Most Popular

  Class Sleeper

  Class Clown

  Best Actress

Rehearsing "Middle School Memoirs."

Production Notes

Each selection is discrete. There are no introductions or transitions. The playing area is set up like a classroom. The seats are set on a slant across the stage so that all the readers are visible. There is a lectern at one side, at which the Narrators and Teachers stand when they are on stage. Otherwise, they may be seated on high stools. Ms. Terranova and Miss Narwin may be played by the same person. The entire cast, with the exception of the teachers, are seated as in a classroom. Students stand at their seats facing the audience as they read their selection(s) unless directed to go Downstage Center. For the segment *How to Eat Like a Child,* students read from their seats, making certain they are seen from the audience. For the segment *Up the Down Staircase,* students stand, say their line(s), and then sit. No special costumes are required. Baseball caps can be worn (one or two backwards) by several of the boys.

From *The D- Poems of Jeremy Bloom*

NARRATOR 1:	Any other day, missing the bus and showing up late would have meant a simple chewing-out by the principal, and maybe a detention or two. But today was the first day of Middle School, which meant that Jeremy Bloom was counting on getting into Music Appreciation.
JEREMY:	Popularly known as "Snooze Patrol." It was a dream course—no homework, no tests—just show up in first period and listen to records.
NARRATOR 2:	Best of all, Mr. DeRobis turned off the lights for better concentration on the music.
JEREMY:	So it was like getting an extra forty-five minutes of sleep every day.
NARRATOR 1:	Besides, all of Jeremy's friends were going to be in that class.
NARRATOR 2:	But he was late, and Snooze Patrol was already full. He panicked, and his eyes flew to the list of classes that were still open.
JEREMY:	Pottery!
NARRATOR 1:	He croaked, signing up in a split-second decision.
JEREMY:	It was not Snooze Patrol, but how hard could it be to make ashtrays?
NARRATOR 2:	It was only when he showed up in Ms. Terranova's room that the truth hit.
NARRATOR 1:	This was not Pottery; it was *Poetry.* Furthermore, they didn't read it, they *wrote* it.
NARRATOR 2:	And no amount of begging and pleading to Ms. Terranova, the Principal, his parents, and God could get him out of it.
NARRATOR 1:	As Ms. Terranova put it,

MS. TERRANOVA.   Anybody who could see *Poetry* and read *Pottery* needs all the English courses he can get.

(Teacher and Narrators exit Left. Jeremy comes Downstage Center.)

JEREMY: WHY I WAS LATE

I was late for school on Monday,
I rolled in at half past nine,
Miss Hackensack demanded
An excuse; I gave her mine.

The house across the street blew up.
The rubble on our lawn
Was twelve feet deep! I worked all night!
I shoveled until dawn!

The school bus made me later!
It was hijacked on the hill.
Dave Brooks was taken hostage,
And I'm sure he's out there still!

Well, then I saw the crater,
And I had to go around it.
I never thought I'd see the school!
I'm quite amazed I found it!

The news made all the papers—
It's not my fault she missed it.
To illustrate this point, I dropped
Down to the ground and kissed it.

My teacher made a face and kicked me out into the hall.
They don't trust a guy at all!

(Jeremy takes a seat. Miss Narwin goes to lectern. Students talk among themselves.)

From *Nothing But the Truth*

MISS NARWIN: Ladies and gentlemen, please settle down. All right. Settle down. For the moment just take any seat you wish. We'll work on the particular problems a bit later on. Yes?

STUDENT 1:   *(Stands.)* Am I supposed to be in this room?

MISS NARWIN:	What's your name?
STUDENT 1:	Lisa Gibbons.
MISS NARWIN:	Lisa? Yes, you're on my list. Just take any seat for the moment.

(Lisa sits.)

STUDENT 2:	Miss Narwin, what about me?
MISS NARWIN:	Is that you, Gloria? No, you're not here. Did you get a notice?
STUDENT 2:	No.
MISS NARWIN:	Oh, dear. Best check in the main office.
ALLISON DORSETT:	*(Screams out.)* What about me?
MISS NARWIN:	You'll have to lower your voices if I'm going to sort things out. Yes, Allison you are here. Yes?
STUDENT 3:	Joseph R. Rippens. Am I?
MISS NARWIN:	Please, let's just get done with the morning business.
PHILLIP MALLOY:	*(Humming.)*
MISS NARWIN:	Do I hear humming. Is that you, Phillip?
PHILLIP MALLOY:	Just humming.
MISS NARWIN:	Please stop it.
PHILLIP MALLOY:	Mr. Lunser doesn't mind. I just . . .
MISS NARWIN:	Stop it now.
PHILLIP MALLOY:	But . . .
MISS NARWIN:	Now! Thank you.

(All freeze in place as Kate Bloomfield 1, 2, and 3, stand and read from black and white notebooks.)

From *Hey World, Here I Am!*

KATE BLOOMFIELD 1:   ABOUT NOTEBOOKS

I love the first page of a new notebook.
I write the date crisply.
My whole name marches exactly along the line.
The spaces are always even.
The commas curl just so.
I never have to erase on the first page.
Never!

KATE BLOOMFIELD 2:

> *When I get to the middle, there are lots of eraser holes.*
> *The corners are dog-eared.*
> *Whole paragraphs have been crossed out.*
> *My words slide off the lines and crowd together.*
> *I wish it was done.*

KATE BLOOMFIELD 3:

> *I have a dream, that, someday, someone will say,*
> *"Here, give me that beat-up old notebook.*
> *You needn't bother filling in all those other zillion pages.*
> *Start a new one this instant*
> *Because its, February, because today's not Wednesday,*
> *Because everybody deserves beginning again more often."*

KATE BLOOMFIELD 1:

> *Yet, crazy as it sounds,*
> *I always like to write the number 8,*
> *Even on the third last page of a messy notebook.*
> *It meets itself so neatly it's almost magic.*
> *And I love swooping big E's and looping small z's.*
> *If, for some reason, I get to write a word*
> *Like "quintessence" maybe or something with lots of m's*
> *Or "balloon" or "rainbow" or "typhoon" or "lollipop"*
> *I forget I'm sick of the book with its stupid margins*
> *And, while I'm writing, I hum inside my head.*

(Kate Bloomfield 1, 2, and 3 return to their seats. Students 1, 2, 3, 4, 5 speak from their seats illustrating their lines with appropriate motions.)

From *How to Eat Like a Child*

STUDENT 1:   HOW TO ACT IF YOU DO NOT WANT TO BE CALLED ON

Make yourself invisible. Align head and shoulders with those of a student directly between the teacher and you. If the teacher moves, adjust alignment.

STUDENT 2:   Make yourself inconspicuous. To accomplish this, assume a casual pose. Concentrate on fitting the top of the pen into the bottom; perhaps even hum to yourself.

STUDENT 3:   Or engage in nonchalant play with a pencil: Hold it upright, point against paper, and slide fingers from eraser to tip. Turn pencil over, slide from tip to eraser. Turn and slide. Turn and slide.

STUDENT 4: Stare down the teacher. Look her confidently straight in the eyes. Pray that she thinks you know the answer and will call on someone else.

STUDENT 5: Wave your arm frantically in the air. Make certain that there are at least four or five other arms frantically waving.

STUDENT 6: Insist that the person who answered before you gave your exact answer.

STUDENT 7: If the teacher calls on you anyway, do not respond im mediately in the hope that a kid with the answer will just yell it out. If no one rescues you and the question calls for a yes or no response, pick one.

STUDENT 8: Pretend the answer just slipped from your mind, being careful not to use this excuse too often to avoid being sent to the school psychologist.

STUDENT 9: Affect a hoarse voice but speak clearly enough to say your doctor advised you not to speak.

STUDENT 10: Otherwise, give a joke answer. The class will laugh. The teacher will say that it won't be so funny when you get your report card.

(Students return to original positions. Eleanor Paine stands.)

From *Class Dismissed!*

ELEANOR PAINE:

When Rhonda read one of her poems in class
I sat there amazed
By a sensitivity I didn't know she possessed.
Isn't it enough for her just to be beautiful?
She talks to boys as easily as if they were her brothers.
She plays tennis as though she were training for Wimbledon.
She tells jokes like a professional comedienne.
A week later, while sitting in the dentist's office,
I saw her poem in a magazine.
Only it didn't have her name on it.
I don't understand.
Why when she has everything
Does she want even more?

(Eleanor Paine sits. Lisa Goodman stands.)

LISA GOODMAN:

Nobody pays attention to me;
I'm average.
If I started to cut class,
Yell at the teacher,
Not do my homework,
Everybody would notice me.
But I don't do these things.
I never get into trouble.
Teachers don't call on me.
I'd like to think that one day
They will all stand up and see me,
But I don't think it will happen.
I once read in a play,
"Attention must be paid."
Not really.

(Lisa Goodman sits. Ellen Winters stands.)

ELLEN WINTERS:

Feeling closed in and cut off from life, I told my
Parents,
Who told me to tell my
Teacher,
Who referred me to my
Guidance counselor,
Who sent me to the
Assistant principal,
Who informed the
Principal,
Who said I should go back to my
Teacher,
Who told me to speak to my
Parents.

(Ellen Winters sits. Lucy 1 and 2 stand and go Downstage Center.)

From *For Your Eyes Only* (Lucy's Notebook)[*]

LUCY 1: *Tuesday, January 23*

Welcome to our class, Mr. Moffat!

Can we really use these notebooks for whatever we want? You said we don't even have to show them to you, but I don't mind if you read mine. As long as it is FYEO (For YOUR Eyes Only).

(Turns page in notebook.)

LUCY 2: *Monday, January 29*

I see that you like poetry, Mr. M.

I confess that I have not read a lot of poetry on my own. Except if you count the funny poems I sometimes read to my five-year-old twin brothers, Victor and Vance, at bedtime.

I also confess that I have not written a lot of poetry on my own. I've written pretty good haiku, but that was only for class. Mrs. Silverberg had us write kazillions of haiku—you know, five syllables in the first line, seven in the next, five in the next.

Here is my best haiku, for your private enjoyment:

Oh, Gladiola! (5)

How iridescent you are (7)

Outside my window (5)

LUCY 1: I like the word iridescent. Believe me, it wasn't easy finding the perfect four-syllable word. And I think gladiola is the most beautiful word in the English language. GLAD-EE-OH-LA. Saying it is just like singing. It must be a beautiful thing in real life.

(Lucy 1 and 2 take seats. Mr. Entwhistle goes to lectern. Kate Bloomfield 1, 2, and 3 go Downstage Center.)

From *Hey World, Here I Am!* (Mr. Entwhistle)

KATE BLOOMFIELD 1: Mr. Entwhistle was our substitute teacher. He had big shoulders and a mean mouth. He knew, before he'd laid eyes on us, that we were out to make trouble.

KATE BLOOMFIELD 2: And he knew how to handle teenagers. Step on them hard, right from the start, and you'd have no discipline problems.

KATE BLOOMFIELD 3: He'd show us who was boss the first time one of us stepped out of line.

KATE BLOOMFIELD 1: Looking back, I can see that was how it started. But at the time, I had not gotten around to noticing him, except to see that he was young.

KATE BLOOMFIELD 2: That's a nice change, I thought, and went back to attempting to show Sandra Mayhew where she'd fouled up in the Math homework.

KATE BLOOMFIELD 3: Mr. Entwhistle had started writing our names in on a seating plan. He knew all the tricks. He wasn't going to put up with desk jumpers.

MR. ENTWHISTLE: *(Sharply)* What's your name?

KATE BLOOMFIELD 1: I didn't look up, let alone answer. Sandra was finally catching on. It never crossed my mind that he was speaking to me.

MR. ENTWHISTLE: I said '*What is your name?*'

KATE BLOOMFIELD 2: He was closer to me. He had started down our aisle. So I glanced up. I still had not realized that I was the one he was addressing.

KATE BLOOMFIELD 3: I sat there, gazing at him, wondering why he was all charged up. I did not tell him my name.

MR. ENTWHISTLE: All right. That does it. You can go to the office.

KATE BLOOMFIELD 1: Me?

MR. ENTWHISTLE: Yes, you. Oh, yes indeed, you! Perhaps next time you'll show respect. On your feet!

KATE BLOOMFIELD 2: I stood up slowly. Outside the open window, the sun was shining. Everything was green, beguiling.

KATE BLOOMFIELD 3: "Come",

KATE BLOOMFIELD 1: it said to me,

KATE BLOOMFIELD 2: "Just come out and away."

KATE BLOOMFIELD 3: I considered it.

(Kate 1, 2, and 3 take seats. Jeremy Bloom comes Downstage Center.)

From *The D- Poems of Jeremy Bloom*

JEREMY BLOOM: REPORT CARD BLUES

My report card is a loathsome thing,
A triumph it is not,
It tells how I am flunking French,
My Math is not so hot.

I got a D in History,
I found the Grammar tough,
I bombed out bad at Reading
And Geography was rough.

I have to show this to my folks
My future will be grim.
It's lucky I can point right to
A brilliant grade in Gym.

(Jeremy takes seat. Patrick DeShannon comes Downstage Center.)

From *My Friend's Got This Problem, Mr. Candler*

PATRICK DE SHANNON:

My little brother, Brendan, is a pain.
He never leaves me alone.
He always messes up my room,
Looking for my magazines, he says.
He makes horrible bird noises,
Which embarrasses me in front of my friends,
And when I scream at him,
Calling him all sorts of names,
He goes running to my mother,
Who says, "Stop teasing him, you're older."
I tell him to get lost,
But he follows me everywhere.
"He wants to be like you," my mother says.
Last week, in order to get Brendan off my back,
I taught him how to ride my bike.
It took the little pain three days to learn.
Now he rides everywhere with his friends.
I miss him.

(Patrick DeShannon takes his seat. Students 1 through 10 stand one after the other. They sit as they finish their line(s).)

From *Up the Down Staircase*

STUDENT 1:   I know homework is essential to our well-being, and I did it but I got into a fight with some kid on the way to school and he threw it in the gutter.

STUDENT 2:	My cat chewed it up and there was no time to do it over.
STUDENT 3:	As I was taking down the assignment my ballpoint stopped.
STUDENT 4:	I had to study French so I didn't have time to study English.
STUDENT 5:	I did it but I left it home by mistake.
STUDENT 6:	The baby spilled milk on it.
STUDENT 7:	My brother took my homework instead of his.
STUDENT 8:	The page was missing from my book.
STUDENT 9:	Someone stole it.
STUDENT 10:	*What* homework?

(All seated. Kate Bloomfield 1, 2, and 3 go Downstage Center.)

From *Hey World, Here I Am!*

KATE BLOOMFIELD 1:	Today I will not live up to my potential.
KATE BLOOMFIELD 2:	Today I will not relate well to my peer group.
KATE BLOOMFIELD 3:	Today I will not contribute in class. I will not volunteer one thing.
KATE BLOOMFIELD 1:	Today I will not strive to do better.
KATE BLOOMFIELD 2:	Today I will not achieve or adjust or grow enriched or get involved.
KATE BLOOMFIELD 3:	I will not put up my hand even if the teacher is wrong and I can prove it.
KATE BLOOMFIELD 1:	Today I might eat the eraser off my pencil.
KATE BLOOMFIELD 2:	I'll look at clouds.
KATE BLOOMFIELD 3:	I'll be late.
KATE BLOOMFIELD 1:	I don't think I'll wash.
ALL KATES:	**I need a rest.**

(Kate 1, 2, and 3 take seats. Jeremy Bloom stands.)

From *The D- Poems of Jeremy Bloom*

JEREMY BLOOM:

I pulled an "A" in math today
It took a bit of work,
I highly recommend it, though—
Your parents go berserk.

It's not enough to buy you stuff
To celebrate your grade,
They also grant you privileges
For this great mark you've made.

Your mom cooks all your favorite foods,
Your dad makes "genius" jokes,
An "A" in math sure makes it tough
To recognize your folks.

Your sister does the dishes, and
Your brother rakes the yard,
I'll get an "A" again one day—
That's if it's not too hard.

(Jeremy Bloom takes seat.)

The Yearbook

EDITOR: Hi, I'm the editor of the yearbook And now that school is ending and many of us will be going on, I thought you might like to meet some of our chosen people. We call them our Senior Superlatives, and here's why.

BEST ATHLETE: I was voted Best Athlete. I think it was because of my sixty-five-yard run. It made me famous. Do you think it's because I went the wrong way? But everyone really loved the way I decorated the basketball hoop in the gym for prom night. My secret? Purple crepe paper.

BIGGEST EGO: They gave me the title of Biggest Ego. It just shows how misunderstood I am. Having the largest ego is the sort of thing one is accused of if you have nothing to back it up with. But I have the evidence. I'm smart. I'm good looking. I have a ready charm. I'm in the know. No, I don't think its ego. I think its, . . . its . . . self-confidence.

MOST POPULAR: It's an honor to be selected as the Most Popular. Yes, everyone wants to be my friend. Don't think its all fun and games. It takes work. I have to write eighty-eight e-mails every day. My father says I tie up the phone, but it isn't my fault if people call. I do have to keep up, don't I?

CLASS CLOWN: Class Clown. Ha, ha! That's a laugh. I just got back from geometry. It's there I get to know all the angles! Hee, hee. I love you guys!

BIGGEST SYCOPHANT:	You voted me the Biggest Sycophant. I had to look it up. It means *flattering for favors.* I don't know why I got this award but just yesterday when I was helping Mr. Bernstein clean up the lab and put away his books and equipment I said, "No matter what it is, recognition is worth something!"
MOST LIKELY TO SUCCEED:	I was glad to get the title of Most Likely to Succeed. Everyone agrees I will be a success one day. Even my parents say I'm going to be a man of letters—C.E.O., Ph.D., D.D.S., M.D., F.A.C.P. As for me, my motto is, buy at the low and sell at the high.
BEST DRESSED:	Yo! I got to be the Best Dressed. Listen, I earned the distinction. If you want to be cool, you've got to have the threads. Baggy pants, funky shirts. It's clothes that make the man, you know.
CLASS SLEEPER:	Class Sleeper? What kinda' category is that? No yearbook has a Class Sleeper. But since you've named me I can defend the title. A guy needs his rest man. Didn't you know that sleep encourages growth? Yeah, it has to do with the pituitary gland. And isn't that what school is supposed to do, encourage growth?
BEST ACTRESS:	Thank you, thank you, thank you academy for this great honor. Best Actress. I could not have done it alone. I want to share this with my director, my fellow actors, my mom, my father, my kid brother, my spiritual leader, my . . .
EDITOR:	Yeah, yeah, we get the idea. Hey guys, the photographer is here. Take your places.

(All take appropriate poses.)

EDITOR:	Now, say cheese!
ALL:	**Cheese!**

(The photographer snaps the picture. The entire cast returns, takes funny poses.)

ENTIRE CAST:	**Cheese!**

(Photographer snaps another shot. All bow and exit Right and Left.)

Notes

1. Materials adapted from the following sources: Gordon Korman and Bernice Korman, *The D- Poems of Jeremy Bloom* (New York: Scholastic, 1992); Avi, *Nothing But the Truth* (New York: Orchard, 1991); Jean Little, *Hey World! Here I Am!* (New York: Harper & Row, 1986); Delia Ephron, *How to Eat Like a Child* (New York: Viking, 1978); Mel Glenn, *Class Dismissed!* (New York: Clarion Books, 1982); Joanne Rocklin, *For Your Eyes Only!* (New York: Scholastic, 1997); Bel Kaufman, *Up the Down Staircase* (New York: Prentice-Hall, 1964); Mel Glenn, *My Friend's Got This Problem, Mr. Candler* (New York: Clarion Books, 1991); Shirlee Sloyer, *The Yearbook*, unpublished.

Bibliography

Readers Theatre Books

Barchers, Suzanne I. *Fifty Fabulous Fables: Beginning Readers Theatre.* Englewood, CO: Libraries Unlimited, 1997.

———. *From Atalanta to Zeus: Readers Theatre from Greek Mythology.* Englewood, CO: Libraries Unlimited, 2001.

———. *Multicultural Folktales: Readers Theatre for Elementary Students.* Englewood, CO: Libraries Unlimited, 2000.

———. *Readers Theatre for Beginning Readers.* Englewood, CO: Libraries Unlimited, 1993.

———. *Scary Readers Theatre.* Englewood, CO: Libraries Unlimited, 1994.

Bauer, Caroline Feller. *Presenting Reader's Theater: Plays and Poems to Read Aloud.* New York: H. W. Wilson, 1987.

Bennett, Gordon. *Readers Theatre Comes to Church.* 2nd ed. Colorado Springs, CO: Meriwether, 1985.

Breen, Robert. *Chamber Theatre.* Ellison Ball, WI: William Caxton, 1986.

Carlsen, James, and Melvin R. White, eds. *Literature on Stage: Readers Theatre Anthology.* New York: Samuel French, 1980.

Coger, Leslie Irene, and Melvin R. White. *Readers Theatre Handbook: A Dramatic Approach to Literature.* 3rd ed. Glenview, IL: Scott, Foresman, 1982.

Dixon, Neill, Anne Davies, and Colleen Politano. *Learning with Readers Theatre: Building Connections.* Grand Forks, ND: Peguis, 1996.

Fredericks, Anthony D. *Frantic Frogs and Other Frankly Fractured Folktales for Readers Theatre.* Englewood, CO: Libraries Unlimited, 1993.

———. *Readers Theatre for American History.* Englewood, CO: Libraries Unlimited, 2001.

Haven, Kendall. *Great Moments in Science: Experiments and Readers Theatre.* Englewood, CO: Libraries Unlimited, 1996.

Kaye, Marvin. *Readers Theatre: What Is It and How to Stage It.* Berkeley Heights, NJ: Wildside Press, 1995.

Latrobe, Kathy H., and Mildred K. Laughlin. *Readers Theatre for Young Adults: Scripts and Script Development.* Englewood, CO: Libraries Unlimited, 1989.

Laughlin, Mildred K., and Kathy H. Latrobe. *Readers Theatre for Children: Scripts and Script Development.* Englewood, CO: Libraries Unlimited, 1990.

Laughlin, Mildred K., Peggy T. Black, and Margery K. Loberg. *Social Studies Readers Theatre for Children: Scripts and Script Development*. Englewood, CO: Libraries Unlimited, 1991.

Ratliff, Gerald Lee. *Beginning Readers Theatre: A Primer for Classroom Performance*. Urbana, IL: ERIC, 1981.

————. *Introduction to Readers Theatre: A Guide to Classroom Performance*. Colorado Springs, CO: Meriwether, 1999.

Shepard, Aaron. *Stories on Stage: Scripts for Reader's Theater*. New York: H. W. Wilson, 1993.

Sierra, Judy. *Multicultural Folktales for the Feltboard and Readers' Theater*. Phoenix: Oryx, 1996.

Sloyer, Shirlee. *Readers Theatre: Story Dramatization in the Classroom*. Urbana, IL: National Council of Teachers of English, 1982.

Tanner, Fran. *Creative Communication*. 4th ed. Topeka, KS: Clark Publishing, 1991, ch. 48.

————. *Readers Theatre Fundamentals: A Cumulative Approach to Theory and Activities*. Topeka, KS: Clark, 1993.

Walker, Lois. *Readers Theatre Strategies in the Middle and Junior High Classroom*. Colorado Springs, CO: Meriwether, 1997.

White, Melvin R. *Mel White's Readers Theatre Anthology: A Collection of 28 Readings*. Colorado Springs, CO: Meriwether, 1993.

Performance Studies and Oral Interpretation Books

Jenkins, Jean R. *Voice, Diction, and Interpretation*. Minneapolis, MI: Burgess, 1981.

Lee, Charlotte, and Timothy Gura. *Oral Interpretation*. 10th ed. Boston: Houghton Mifflin, 2001.

Lewis, Todd V. *Communicatin Literature: An Introduction to Oral Interpretation*. 3rd ed. Dubuque, IA: Kendall/Hunt, 2000.

Long, Beverly Whitaker. *Performing Literature: An Introduction*. 2nd ed. Dubuque, IA: Kendall/Hunt, 1997.

Pelias, Ronald J. *Performance Studies: The Interpretation of Aesthetic Texts*. Dubuque, IA: Kendall/Hunt, 1999.

Yordon, Judy. *Roles in Interpretation*. 2nd ed. Dubuque, IA: William Brown, 1989.

Theatre Arts Books

Apperson, Linda. *Stage Managing and Theatre Etiquette: A Basic Guide*. Chicago: Ivan R. Dee Publisher, 1998.

Berger, Melvin. *Putting on a Show*. New York: Franklin Watts, 1980.

Bordan, Sylvia Diane. *Plays as Teaching Tools in the Elementary School*. West Nyack, NY: Parker, 1970.

Cassady, Marsha. *The Theatre and You: A Beginning.* Colorado Springs, CO: Meriwether, 1992.

Durland, Frances Caldwell. *Creative Dramatics for Children.* Kent, OH: Kent State University Press, 1975.

Haycock, Kate. *Plays Media Story.* Ada, OK: Garrett Educational Corp., 1990.

Judy, Susan, and Stephen Judy. *Putting on a Play.* New York: Charles Scribner's Sons, 1982.

LeRoy, Robert. *Everything About Theatre: The Guidebook of Theatre Fundamentals.* Colorado Springs, CO: Meriwether, 1996

McCaslin, Nellie. *Act Now!* New York: S. G. Phillips, 1975.

McSweeny, Maxine. *Creative Children's Theatre.* New York: A. S. Barnes, 1974.

Pryor, Nick. *Putting on a Play.* New York: Thomson Learning, 1994.

Schotz, Amiel. *Theatre Games and Beyond: A Creative Approach for Young Performers.* Colorado Springs, CO: Meriwether, 1998.

Sternberg, Patricia. *On Stage: How to Put on a Play.* New York: Julian Messner, 1983.

Williamson, Walter. *Early Stages: The Professional Theater and the Young Actor.* New York: Julian Messner, 1983.

Wood, David, and Janet Grant. *Theatre for Children: A Guide to Writing, Adapting, Directing and Acting.* Chicago: Ivan R. Dee, 1999.

Journal Articles

Forsythe, Sheri J. "It Worked! Readers Theatre in Second Grade." *The Reading Teacher* 49, no. 3 (November 1995): 264.

Hoyt, L. "Many Ways of Knowing: Using Drama, Oral Interactions, and the Visual Arts to Enhance Reading." *The Reading Teacher* 45, no. 8 (April 1992): 580.

Martinez, Miriam, Nancy L. Roser, and Susan Strecker. "I Never Thought I Could Be a Star: A Readers' Theatre Ticket to Fluency." *The Reading Teacher* 52, no. 4 (December 1998/January 1999): 326.

Shepard, Aaron. "From Script to Stage: Tips for Readers Theatre." *The Reading Teacher* 48, no. 2 (October 1994): 194.

Stewart, Loretta. "Readers Theatre and the Writing Workshop Using Children's Literature to Prompt Student Writing." *The Reading Teacher* 51, no. 2 (October 1997): 174.

Wolf, Shelby Anne. "What's in a Name? Labels and Literacy in Readers Theatre." *The Reading Teacher* 46, no. 7 (April 1993): 540.

Young, Terrell A., and Sylvia Vardell. "Weaving Readers Theatre and NonFiction into the Curriculum." *The Reading Teacher* 46, no. 5 (February 1993): 396.

Readers Theatre Scripts for Sale

Readers Theatre Script Service
P.O. Box 178333
San Diego, CA 92117
(619) 276-1948
(Scripts for elementary grades and bilingual scripts)

Contemporary Drama Service
Box 7710-C
985 Elkton Dr.
Colorado Springs, CO 80933
(719) 594-4422
(Readers theatre scripts for schools)

Samuel French
45 West 25 St.
New York, NY 10010-2751
(212) 206-8990
(Professional readers theatre scripts)

Readers Theatre Scripts on the Web

Aaron Shepard's R.T. Page
www.aaronshep.com/rt
(Resources for readers theatre including multicultural script series for young people,
    Readers Theatre Editions)

Readers Theatre Online Canada
www.scriptsforschools.com
(Markets readers theatre scripts and choral speaking scripts for schools and libraries;
    provides free online samples)

Storycart Press
www.storycart.com
(Books and free sample scripts)

Index

About the Author

Shirlee Sloyer is a professor of speech and rhetorical studies at Hofstra University, Long Island, New York. She teaches courses in readers theatre, performance studies, communication theory, argumentation and debate, and small group communication. She also lectures at all school levels on readers theatre in education. Her doctorate in speech and rhetoric was earned from New York University.

Dr. Sloyer was Hofstra's debate and forensic coach for many years and originated the Hofstra University Readers Theatre, which performed throughout Long Island and New York City. She appeared with her readers on CBS and NBC television.

Prior to her college career Dr. Sloyer was the director of children's drama at the Five Towns Music and Art Foundation on Long Island and founded and directed The Downstairs Theatre for Children in Lawrence, New York. Her first book, *Readers Theatre: Story Dramatization in the Classroom,* received critical acclaim from the National Council of Teachers of English. Other publications include articles on the relationship of readers theatre and reading motivation.

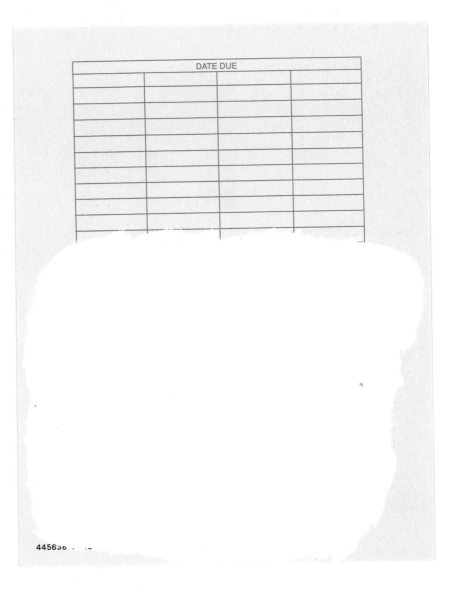

DATE DUE

445658